PRESTEL

Prague

by
Anneliese Keilhauer

Photographs by Hermann Josef Wöstmann

Prestel
Munich – New York

This guide contains 137 full-color and 125 black-and-white illustrations, 2 double-page color maps, 7 plans, and a map of the metro system.

Front cover:
View across the Vltava River, with Charles Bridge and Prague Castle in the background [No. 49]
Photographer: Werner Neumeister, Munich

Inside front cover:
View of the Old Town Bridge Tower from Charles Bridge [No. 50]
Photographer: Hermann Josef Wöstmann, Kerpin-Buir

Back cover:
The Hanau Pavilion on Letná Hill [No. 123]
Photographer: Hermann Josef Wöstmann

Page 3:
Prague's Old Town coat of arms

Page 5:
The Golden Well house on Charles Street [No. 56]
Photographer: Hermann Josef Wöstmann

Originally published as *Prestel Führer Prag,* © 1993 Prestel, revised edition
Other Prestel Guides in this series: **Berlin, Munich,** and **Vienna**

Edited by Michael Robertson, Augsburg
Translated from the German by Ian Robson, Merklín u Přeštic

Prestel-Verlag, 16 West 22nd Street, New York, NY 10010, USA
Tel. (212) 6 27 81 99; Fax (212) 6 27 98 66
and Mandlstrasse 26, 80802 Munich, Germany
Tel. (89) 3 81 70 90; Fax (89) 38 17 09 35

The concept, format, and layout of this book have been developed specially for the series *Prestel Guides.* They are subject to the laws protecting intellectual property and may not be copied or imitated in any way.

Distributed in continental Europe by Prestel-Verlag
Verlegerdienst München GmbH & Co. KG, Gutenbergstrasse 1, 82205 Gilching, Germany
Tel. (81 05) 38 81 17; Fax (81 05) 38 81 00

Distributed in the USA and Canada on behalf of Prestel by te Neues Publishing Company,
16 West 22nd Street, New York, NY 10010, USA
Tel. (2 12) 6 27 90 90; Fax (2 12) 6 27 95 11

Distributed in Japan on behalf of Prestel by YOHAN Western Publications Distribution
Agency, 14-9 Okubo 3-chome, Shinjuku-ku, Tokyo 169, Japan
Tel. (3) 32 08 01 81; Fax (3) 32 09 02 88

Distributed in the United Kingdom, Ireland, and all remaining countries on behalf of Prestel by
Thames & Hudson Limited, 30-34 Bloomsbury Street, London WC1B 3 QP, England
Tel. (71) 6 36 54 88; Fax (71) 6 36 16 95

Photograph credits: Peter Keilhauer, Salzburg: pp. 69, 79 (top), 103 (left), 104 (top), 108 (2), 140 (right), 148 (bottom); Werner Neumeister, Munich: pp. 43, 44, 169

Design: Norbert Dinkel, Munich
Maps: Franz Huber, Munich
Color separations: PHG Lithos GmbH, Martinsried
Typesetting, printing, and binding: Passavia Druckerei GmbH, Passau

Printed in Germany

ISBN 3-7913-1276-6 (English edition)
ISBN 3-7913-1273-1 (German edition)

Contents

Contents

Staré Město (Old Town) *map on page 7* 93

Josefov (The Former Jewish Quarter) *map on page 7* 128

Nové Město (New Town) *map on pages 8-9* 134

Outskirts *map on pages 8-9* *155*

Practical Tips *170*

Index *188*

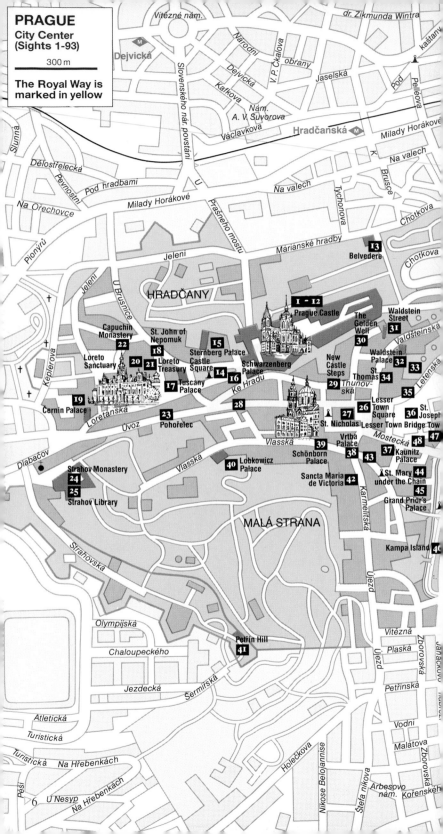

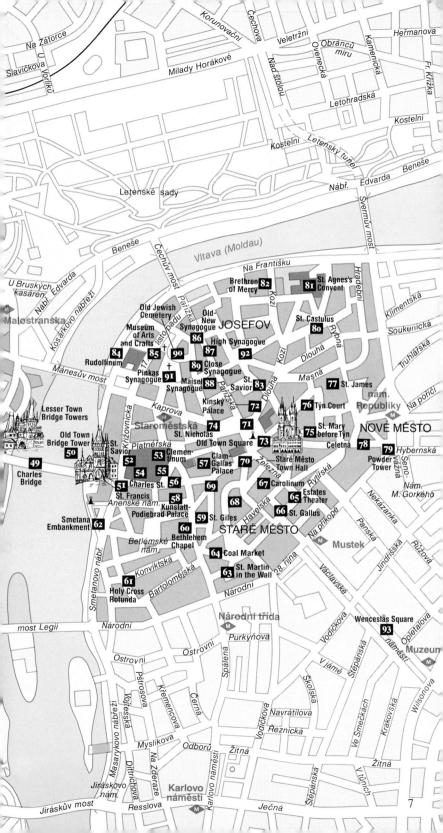

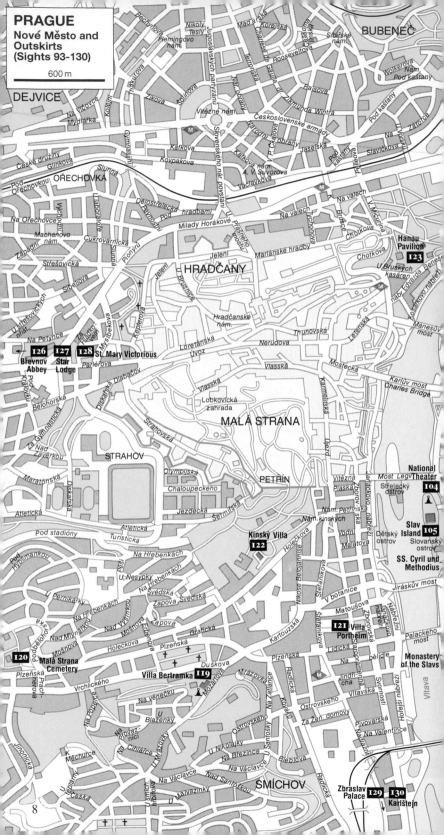

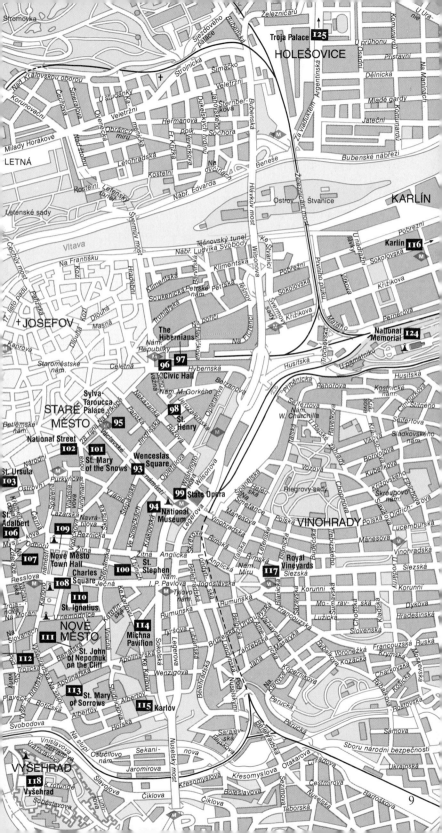

Prague – The Golden City

"I see a city whose glory will one day reach to the stars" – thus, in a Czech saga, begins the prophecy of Libuše, visionary founder of the House of Přemysl. This glorious city, which was to arise to the north of her seat at Vyšehrad, the "High Castle" on the right bank of the Vltava, did indeed become reality: in the late ninth century, the Přemyslid rulers founded Prague Castle on a ridge commanding the left bank of the river and a ford where international trade routes converged, and the market settlements that sprang up at this strategic site soon evolved into "one of the most prosperous trading centers far and wide."

Prague's "Golden Age," in the literal sense of the term, began with the reign of Charles IV in the mid-fourteenth century. The second of the Luxemburg monarchs, who was descended from the Přemyslid line through his mother, made Prague the capital of the Holy Roman Empire, and as an outward sign of the city's new status and as a reflection of its wealth and cultural significance he ordered the gilding of the lead roofs of its towers and defensive walls. Travelers and chroniclers from all over Europe enthused about "hundred-spired, golden Prague." Later, during the reign of the Habsburg emperor Rudolf II at the end of the sixteenth century, the city was again a glittering imperial metropolis.

Right: *View of Prague Castle over the roof of St. Thomas. The towers of St. George's Basilica can be seen in the background*

Below: *The narrow lane leading up to the castle is a favorite spot for street musicians*

Even without the golden roofs, Prague is today still a jewel in the heart of Europe, captivating millions of visitors every year with its timeless beauty. One can stroll endlessly through the picturesque lanes of this unique open-air museum, imbibing history at every turn; and should the dust of centuries begin to tickle one's throat, a refreshment stop need not break the spell – beer and wine are dispensed in medieval vaults, garden restaurants nestle in the shadow of stately Baroque mansions, Art Nouveau cafés still retain something of their fin-de-siècle touch.

This guide leads us in turn through the four historic townships that were only amalgamated to form the city of Prague in the late eighteenth century. Each of these quarters has its own specific character: Hradčany, or "Castle Ward," bears the stamp of Bohemia's monarchs, of the princes, kings, and emperors of the Přemysl, Luxemburg, Jagiellon, and Habsburg lines; at its foot, in the hollow between the castle ridge, Petřín Hill, and Vltava River, lies Malá Strana, the "Lesser Town," once residence of the high nobles of the realm and now a favored address for embassies; across Charles Bridge, in Staré Město ("Old Town"), we can gain an idea of how the proud burghers and humbler folk lived, not least in Josefov, once the Jewish ghetto; and then Nové Město, to the south and east, is only in a relative sense the "New Town," having been founded by Emperor Charles IV. Palaces, abbeys, and other points of interest are also to be found in the more outlying districts, although for a day trip out of Prague, most visitors will first head for Karlštejn Castle.

The Royal Way

Prague is probably unique in that its main tourist route was marked out hundreds of years before guidebooks were invented; today it provides an optimal overview of the city's history and of the evolution of European architecture. The Royal, or Coronation, Way leads from the site of the old royal palace in Staré Město to St. Vitus's Cathedral in Prague Castle. The sovereigns traveled this route on the day of their coronation, even in later times when they resided in the castle or in Vienna. Old engravings give an idea of the pomp of these coronation processions. The stream of tourists today may be less spectacular, but there is still no better way to get a first impression of Prague.

The route begins at Powder Tower, the Gothic tower on the edge of the old town.

Left: *View of St. Wenceslas Square from the National Museum. In the foreground the equestrian statue of St. Wenceslas*

Below left: *Relics of socialism are now on sale at bargain prices*

Below center: *Detail of a facade in Malá Strana. Stucco relief depicting Our Lady*

Below right: *Traders, painters, and musicians on Charles Bridge, seen here in front of one of the sculptural groups by M. W. Jäckel*

U Fleků, a traditional pub in Staré Město

The site of the old palace is now occupied by the Civic Hall, a masterpiece of Czech Art Nouveau. Proceeding along Celetná, between rows of impressive patrician mansions, we soon find ourselves on Staroměstské náměstí, the grand square that has witnessed so many momentous events in the city's history; the inscription on a window of the town hall proudly affirms Prague's status as *caput regni*, "capital of the realm." We follow the royal procession across Malé náměstí into Karlova, one of the most characteristic Old Town lanes, with the seemingly endless facades of the Clementinum, the old Jesuit institute. The Baroque splendor of the Counter-Reformation era is also the keynote of Křižovnické náměstí, where the Royal Way emerges onto the bank of the Vltava to confront the eye with Prague's finest panorama: the Gothic Charles Bridge with its gallery of dramatic statues before the backdrop of the castle and Malá Strana, where the majestic dome of St. Nicholas adds a note of Roman grandeur. Crossing

Riding in a hackney carriage on Old Town Square with St. Nicholas in the background

the river and proceeding up Mostecká, we follow in the footsteps of the merchants who a thousand years ago traveled the east-west trade route. From Malostranské náměstí on, the way becomes steeper as it ascends the castle hill; Nerudova is lined with aristocratic mansions and fine burgherhouses, and heraldic figures and typical Prague house emblems abound. The castle ramp (Ke Hradu) presented the final challenge to the royal coach and horses before they reached Hradčanské náměstí, with the archbishop's palace and the main gate to the castle – the sentries today guard the president of the Czech Republic, who has his official residence in the former royal palace. The Royal Way leads through three courtyards to the Golden Gate of St. Vitus's Cathedral, by which the king entered Wenceslas Chapel; here the crown reposed on the hallowed reliquary bust of the tenth-century prince and patron saint of Bohemia. Walls studded with precious stones are no more than fitting for a room that housed the insignia of a divinely ordained monarch. The coronation itself took place in the soaring chancel of the cathedral, a jewel of Gothic architecture and sculpture.

The latter-day follower of the Royal Way can now pause to survey the Golden City spread out before him, and with the aid of the following pages plan a more intensive journey of discovery.

Right: *The choir vaulting in St. Vitus's Cathedral. On the capital of the column, an impressive depiction of the Fall of Man*

Below: *Exterior view of the Golden Gate, leading to the famous chapel of St. Wenceslas*

Prehistory Evidence of settlements in the Prague basin since the middle Stone Age.

4th century B.C. Arrival of the Boii, a Celtic tribe from Bononia (Bologna), giving origin to the name "Bohemia."

1st-5th century A.D. Colonization by Germanic tribes.

6th century Fleeing from the advancing Avars, Slavic peoples migrate to central Bohemia.

623-58 League of the Slavic tribes under the Franconian or north German merchant Samo.

9th century Emergence of the Greater Moravian Empire. The western Slavs, the Czechs (named after their legendary ancestor Čech), are ruled by the House of Přemysl. Princess Libuše allegedly prophesies the founding and the fame of the city of Prague (Praha, related to the word for "threshold" or "river rapids").

871-94 Bořivoj I, the first historically attested prince of the Czechs, and his wife

Tomb of Ottokar I (detail), St. Vitus's Cathedral

View of Prague, from Schedel's World Chronicle *(1493)*

Libuše prophesies the glory of Prague. Mosaic designed by Mikoláš Aleš, in the vestibule of the Staré Město Town Hall

Ludmila (of the Pšovs, a people of northern Bohemia) are baptized by Methodius, archbishop of the Greater Moravian Empire and "Apostle to the Slavs"; they adopt the Slavonic-Byzantine liturgy. The princely residence is moved from Levý Hradec (near Roztoky, north of Prague) to the Hradčany hill, where Prague Castle is founded and a first stone church is dedicated to Our Lady.

10th century Prague begins to flourish: the merchant Ibráhím ibn Ya'qūb, a Spanish Jew, describes it as "built of stone and lime and one of the most prosperous trading-centers far and wide."

920-35 Prince Wenceslas (Václav) acknowledges the primacy of the German kings and introduces the Latin liturgy; Prague is assigned to the diocese of Regensburg. Wenceslas is murdered by his brother, Boleslav I the Cruel, in Stará Boleslav, and becomes (after his grandmother Ludmila) the second Czech martyr and patron saint.

Seals with effigies of the Bohemian kings Wenceslas II and Vladislav II

973 Prague is elevated to the status of a bishopric, attached to the archdiocese of Mainz.

972-99 Prince Boleslav II founds the Benedictine convent of St. George in the castle, Bohemia's first religious institution.

993 Adalbert (Vojtěch), bishop of Prague, founds the first monastic community, the Benedictine abbey of Břevnov.

1061-92 For his support in the Investiture Controversy, Prince Vratislav II is rewarded by Emperor Henry IV with the

The burning of John Huss. Miniature from the Leitmeritz Gradual, *before 1517, Litoměřice County Museum*

title of King Vratislav I (1085). German, French, and Jewish merchants and artesans establish themselves on the banks of the Vltava.

1140-72 Prince Vladislav II (from 1158 King Vladislav I) founds the Premonstratensian abbey at Strahov, which becomes an important cultural center. The river is spanned by the stone Judith Bridge.

1197-1230 King Ottokar I (Přemysl I Otakar). Thanks to the silvermines at Kutná hora, Bohemia has a sound economic basis; it is confirmed as a hereditary kingdom in 1212.

1230-53 King Wenceslas I orders the expansion and fortification of the "First" or "Old Town of Prague" (Staré Město).

1253-78 Under Ottokar II (Přemysl II Otakar), the "Iron" or "Golden King," Bohemia becomes a major power. The "Lesser Town of Prague" (Malá Strana) receives its charter in 1257. In the war against Rudolf of Habsburg, Ottokar is killed at the battle of the Moravian Plain.

1306 The seven-year-old King Wenceslas III is murdered; the Přemysl dynasty has no male heir.

1310-46 John the Blind of Luxemburg, married to Elizabeth, the last of the Přemysl line. In 1244 Prague is made an archbishopric; work commences on St. Vitus's Cathedral.

1346-78 Charles I, crowned king of Germany and Rome in 1346, from 1355 Emperor Charles IV. Prague, known as the "Golden City" for the shimmer of its gilt lead roofs, becomes the political and cultural hub of the Holy Roman Empire, and with its forty thousand inhabitants is the biggest city in central Europe. Karlštejn castle is built for the safekeeping of the imperial insignia. Brilliant artists such as Peter Parler and Master Theoderich achieve a culmination of European Gothic in Prague.

The emperor, who had been brought up at the French court, changed his name from Wenceslas to Charles to place himself in the tradition of Charlemagne. He traveled widely, especially in Italy, and was a man of great learning. His humanist cast of mind was strongly tinged with medieval mysticism (the cult of relics as a supernatural justification of worldly power). He was one of the greatest collectors and patrons of the arts since antiquity. Petrarch was an honored guest at court.

Votive panel of Jan Očko of Vlašim, archbishop of Prague, before 1371, National Gallery in St. George's Convent

1393   John of Nepomuk, vicar-general of the archbishopric of Prague, is drowned in the Vltava by order of the king; canonized in 1729.

1409   The Kuttenberg (Kutná hora) Decree gives the main say in the running of the university to the Czech members, led by the rector, John Huss (Jan Hus). The

Fifteenth-century Hussite shield with the coat of arms of the Old Town, Prague City Museum

Renaissance tile with profile portrait of John Huss, Prague City Museum

1348   The Collegium Carolinum is founded on the model of Paris and Bologna as the first university in central Europe. Craftsmen are encouraged to settle in a "New Town" (Nové Město).

1356   The Golden Bull asserts the independence of the sovereign state from the pope and regulates the procedure for the election of the kings.

1378-1419   Wenceslas IV (king of Germany 1376-1400). Conflicts with the nobility and clergy, social unrest. Beginnings of a movement for ecclesiastical reform. Friction between Czechs and Germans over questions of religion and nationality.

The Second Defenestration of Prague, 23 May 1618

German professors and students resign in protest and move to Leipzig.

1415 Huss appears before the Council of Constance to defend his reformist theses, and is burned as a heretic. His followers demand the right to communion in both kinds *(sub utraque specid)*; the lay chalice becomes the symbol of the Hussite revolution.

1419 First Defenestration of Prague at the town hall of Nové Město on 30 July marks the beginning of the Hussite wars.

Emperor Rudolf II,
etching by Ägidius Sadeler, 1609

The Hussites split into two camps: the moderates (Utraquists, Calixtines), supported by the higher aristocracy and the university, and the radicals (Taborites), with a strong following among the peasants.

1420 Victory of the Taborites under Jan Žižka at Vítkov (Žižkov) outside Prague (14 July). Emperor Sigismund (brother of Wenceslas IV) is deposed as king of Bohemia.

1433 Council of Basel: the Utraquists agree to a compromise with the Catholic church that allows them the lay chalice and considerable freedom of religion (Compacts of Basel).

1434 Battle of Lipany: the Utraquist nobles defeat the people's army of the Taborites.

1436 Emperor Sigismund is crowned king of Bohemia.

1458-71 George of Poděbrady (Jiří z Poděbrad), the "People's" or "Hussite King."

1471-1526 The Polish-Lithuanian Jagiellon dynasty rules in Bohemia. Vladislav II is succeeded by Ludvík, who is killed fighting the Turks at Mohacs in 1526. The Habsburgs inherit the realms of Bohemia and Hungary.

1526-64 Ferdinand I. The Belvedere pavilion (1538-60) is the first pure Renaissance building north of the Alps. The Jesuits are invited to Bohemia in 1556.

1564-76 Maximilian II.

1576-1612 Rudolf II makes Prague once again the imperial capital and ushers in a new blossoming of culture. The emperor's collection of pictures is world-renowned, Prague is a magnet for late Renaissance (Mannerist) and early Baroque artists, architects, and men of learning from all over Europe, such as the astronomers Tycho de Brahe and Johannes Kepler. Mordechai Maisel and Rabbi Löw are the leading lights of a flourishing Jewish community. The Majesty Charter of 1609 grants freedom of religion. In the latter years of his life Rudolf falls out with his brothers and is effectively deposed.

1612-19 Matthias, brother of Rudolf II. The Second Defenestration of Prague (23 May 1618) is a protest against infringement of the Majesty Charter, and sparks off the Thirty Years' War. In 1619 Elector Frederick V of the Palatinate is chosen by the Protestants as king of Bohemia (the "Winter King").

1619-37 Ferdinand II.

1620 On 8 November, at the battle of Bílá hora (White Mountain, outside Prague), the Protestant army of the Bohemian and Moravian estates under Christian of Anhalt suffers a crushing defeat at the hands of the imperial army and the Catholic League under Maximilian of Bavaria and generals Buquoy and Tilly. Massive reprisals follow: 150,000 have to flee the country, one-half of all landed property is confiscated, and the Czech aristocracy is largely replaced by loyal Catholic nobles from the Habsburg lands. Bohemia is forcibly re-catholicized under the Counter-Reformation.

1621 The twenty-seven ringleaders of the 1618 rebellion are executed in front of Staré Město town hall on 21 June.

1623 The Bohemian Court Chancery is moved to Vienna, depriving Prague of political significance. Bohemia is demoted to "hereditary land" of the Habsburgs. Commander-in-chief Albrecht von Waldstein commissions the first Baroque mansion in Prague.

1648 Swedish troops occupy Hradčany and Malá Strana. The Peace of Westphalia ends the Thirty Years' War.

1650-1700 Migrant artists from Italy help to shape the Baroque face of Prague; the city's economic fortunes begin to revive.

Albrecht von Waldstein as Mars, detail of a ceiling fresco by Baccio del Bianco in Waldstein Palace, c. 1630

1700-40 The era of high Baroque sees major architects (C. and K. I. Dientzenhofer, Fischer von Erlach, Santin-Aichel) and sculptors (M. Braun, F. M. Brokoff) at work in Prague.

1740-80 Maria Theresa, queen of Bohemia and Hungary, regent of the Habsburg empire (her husband Francis I is emperor). Prague is besieged by the French and the Prussians three times in the course of the

Josef Václav Myslbek: Libuše and Přemysl, first plaster model

Josef Dietzler: Maria Theresa's Coronation Procession through Prague *(detail), 1743; on the right the tower of Staré Město Town Hall*

War of the Austrian Succession and the Seven Years' War. Enlargement and re-modeling of Prague Castle.

1780-90 Joseph II, the "enlightened" emperor, abolishes feudalism and secularizes many religious institutions. His Edict of Tolerance of 1781 accords a measure of freedom to non-Catholic faiths; life becomes easier for the Jews; the ghetto is now known as "Josefov."

1784 Hradčany, Malá Strana, Staré Město, and Nové Město are amalgamated into the City of Prague (72,000 inhabitants). Tension between Germans and Czechs is again on the increase.

1792-1835 Francis II, from 1804 Francis I of Austria. Chancellor Metternich clamps down on emancipatory movements. During the Napoleonic wars Prague is occupied by French and Russian troops.

Rudolf von Alt: The Old Council Chamber in Staré Město Town Hall, *watercolor (1858)*

1845 Opening of the Prague-Vienna railroad. The process of industrialization gains pace, and working-class suburbs take shape.

1848-1916 Francis Joseph's reign sees the upsurge of Czech nationalism, typified by the "National Theater Generation" of patriotic writers and artists. In the field of architecture, Historicism and Secessionism (Art Nouveau) dominate.

Emil Zillich: The Laying of the Foundation Stone of the National Theater *by František Palacký, the "Father of the Nation," (1868)*

1848 The historian František Palacký organizes the Slav Congress. The "Whit Uprising" of Czech radicals is crushed.

1861 The Germans lose their majority in the municipal parliament.

1866 The Peace of Prague (23 August) marks the end of hostilities between Austria and Prussia and the end of the German League.

1868 The National Theater is founded.

1882 The university is split into two, one Czech and one German.

1891 The Jubilee Exhibition presents Bohemia as the industrial heart of the Austro-Hungarian monarchy.

1918 The Czechoslovak Republic is proclaimed in Prague on 28 October; its first president is Tomáš G. Masaryk.

1920 Greater Prague is created (by 1930 the population is 850,000, nearly double that of 1914).

Josef von Hellich: Portrait of Božena Němcová, *oil on canvas (1845)*

1939 German troops march in to occupy the "Reich Protectorate of Bohemia and Moravia."

1942 On 27 May Deputy Reichsprotektor Reinhard Heydrich is assassinated in the suburb of Libeň; as a reprisal, the village of Lidice, northwest of Prague, is wiped off the face of the earth. Thirty-six thousand Prague Jews are murdered by the Nazis up to the end of the war.

1945 The people of Prague stage an uprising against the Germans on 5 May; four days later the Red Army enters the city.

1948 Czechoslovakia is declared a "People's" (Communist) Republic; its first president is Klement Gottwald (to 1953).

1954 The population of Prague reaches the million mark.

The former Federal Parliament, built in 1967-73 by a team of architects under Karel Prager

In autumn 1989 the call goes forth: "Havel to the castle!"

1960 Under a new constitution the Czechoslovak Socialist Republic comes into being, but the powers that be remain the same.

1968 Party leader Alexander Dubček introduces reforms, aiming to create "socialism with a human face." The "Prague Spring" of liberalization comes to an abrupt end on 21 August when Warsaw Pact troops march in.

1969 The ČSSR becomes a federal entity. Gustav Husák is elected party leader, from 1975 also president.

1974 Prague's first metro line opens.

1977 Charter 77, a campaign for civil rights, is founded.

The John Huss memorial on Staroměstské náměstí is a popular meeting place

1987 Reconstruction of the "Royal Way" is completed.

1988 In the wake of Gorbachev's Perestroika program a government reshuffle takes place in Prague.

1989 In October and November, demonstrations for democracy on Wenceslas Square are broken up by the police. Twelve opposition groups unite as the Civic Forum. On 24 and 25 November, Alexander Dubček and Václav Havel, a famous author and longtime dissident, address a mass rally of half a million people. The presidium and secretariat of the Communist party resign. A general strike is called. On 10 December Marián Čalfa forms a cabinet with a non-Communist majority. On 28 and 29 December Dubček is elected President of the Federal Assembly, and Havel is elected the first non-Communist president since 1945.

1990 The Czech and Slovak Federative Republic is proclaimed on 20 April. Pope John Paul II visits Prague. In June, the Civic Forum wins an overwhelming victory in the first free elections since 1946.

1992 The conservative Civic Democrats emerge as the strongest party in the June elections and form a coalition government under premier Václav Klaus; the strongest Slovak party calls for independence.

1993 After the secession of Slovakia, Prague becomes the capital of the independent Czech Republic on 1 January. Václav Havel is elected president.

Prague: Facts and Figures

Population: 1,300,000 (January 1993)
Area: 192 square miles
Location: 50° 05' north, the same as Bonn, Cracow, Kharkov, Winnipeg, and the southern tip of England; 14° 27' east
Height above sea level: 580-1302 feet
Climate: average annual temperature 9°C (48°F); June 17° (63°F); July 19° (66°F); December 0° (32°F); January –1° (30°F)
Average annual precipitation: 19 inches – driest month February, wettest month July
The **Vltava** flows through Prague from south to north over a distance of 19¼ miles; it has ten islands and is spanned by eighteen bridges
Administrative divisions: ten municipal districts

Hradčany

Prague Castle and District

Besides the complex of Prague Castle itself (Pražský hrad) and the Belvedere pavilion, the Hradčany quarter also includes the former suburbs reaching as far as Strahov Monastery. The impressive palace buildings, churches, monasteries, and mansions of the nobility and bourgeoisie bear witness to more than a thousand years of Czech history.

Prague Castle has its origins in the late ninth century. Around 875 Bořivoj I, the first historically recorded Bohemian ruler, moved the residence of the House of Přemysl from Levý Hradec, about seven miles to the north, to the ridge overlooking the Vltava ford. He had a fort built of wood and protected by earthworks and palisades, and under his aegis the first stone church, dedicated to the Virgin Mary, was erected within the precinct around 890. The first stone escarpments were built in the eleventh century, and during the reign of Prince Soběslav I (1125-40) a Romanesque castle complex arose, which was modified but not appreciably enlarged over the next five hundred years. Emperor Charles IV (1346-78) of the House of Luxemburg made Prague Castle the hub of the Holy Roman Empire, and established the Gothic cathedral of St. Vitus as the mother church of the new archbishopric of Prague. Soon after his death the castle fell into disrepair; his successors preferred to reside in the Old Town, near Powder Tower. It was not until 1484, after the ravages of the Hussite wars, that the castle again saw the splendors of court life with the monarchs of the Jagiellon dynasty. Vladislav II, king of Bohemia and Hungary, had the Old Palace rebuilt on a grand scale, in a late Gothic style with incipient Renaissance elements. The first Habsburg emperors improved the quality of life in Hradčany by adding extensive gardens and the Belvedere pavilion, and Rudolf II (1576-1612) once again restored the castle to the status of imperial residence and made it a cosmopolitan center of late Renaissance culture. Reconstruction in the middle of the eighteenth century, under Empress Maria Theresa, removed the last traces of the medieval fortress. Only with the completion of the cathedral, less than a hundred years ago, did the castle complex acquire its present-day appearance. Since 1918 it has been the official residence of the president of Czechoslovakia, and since 1993 of the Czech Republic.

One of Prague's finest views: from Smetanovo Nábřeží to Charles Bridge, Lesser Town,

I First Courtyard

První nádvoří

Hradčanské náměstí

After the Seven Years' War against Prussia, Empress Maria Theresa ordered the filling in of the deep moat that had hitherto marked the western end of the castle precinct, and the demolition or total reconstruction of existing medieval buildings to create a new "Royal Palace." The work was carried out between 1756 and 1774 to a plan by the royal architect from Vienna, Nicolo Pacassi. The **west and south wings** ("Theresian" or "Pacassi" wings) of the new palace complex mark the end of Prague Baroque and the transition to a sober Neoclassicism. Ignaz Platzer, the leading sculptor of Prague Rococo, was entrusted with the sculptural work: battling titans flank the outer gateway, and vases and martial emblems adorn the attic story (most of these have been replaced by replicas).

Entrance to the castle; in the background the Matthias Gate, leading to the second courtyard

The **Matthias Gate** (1614), built as part of the fortifications during the reign of Emperor Matthias, was incorporated by Pacassi into the main frontage. With its broad expanse of masonry and horizontal courses of rustication, it is reminiscent of the Manneristic late sixteenth-century citadels of northern Italy; the pronounced vertical emphasis – cutting through four floors of Pacassi's facade – and the curving sides of the superstructure, on the other hand, foreshadow Baroque church facades of decades later (e.g., St. Savior's in Staré Město). The Matthias Gate may thus be regarded as the earliest example of Prague Baroque, opening up Bohemia to the new style. Formerly attributed to Vincenzo Scamozzi, it is now considered to be the work of Giovanni Maria Filippi, court architect in Prague.

and Castle Ward; at left, Liechtenstein Palace on Kampa Island

View from Strahov Monastery to the palace wings of the castle and St. Vitus's Cathedral; at left, above the ramp, Schwarzenberg Palace and Salm Palace, behind them the Archbishop's Palace and the arcaded Riding School

2   Second Courtyard, Castle Gallery

Druhé nádvoří, Obrazárna
Pražského hradu

The wings lining the courtyard, mainly of sixteenth-century origin, were given their present facades by Pacassi. The early Baroque **sandstone fountain**, by the Prague sculptor Hieronymus Kohl and the Italian stonemason Francesco della Torre, is based on the classical mussel-shell motif. The central column is decorated with figures of ancient gods (Mercury, Neptune, Hercules, and Vulcan, dated 1686), tritons, and lions; the imperial eagle that crowned it was removed in 1918.

The **Castle Gallery** in the old stables (north wing) displays some of the works of art that once made up the collections of the Habsburg emperors of the sixteenth and seventeenth centuries, the most renowned of which was assembled by Rudolf II. There are paintings by Spranger, Titian, Tintoretto, Bassano, Veronese, Reni, Brandl, Kupecký, and others. **Major works**: Hans von Aachen (1552-1615) of Cologne, court painter from 1596 on: *Emperor Matthias* and *Head of a Girl* (**Room 1**); Adriaen de Vries (ca. 1560-1626): bust of Emperor Rudolf II (**Room 2**), bronze horse (**Room 3**); and Peter Paul Rubens (1577-1640): *Assembly of the Olympian Gods* (**Room 4**), an important early work, probably painted in Mantua in 1602 in homage to the ducal family of the Gonzagas (restored 1963-64). In **Room 6** an attempt has been made to reconstruct the Rudolfine collection using photographs illustrating works recorded in old inventories. Behind glass, the foundations (excavated 1950) of the oldest church in the castle precinct, St. Mary's, founded by Prince Bořivoj I around 890, can be seen. It was Bořivoj and his wife Ludmila (later canonized) who adopted the Slavonic-Byzantine liturgy from the Greater Moravian Empire; early in the tenth century the Latin rite was brought to Bohemia by priests from the bishopric of Regensburg,

The sandstone fountain in the second courtyard dates from 1686

to which Prague belonged until 973. The layer above it probably dates from the eleventh century.

On the upper floor of the north wing are the **Spanish Hall** (Španělsky sál) and the former Rudolf Gallery (Rudolfova galerie), today used for state occasions and not accessible to the public. It was here that Rudolf II installed his celebrated collection of works of art and curios, one of the largest and most valuable in Europe. Soon after his death the contents were dispersed far and wide, some objects ending up in Vienna, others in Sweden.

3 Holy Cross Chapel
Kaple Svatého Kříže

The late Baroque chapel in the southeast corner of the second courtyard was built by Anselmo Lurago around 1760 to a design by Pacassi; the interior was renovated in a neo-Baroque style in the middle of the nineteenth century. The wealth of marble and gilt ornamentation effectively sets off the generously proportioned space; the vault is frescoed with Old Testament scenes by V. Kandler.

4 Third Courtyard
Třetí nádvoří

Emerging from the gateway of the second courtyard, we are confronted by the neo-Gothic **west facade of St. Vitus's**, on completion of which the cathedral was consecrated in 1929. The bronze doors depict the building history of the edifice (center) and the legends of St. Wenceslas (right) and St. Adalbert (left); the tympanum reliefs were completed as recently as 1952. To the right, the **Provost's House** has a statue of St. Wenceslas in a corner niche, executed in 1662 by Johann Georg Bendl, Bohemia's first major Baroque sculptor. In the east wall of the house, masonry and a window can be seen that have survived from the Romanesque bishop's palace. Under a sheltering roof lie the **foundations** of the old bishop's chapel, dedicated to St. Maurice, and the eleventh-century basilica of St. Vitus, predecessor of the cathedral. The granite obelisk, over 55 feet high, was erected in 1928 to commemorate the fallen of World War I.

The Gothic **equestrian statue of St. George** (1373), a masterpiece by the brothers Martin and Georg of Cluj (Transylvania), stood on various sites before being used as part of a fountain (original in St. Georg's Convent). The first freestanding equestrian sculpture since the "Magdeburg Rider" of 1240, it represents a great step forward: the two artists, Hungary's leading High Gothic sculptors, translated the goldsmith's craft of their homeland into large-scale sculptural form, anticipating the stylish elegance of courtly art around 1400 – even Renaissance elements can be detected. An Italian influence was no doubt already at work, for Hungary was then ruled by monarchs of the Neapolitan Anjou line. With an easy grace, the saint is captured in the moment of spearing the dragon. The powerful horse, with its pronounced turn of the head toward the dragon, may not, however, be exactly as the brothers intended: an eyewitness account of 1562 relates how during a tournament the "magnificent horse" was shattered, and had to be recast. In its present state it bears a striking resemblance to equestrian studies from the pen of Leonardo da Vinci.

To the north of St. Vitus's the **Mihulka**, or **Powder Tower**, rises from the moat below the ramparts. Built in 1496 by Benedikt Ried as part of the Late Gothic fortifications, it was used as a laboratory by the alchemists and sorcerers of Rudolf II in their search for the philosopher's stone and the elixir of youth. Today it houses an exhibition of the handicrafts of Rudolf's time.

5 Garden on the Ramparts, Paradise Garden
Zahrada na valech, Rajská zahrada

A covered stairway leads from the southeast corner of the third courtyard to a delightful terrace of art and greenery, which affords breathtaking views down to the river, with the Malá Strana quarter straggling up the slopes between the castle and Petřín Hill. The **Garden on the Ramparts** (Zahrada na valech), created in the mid-nineteenth century when the moat was filled in with earth, was given its present form in the 1920s by the Slovenian architect Josip Plećnik, first castle architect of the republic, whose renovating and remodeling hand can be seen at various points. Below the Ludvík Wing of the Old Palace stand two obelisks to mark where the victims of the 1618 defenestration landed. The smaller **Paradise Garden** (Rajská zahrada) leads back toward Hradčanské náměstí; it was created in 1562 by the governor of Bohemia, Archduke Ferdinand of Tyrol.

Equestrian statue of St. George, by Martin and Georg of Cluj – a masterpiece of Gothic sculpture (1373)

6 Old Palace

Starý palác

The Pacassi facade (with putti by Ignaz Platzer, 1760) on the eastern side of the third courtyard marks the entrance to the three-story **Old Royal Palace**. Above the remains of the first, ninth-century structure, which extend under the courtyard, Romanesque and Gothic stories were built

in the times of the Přemysl and Luxemburg kings, between the eleventh and fourteenth centuries. The upper story represents the final, Late Gothic phase of the building's history, dating from the reign of King Vladislav II of the Jagiellon dynasty, at the end of the fifteenth century. The side of the palace facing the east end of the cathedral provides an instructive lesson in architectural style: the open arcades are early Gothic, stemming from the palace of King Ottokar II (1253-1278), the buttresses are Late Gothic, and the windows of the Vladislav Hall are pure Renaissance – the first appearance of this style in Prague and Bohemia. The left window bears the inscription "Wladislaw rex Ungariae et Bohemiae 1493." No doubt the royal residence in Buda (today Budapest) had served as the model, for there, under King Matthias Corvinus, Italian architects had introduced the new style. In the fire of 1541 the Vladislav Hall lost its steeply pitched roofs, of the type that can still be seen at St. Barbara's, Kutná Hora.

The lobby, where the ticket office is situated, incorporates parts of the wall of the Romanesque palace built by Prince Soběslav I before 1140. The Green Chamber to the left (now the bookshop) was used in early times for sessions of court, and under Emperor Ferdinand I as an audience chamber; the Baroque ceiling fresco of the Judgment of Solomon was originally in the

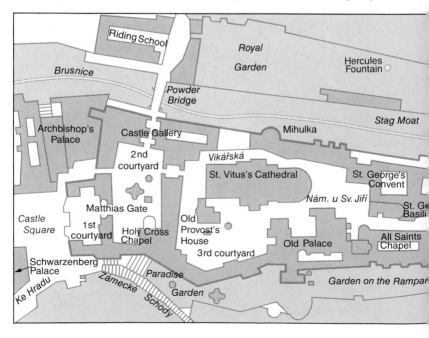

Vladislav Hall in the Old Palace is the largest and finest secular hall of the late Middle Ages

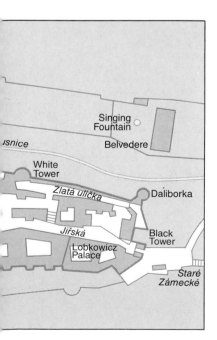

Burgrave's Chancery. The adjacent Vladislav Chamber (not usually accessible), the bedchamber and audience chamber of Vladislav II, is a charming room with a rhomboid stellar vault lined with blue, red, and gold, by Benedikt Ried (1493).

Vladislav Hall, a pierless room of majestic dimensions – 203 feet long, 53 feet wide, and up to 43 feet high – is both technically and artistically a masterpiece. It was built between 1493 and 1502 by Benedikt Ried, from Piesting in Austria, court architect to Vladislav II, who brought Prague Gothic to its climax and to the threshold of the Renaissance. In bygone days it saw rumbustious equestrian tournaments, sumptuous coronation banquets, and bustling markets; today, the president of the republic is elected here. The hall is most renowned for its delicately intertwining ribbed vaulting, which emanates from six pairs of buttresses that rise through three floors (the Romanesque and early Gothic stories are directly beneath). The curvilinear ribbing is characteristic of the final, "Baroque" phase of Gothic, as exempli-

31

Land-Table Chamber in the Old Palace

fied in many hall churches; making its first appearance in Kutná Hora, where Ried was in charge of work on St. Barbara's, it spread deep into Austria, where it markedly influenced the "Danube" school. The windows and portals, on the other hand, remind us that a new wind was already blowing, bringing with it Renaissance ideals.

The **Ludvík Wing**, which projects to the south, demonstrates how Ried quickly made the new style his own. It is named after Ludvík, the son of Vladislav II, who was crowned king of Bohemia in 1509, at the age of three; the monogram above the doorway of the secretary's office in the Bohemian Chancery recalls the event.

The next room, **Governor's Hall**, has gone down in history for a much more significant event. It was from the window in the east (left) wall that on 23 May 1618 representatives of the Protestant estates threw the imperial councillors Jaroslav Martinic and Vilém Slavata, with their secretary Philipp Fabricius, into the ditch 50 feet below – such was the "traditional" punishment for traitors! Although Martinic and Fabricius suffered barely a scratch, Slavata was badly hurt, but survived to write a vivid report of his experience. This, the "Second Defenestration of Prague," sparked off the Thirty Years' War.

A narrow, enclosed footbridge leads from the Ludvík Wing, next to the spiral staircase, to the royal oratory in St.Vitus's. The **Imperial Court Chancellery** (upstairs, not usually accessible) has retained its furnishings from the time of Rudolf II, when it was the administrative center of the Holy Roman Empire.

At the east end of Vladislav Hall a terrace opens, offering a fine view of the city. A Renaissance portal by Giovanni Gargiolli leads to the gallery of the royal **All Saints' Chapel**. The original Romanesque structure was gothicized by Peter Parler, and later (1570-71) remodeled by Udalrico Aostalis in the Renaissance style and extended to connect with Vladislav Hall; after 1755 it was used by the Institute of Noblewomen. The oldest painting is a Deposition by Hans von Aachen (turn of the sixteenth century) on the right-hand side altar. The Baroque depiction of All Saints on the high altar was painted by Wenzel Lorenz Reiner in 1729; the frame was carved by Peter Prachner around 1765. A Baroque reliquary on the north wall of the nave houses the remains of St. Procopius, abbot of the Benedictine monastery in Sázava (died 1052) and one of the patron saints of Bohemia; a cycle of paintings by Christian Dittmann (1699) illustrates his life.

To the left of the chapel entrance a Renaissance portal leads to the **Diet Chamber**, former meeting-place of the estates assembly and venue for the election of the king; later, up to 1847, it was the chamber of sessions of the Bohemian Supreme Court. The late Gothic rebuilding of the hall was supervised by Ried; Bonifaz Wolmut contributed the Renaissance podium for the chief registrar. On the right of the royal throne sat the archbishop and the prelates, on the left the officials of the Bohemian administration, while the other benches were reserved for the lords and cavaliers; the representatives of the cities with special privileges (but without voting rights) took their place on the gallery. The paintings portray Habsburg monarchs: Maria Theresa and her consort, Francis Stephen of Lorraine (Emperor Francis I), their sons Joseph II and Leopold II, and Francis II (Francis I of Austria).

On the first floor (doorway to the left of the equestrian stairwell) are situated the **Land-Table Chambers**, where registers were kept of the property of the nobility, the clergy (churches and monasteries), and the municipalities, and where the most important decisions of the diet were recorded. The old land registry from the thirteenth century, on the ground floor, was destroyed by fire in 1541; of the "land-tables" subsequently filed, 1,714 folios have survived, most of which are now kept in the Central State Archives. In 1838 the presidium chamber, which is decorated with the coats of arms of the high officers, became the home of the Crown Archive, which had previously been installed in Karlštejn Castle and in the cathedral.

The **equestrian stairwell** was built with very low steps to enable knights to ride in full armor from the courtyard up to Vladislav Hall for the tournaments held there. The truncated twining ribs of Ried's magnificent vaulting spring directly from the walls, without consoles.

One of the halls of the Old Palace will in future house the **treasury of St. Vitus's Cathedral**, which comprises such priceless objects as reliquaries, liturgical vessels, and vestments from the eighth to the nineteenth centuries. Among the most notable items are: the so-called Holy Lance; Gothic reliquary busts of SS. Ludmila, Adalbert, Wenceslas, and Vitus; the armor of St. Wenceslas; the sword of St. Stephen, king of Hungary; the coronation cross (thirteenth/fourteenth century, presumably of French origin, with fragments of the Cross, antique gems and cameos, addi-

The equestrian stairwell leading from the courtyard to Vladislav Hall

tional relics of Christ donated by Charles IV in 1354, and the base dating from 1522); the reliquary cross of Pope Urban V (1368-76, niello engraving); an onyx chalice, gift of Charles IV (1350); the so-called Parler Monstrance, a reliquary with the emblem of the master mason Peter Parler of Schwäbisch Gmünd (late fourteenth century); a jewel-casket with Venetian ivory carving (c. 1360; it originally held the bones of St. Sigismund, king of Burgundy, which were acquired by Charles IV in St. Moritz); the Záviš Cross, donated by Zawisch von Falkenstein of the Rosenberg family (late thirteenth century).

7 St. Vitus's Cathedral
Katedrála svatého Víta

Coronation and burial church of the Bohemian monarchs; chancel featuring the first net vaulting, triforium busts and royal tombs by Parler: major works of Gothic architecture and sculpture.

Vitus, a fourth-century Sicilian martyr, was a popular saint in Slavic lands. Emperor Henry I presented Prince Wenceslas (who was himself later canonized) with a precious arm relic, which was venerated in the Vitus Rotunda, a round church built around 930. And when Charles IV acquired the saint's bones in Pavia and brought them to Prague, the city became a veritable center of the Vitus cult.

When Prague became an archbishopric in 1344 Charles IV laid the foundation

The south tower of St. Vitus has a Renaissance gallery offering a fine panorama of the city

stone of the Gothic cathedral. The design and supervision of the works was entrusted to Matthias of Arras, who took his inspiration from the chancels of Narbonne and Rodez cathedrals in the south of France. By the time of his death, in 1352, he had completed the eight polygonal radiating chapels and the adjacent sections of the ambulatory. For the next forty-seven years, until his death in 1399, the master in charge was Peter Parler. Hailing from Swabia, the various architects and sculptors of

The Golden Gate, through which the monarchs entered the cathedral to be crowned

the Parler family were of epochal influence in central and southern Germany and Bohemia in the second half of the fourteenth century (the name probably derives from the French *parlier*, the "spokesman" of a stonemasons' lodge). Peter's father, Heinrich, inaugurated the specifically German mode of Late Gothic around 1350, with the hall chancel of Holy Cross Church in his home town of Schwäbisch Gmünd. In Prague, Peter had to follow the basic plan laid down by his predecessor, but allowed himself liberties with the classic cathedral model and engendered a marked shift of style toward Late Gothic, especially in the vaulting and the design of the south facade. He first completed the remaining radiating chapels on rectangular plans and proceeded to build the Old Sacristy, the main superstructure of the chancel (consecrated in 1385), the south facade with the Golden Gate, and the St. Wenceslas chapel. In 1421, the Hussite wars stopped work on the cathedral, which remained a torso for several hundred years, until between 1872 and 1929 cathedral architects Josef Mocker and Kamil Hilbert completed nave and aisles in a conservative neo-Gothic style, adding the west facade with its three portals and twin spires.

Artistically, the most interesting exterior feature is the south side, which Parler saw as the principal facade, relating to both the Old Palace and the city below. The **Golden Gate** (Porta Aurea) was the doorway by which the kings entered on coronation day. Because of the obtruding St. Wenceslas

The chancel of St. Vitus is Peter Parler's chef-d'œuvre; the nave is neo-Gothic, with ▷
triforium busts continuing Parler's original sequence (see also p. 37)

chapel the triple-arched outer face had to funnel into only a single inner door, and the trumeau that would have served as central mullion in a French double portal was advanced to constitute a freestanding pillar. Without parallel in central Europe at the time (1370-71) was the depiction of the Last Judgment in Bohemian glass mosaic, from a cartoon by Nicoletto Semitecolo; the work, which shows Venetian and Byzantine influence, has been restored several times. Before Christ in the mandorla, Mary and John the Baptist kneel in intercession, with the nationally venerated saints Procopius, Sigismund, Vitus, Adalbert, Ludmila, and Wenceslas arrayed below; in the spandrels of the central arch we see Charles IV and his fourth wife, Elizabeth of Pomerania.

The Gothic section of the **Bell Tower,** or Wenceslas Tower, was built by 1406, and is the work of Johann and Wenzel Parler, Peter's sons. In 1562 Bonifaz Wolmut added a gallery and spire in Renaissance style; after coming under Prussian artillery fire during the Seven Years' War it was given a Baroque facelift around 1770. The gallery (open summer only) affords a magnificent view.

Peter Parler's abundant creative genius can best be admired in the **chancel**. The "earthly" zone of the ambulatory blends into the soaring, radiant space of the "heavenly Jerusalem," with its intricate tracery and marvelous culmination of net vaulting. For all its vertical momentum, the horizontal is also emphasized: above the arcade sector Parler inserted a triforium, a narrow gallery that is in turn marked off by a cornice that juts out around the vaulting shafts. The divisions between the triforium bays constitute a unique gallery of **portrait busts**, sculpted between 1374 and 1385 by Parler himself and his assistants, and perpetuating in stone the founders, sponsors, canons, and the two master masons of the cathedral. Here, for the first time, Gothic sculpture casts off the shackles of medieval stereotypes and infuses its subjects with an individualism that heralds the Renaissance spirit. The "royal gallery" of the house of Luxemburg begins at the apex of the chancel with the busts of Charles IV and his fourth wife, Elizabeth of Pomerania; to the left follow the emperor's three previous wives and his two brothers, to the right his parents, and his son Wenceslas IV and wife; archbishops and clerks of the works make up the rest of the figures, with a partition being reserved for a bust of Matthias

of Arras and a Parler self-portrait. The triforium is not accessible, but casts of some of the busts are on display at Karlštejn and in Lobkowicz Palace, and occasionally in the Old Sacristy or the Old Palace.

The **Habsburg Mausoleum** in the choir was commissioned by Rudolf II from the Dutch sculptor Alexander Colin, who between 1570 and 1589 collaborated on the tomb of Emperor Maximilian I in Innsbruck. The reclining figures of Ferdinand I, his wife Anna Jagiello, and their son Maximilian II are carved on the marble tombs. The relief panels on the sides carry portraits of those buried in the

Scheme of the triforium busts in the chancel of St. Vitus's

1 Václav Hradec	12 Charles IV
2 Matthias of Arras	13 John
3 Peter Parler	of Luxemburg
4 Andreas Kottik	14 Elizabeth
5 Beneš	of Bohemia
of Weitmühl	15 Wenceslas IV
6 Wenceslas	16 Joan
of Luxemburg	of Bavaria
7 John Henry	17 Arnošt
of Moravia	of Pardubice
8 Blanche of Valois	18 Jan Očko
9 Anne of the	of Vlašim
Palatinate	19 Johann
10 Anne	of Jenzstein
of Schweidnitz	20 Mikuláš
11 Elizabeth of	Holubec
Pomerania	21 Leonhard Busko

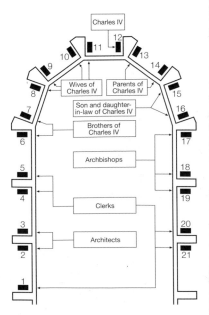

Sequence
of pictures:

	11
9	10
7	8
5	6
3	4
1	2

Sequence
of pictures:

	12
13	14
15	16
17	18
19	20
21	

The triforium busts, which show an individuality of human expression unprecedented in Gothic sculpture

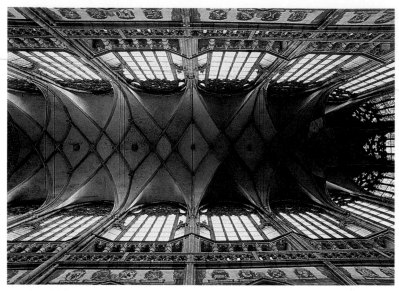

A novelty in late Gothic architecture is the net vault created by Parler for the majestic chancel of St. Vitus

Royal Crypt. The splendid Renaissance grille is by Georg Schmidthammer, artisan to the Prague court.

The **Royal Crypt** (access via Holy Cross Chapel) was refurbished for the thousand-year anniversary of St. Wenceslas in 1929. To the left and right of the bronze sarcophagus that holds the remains of Charles IV ("Karel") are King Ladislaus Postumus (1439-57) – son of Elizabeth of Luxemburg and King Albrecht of Habsburg – and

the "people's king" George (Jiří) of Poděbrady (1458-71); behind lie Charles's two sons Wenceslas IV and Johann of Görlitz; his four wives (Blanche of Valois, Anna of the Palatinate, Anna of Schweidnitz, and Elizabeth of Pomerania) each share a common casket with their children; an original Renaissance pewter sarcophagus holds the remains of Rudolf II, and a casket in Empire style those of Archduchess Maria Amalia of Parma (died 1804), a

Plan of St. Vitus's Cathedral

1 Tomb of Count Leopold Schlick **2** Vladislav Oratory **3** Mary Magdalen Chapel **4a, b** Wood reliefs by Kaspar Bechterle **5** Altar of St. John of Nepomuk **6** John of Nepomuk Chapel **7** Reliquary (Saxon) Chapel **8** Lady Chapel **9** Chapel of St. John the Baptist

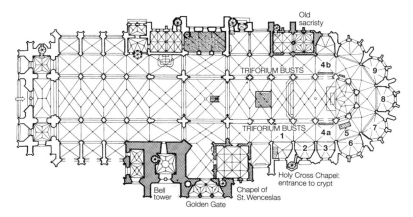

daughter of Maria Theresa. **Excavations** have revealed fragments of the Vitus Rotunda, in which Prince Wenceslas was buried in 935, and remains of the Romanesque basilica of the eleventh century.

The **ambulatory and radiating chapels** harbor a wealth of art from the Gothic to the Baroque eras. The **marble memorial** to **Count Leopold Schlick [1]**, field marshal and lord chancellor of Bohemia, is one of the finest examples of Bohemian High Baroque portraiture; it was fashioned around 1723 by the Tyrolean sculptor Matthias Bernhard Braun to a design by Joseph Emanuel Fischer von Erlach (son of the Vienna court architect Johann Bernhard Fischer von Erlach), who took his inspiration from Bernini's funerary sculptures in Rome. The **Vladislav Oratory [2]** was the king's private gallery, built in 1493 with direct access from the Old Palace. The pendant bears the monogram of Vladislav II, the commissioning monarch, the projecting balustrade the arms of Hungary and Bohemia, and the balustrade (from left to right) those of Dalmatia, Lower Lusatia, Slavonia, Poland, Moravia, Luxemburg, Silesia, and Upper Lusatia. This magnificent example of a Late Gothic style originating in southern Germany and characterized by filigree "branch-and-twig" work was once ascribed to Benedikt Ried, but is now considered to be the work of Hans Spiess of Frankfurt. The **Mary Magdalen chapel [3]** contains the tombstones of the cathedral architects Matthias of Arras and Peter Parler, from around 1400. Two large-scale **wood reliefs [4]**, carved to the order of Emperor Ferdinand II around 1630 by Kaspar Bechterle or Bechteller (the court cabinet-maker) or possibly by Kajetan Bendl (Georg Bendl the Elder?), are intriguing contemporary illustrations of events from the Thirty Years' War: in the south aisle the vandalizing of the cathedral by Calvinist iconoclasts in 1619, and in the north aisle the flight of the "Winter King" Frederick V of the Palatinate after his defeat at Bílá hora in 1620.

The silver **reliquary altar** of St. John of Nepomuk **[5]** was donated by Emperor Charles VI to mark the canonization of the former vicar-general of the archdiocese of Prague, who in 1393, having aroused the ire of King Wenceslas IV in a dispute over ecclesiastical privilege, was drowned in the Vltava; he was only canonized in 1729, after the Jesuits had taken up his cause. The sarcophagus contains the saint's bones and his tongue, which reputedly showed no signs of decay when exhumed many years

The Habsburg Mausoleum in the choir, with the reclining figure of Emperor Ferdinand I flanked by his son, Maximilian II, and his wife Anna

after his death (according to legend, John refused to betray the queen's confession, even under torture). The ornamental metalwork was executed by the Vienna silversmith Joseph Johann Würth after sketches by J. E. Fischer von Erlach and a wooden model by Antonio Corradini. The marble balustrade, allegorical figures, baldachin, and hovering angels are late Baroque, and

Tomb of Count Leopold Schlick

The silver reliquary altar of St. John of Nepomuk in the ambulatory

were added by Ignác Novák, a Malá Strana silversmith, around 1770.

The **chapel of St. John of Nepomuk [6]** holds the tomb of Jan Očko of Vlašim, cardinal archbishop of Prague and longstanding counselor to Charles IV. Relics of St. Adalbert are here preserved in a glass shrine, and Gothic **murals** by the court painter Oswald depict the decapitation of St. Catherine and the baptism of St. Ottilia by St. Erhard, bishop of Regensburg, to whom the chapel was originally dedicated.

The three chapels at the apex contain limestone sarcophagi with the remains of **Přemyslid** rulers, works of expressive piety by Parler and his assistants (later damaged by the Calvinists). Charles IV had the bones of his predecessors transferred from the Romanesque crypt of the cathedral to their present resting-place. The most impressive figural carving is to be found in the **Reliquary**, or **Saxon Chapel [7]**, dedicated to SS. Adalbert and Dorothy, where Ottokar I (right) and Ottokar II (left) recline. The *Adoration of the Magi* fresco by Master Oswald (c. 1372) is one of the largest murals of Bohemian High Gothic. **Lady Chapel [8]** and the **chapel of St. John the Baptist [9]** are the resting-places of the

eleventh-century rulers Břetislav I, in full armor, Spitihněv II, Břetislav II, and Bořivoj II.

8 Chapel of St. Wenceslas
Svatováclavská kaple

Reliquary chapel of the Bohemian national saint, one of Europe's most awesome High Gothic interiors, studded with a thousand precious stones.

Prince Wenceslas, or Václav (reigned 920-35), who was murdered in Stará Boleslav by order of his brother Boleslav, was soon venerated as the major martyr of the house of Přemysl. To atone for his crime, Boleslav I ("the Cruel") had the body of his brother brought to Prague Castle and buried in the Vitus Rotunda, which Wenceslas had begun to build. On this site, at the southwest corner of the choir of the new cathedral, Charles IV commissioned from Parler a funerary and reliquary chapel for his revered ancestor, which was erected between 1358 and 1367 and furnished "with such exquisiteness as the world has never seen." The emperor, who regarded relics and precious works of art as important accoutrements of his "God-given" position, had founded Karlštejn Castle as a repository for the relics of the Savior and the imperial crown jewels; now he wished for a chapel shrine in which the bones of the patron saint might rest as close as possible to the altar and the Bohemian coronation insignia. As in Karlštejn, the walls gleam with gold leaf and polished semiprecious stones of Bohemian provenance – over thirteen hundred amethysts, agates, cornelians, and chrysoprases. Only the favored few were allowed to set foot in these chambers, which were infused with an aura of the supernatural, and seemed mystically to foreshadow the New Jerusalem of St. John's apocalyptic vision.

The furnishings and decoration of the Wenceslas chapel are some of the finest specimens of medieval art to be found in Prague. On the round-arched **north doorway** opening from the choir, on the left-hand impost of the cusped arch, Parler has immortalized himself as an old man with a beard; the figure has been interpreted as Socrates, in the parable of the liberation of the soul (the female figure is almost totally destroyed), or as Peter denying Jesus in the exchange with the maid. On the right-hand impost we find the traitor Judas, whose tongue (soul) is being ripped out by the devil. The Gothic door, by a Master Wenzel or Václav, boasts a splendid knocker in the form of a late Romanesque

lion's head (c. 1200). The tympanum of the pointed-arched doorway leading from the transept portrays Christ as savior of the world. The **tomb of St. Wenceslas** dates from the fourteenth century, and was restored in modified form in 1911, to compensate for the loss of the original gold sarcophagus, a priceless artifact studded with gems, pearls, and cameos, which King Sigismund had plundered to fund his army in the war against the Hussites.

The **murals** on the lower section of the wall, amid the decoration of precious stones, were executed by court artist Oswald around 1378 and depict the Passion; behind the altar is a Crucifixion scene with the Virgin and St. John, and Charles IV and Elizabeth of Pomerania kneeling at the sides. The fine limestone **statuette of St. Wenceslas**, sculpted in 1373 by Heinrich Parler, a nephew of Peter (the base has the family emblem, an angled hook), corresponds to the stereotype of the noble knight, but adds more lifelike touches: the mild countenance and the inclination of the head almost contradict the military spirit of the armor.

The **fresco cycle** in the upper zone – painted around 1506 by the Master of the Leitmeritz Altar – relates the Wenceslas legend, which as early as the tenth century had come to be regarded as a typological parallel to Christ's Passion. The donors are commemorated on the altar wall (heavily

Late Gothic panel painting and bronze lantern from the Wenceslas chapel: workshop of Peter Vischer

The murals in the Wenceslas chapel:

The legend of St. Wenceslas (chronological numbering by J. Krása)

1 The ransoming of heathen children
2 The heathen children are baptized
3 Wenceslas demolishes a gallows
4 He visits those in jail
5 He releases prisoners
6 He offers a wanderer hospitality
7 He digs a grave
8 He serves at mass
9 He brings a widow wood and is accosted by foresters
10 He exhorts his servant Podiven to follow his footprints in the snow

11 He tills a field
12 He sows corn
13 He reaps and threshes the corn
14 He bakes wafers for the communion
15 He presses grapes to make wine
16 He arrives at the Imperial Diet
17 He is greeted by King Henry
18 The assembly of the electors
19 Henry presents Wenceslas with the arm relic of St. Vitus
20 Wenceslas places the relic in a chest
21 A duel is arranged with Radslav
22 Radslav is defeated
23 Wenceslas is welcomed by his brother Boleslav in Stará Boleslav
24 The banquet in Stará Boleslav

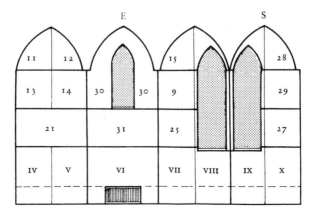

Passion cycle

25 Wenceslas is murdered on the orders of his brother
26 A miracle happens as the body is brought back to Prague
27 Podiven kills his master's murderer and is hanged
28 Christ appears to King Erik of Denmark
29 Erik visits a church built in honor of Wenceslas
30 King Vladislav II and his wife, Anne de Foix, with their coats of arms above
31 Parler's statue of St. Wenceslas between two angels, flanked by patron saints of Bohemia: Sigismund and Vitus (left) and Adalbert and Ludmila (right)

   I Jesus on the Mount of Olives
  II The Judas kiss
 III Jesus before Caiphas
  IV The flagellation
   V The crown of thorns
  VI The crucifixion, with SS. Mary and John and (to left and right) Emperor Charles IV and an empress (Elizabeth of Pomerania?); at the foot of the cross two female figures wearing crowns
 VII Jesus on the cross
VIII Jesus in the tomb
  IX The Resurrection
   X The Ascension
  XI The feast of Pentecost
 XII St. Paul
XIII St. Peter

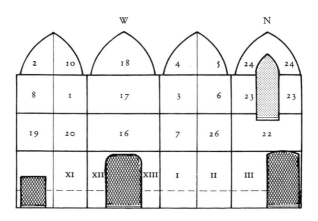

The statue of St. Wenceslas, a masterpiece of Bohemian Gothic art, sculpted by Heinrich Parler in 1372

jewels. The door to it is locked with seven keys, each in the charge of a different high-ranking personage. Before the coronation of a new king, the ritual dictated that the Bohemian crown be placed upon the reliquary bust of St. Wenceslas, whence it came to be known as the "Wenceslas Crown." It was adapted from the old Přemyslid crown for the coronation of Charles IV in 1346, and incorporates a fragment of Christ's crown of thorns in a fabulous setting of gold fleurs-de-lis, pearls, and ninety-one jewels (rubies, sapphires, emeralds, and spinels).

9 St. George's Basilica

Svatý Jiří

Náměstí u Svathého Jiří

Prague's most important Romanesque church, fronted by a Baroque facade.

overpainted): Vladislav II and his wife, Anne of Foix-Candale. The murder of St. Wenceslas is also depicted in the fine **panel** near the north door, painted in 1543 by an unknown Bohemian artist. The ornate **bronze lantern** is from the workshop of Peter Vischer in Nuremberg.

Above the chapel is the **Crown Chamber** (not accessible) containing the crown

Sometime before the year 921, Prince Vratislav I, father of St. Wenceslas, built the second stone church within the castle precinct, probably as a place of burial for the Přemyslid rulers. When the diocese of Prague was created in 973, Boleslav II, known as "the Pious," had the church enlarged into a modest basilica. His sister Mlada founded the first Benedictine convent in Bohemia on an adjacent site, and was herself its first abbess. The daughters of the nobility were educated here as Christian missionaries. Charles IV endowed the abbesses with the rank of princess and the privilege of crowning the

Scenes from the Passion cycle by Master Oswald in Wenceslas chapel; the wall is inlaid with semiprecious stones

queen during the coronation ceremony. Upon the dissolution of the convent in 1783, in the reign of Joseph II, these privileges passed to the Institute of Noblewomen in nearby Jiřská Street, founded by Maria Theresa, which was accommodated in the former Renaissance palace of the Rosenberg princes (the picturesque facade with towers and onion domes fell victim to the empress's scheme to harmonize the castle buildings).

The present church of **St. George** stems basically from the period after the castle fire of 1142, when Abbess Berta refounded the religious community and engaged a master mason named Wernher to plan the new church. The two Romanesque east spires tower above the early Baroque west front, which was added around 1670 by Carlo Lurago – this is one of the first two-story facades of the Roman type in Prague. Johann Georg Bendl was responsible for the upper-zone statues depicting the founders of the church and convent, Vratislav I and Mlada. On the Jiřská corner stands the Baroque Nepomuk chapel; the statue of the saint is by Ferdinand Maximilian Brokoff. The magnificent **south portal** of St. George's was fashioned as an aedicule with demicolumns on classical lines by Benedikt Ried's lodge around 1515, and represented a totally new departure in the Prague of the late Middle Ages. The tympanum relief of St. George and the Dragon, on the other hand, combines the awakening naturalism of the Renaissance with elements of declining Gothic (original in St. George's Convent).

The Baroque west facade of St. George's Basilica, with the chapel of St. John of Nepomuk (right)

Following two restorations, the **interior** has recovered its original austere beauty. The nave arcades and the nuns' galleries above the aisles derive from the tenth-century structure, while the raised square of the choir and the three semicircular apses date from the mid-twelfth century. The curving double staircase to the choir, with its Baroque railing, makes for a pleasantly effective transition to the east end. Before

St. George's Basilica, showing the nuns' galleries and the raised choir

The Ludmila chapel in St. George's Basilica

the entrance to the crypt are the founders' tombs: on the right, Vratislav I (died c.920), whose tomb has a Late Gothic superstructure from 1438; on the left – guarded by a wrought-iron grille – Boleslav II (967-99), or possibly Oldřich (1012-37); in the center is the original tombstone of Boleslav II, which was unearthed in the course of excavations. In the crypt, which is divided by columns into three bays, there is an impressive piece of late Romanesque stone carving from around 1220, which probably originally belonged in the chapel of St. Anne (formerly Lady Chapel) in the convent cloisters: the triptych depicts the Madonna and Child enthroned, with the abbesses Mlada and Berta kneeling at her feet and, in the lateral panels, King Ottokar I and his daughter, Abbess Agnes.

Fragments of **Romanesque murals** are preserved in the north bay of the choir (Christ in a mandorla, and other motifs), in the chapel beneath the south tower, and in the central choir area (the Heavenly Jerusalem, first half of thirteenth century). The other frescoes are mainly Gothic, some having been restored after the fire of 1541. Late Gothic panel-paintings are displayed in the nave (Crucifixion, Legend of St. Ursula), fifteenth-century sculptures in the aisles (a headless Pietà with soft contours, a wood-carving of a saint in an old frame, and a relief depicting the Three Wise Men).

The **St. Ludmila chapel** (accessed via the choir podium) is of early tenth-century origins. Around 1370 Charles IV ordered the Gothic conversion of the early Romanesque structure and commissioned the imposing tumba from the Parler workshop. Ludmila had brought up her grandson, the future St. Wenceslas, in the Christian faith; after the death of her son Vratislav I, she fell foul of her daughter-in-law, the heathen princess Drahomira, who had long been resentful of the older woman's influence at court; in 921, at Drahomira's behest, Ludmila was strangled in Tetín Castle, and soon after was venerated and canonized as Bohemia's first martyr.

Before proceeding further, it is worth taking a look inside the chapel of St. John of Nepomuk: the high-altar painting of the transfiguration of the saint is a 1722 work by Wenzel Lorenz Reiner.

10 St. George's Convent (National Gallery)

Jiřský klášter

Náměstí u Svatého Jiří 5

The National Gallery's magnificent collection of Bohemian painting and sculpture, from Gothic to Neoclassical times.

The convent owes its present form to an early Baroque conversion carried out by Carlo Lurago around 1670. The oldest part is the **chapel of St. Anne** (formerly Lady Chapel) in the east wing of the cloisters, with a Romanesque and Gothic core; in a barred niche lies the glass coffin of Mlada (died 994), the foundress of the convent.

The basement and ground floor are devoted to **Gothic art**, covering the period from the late thirteenth century to around 1520. Among the highlights of this section are: a tympanum from the Church of St. Mary of the Snows, pre-1346 (Throne of Grace, Coronation of the Virgin, King John of Luxemburg and his son, the future emperor Charles IV); the tympanum by the Parler workshop from the north portal of the Týn Church, c. 1390 (the Passion); a winged altar from Velhartice, c. 1500 (Life of the Virgin Mary); the Leitmeritz, or Litoměřice Altar, c. 1505, an early example of landscape painting that has affinities with the Danube School (the "swan-song" of Late Gothic) but with a treatment of na-

The Nativity, *a Gothic panel by the Master of Hohenfurt (Vyšší Brod), with (bottom right) portrait of the donor and coat of arms of the Rosenberg family*

The Resurrection, *from the cycle by the Master of Wittingau, painted c. 1380 in the Augustinian abbey at Třeboň in southern Bohemia*

ture and light in the Renaissance spirit; a bronze statue of St. George and the Dragon (see p. 29); a tympanum relief on the same theme (see p. 45); five panels from Karlštejn Castle by Theodoricus Zelo ("the Zealous"), painter to the imperial court, pre-1367 (St. Elizabeth, St. Vitus, St. Jerome, Pope Gregory, St. Matthew); a Madonna from Most, the oldest Bohemian painting of the Virgin, post-1340; a crucifixion from Emmaus Abbey in Prague, c. 1370; a Madonna from Roudnice nad Labem, the oldest example of the Bohemian type with a frame of medallions, pre-1400; the pre-1371 votive panel of Archbishop Očko, divided into two parts: above, the Virgin and Child between Emperor Charles IV and his son Wenceslas IV, who are sponsored by St. Sigismund of Burgundy and St. Wenceslas, and (below) the kneeling figure of the donor between the national saints Abbot Procopius and Bishop Adalbert and SS. Vitus and Ludmila.

Pride of place in the collection must go to the treasures from monasteries, castles, and palaces of the **Rosenberg princes** of southern Bohemia (their emblem is a five-petaled rose) that survived the Hussite wars: The Master of Hohenfurt, who developed the "Byzantine" elements of Sienese painting (Giotto, Martini) and was a major influence in Bohemian art, is here represented by the nine panels of an altar cycle commissioned around 1347 by Peter I of Rosenberg, lord chamberlain of the kingdom of Bohemia, for the Cistercian monastery in Vyšší Brod (Hohenfurt); painted on a gold ground, the scenes range from the Annunciation to Pentecost. Dating from around 1380, the six panels were painted by the Master of Wittingau for an altar in the congregation of Augustinian canons in Třeboň (Wittingau): the three Passion scenes were displayed on Sundays and other holy days, while the portraits of saints made up the weekday side of the altar. The Master of Wittingau, who probably worked at Karlštejn during the 1360s along with Charles IV's other artists, represents the golden age of Bohemian Gothic painting; his work foreshadows the "soft style" and the realistic trend that began to assert itself around 1400, and had a lasting influence on German Late Gothic art; the tenderly lyrical "Fair Madonnas" were also influenced by him. The Rosenberg section also includes sculptures in the style of the Krumau Madonna (from Český Krumlov, c. 1400), which is now in the Kunsthistorisches Museum in Vienna.

The exhibits on the first floor commence with **late Renaissance or Mannerist works**, mostly by artists associated with the court of Emperor Rudolf II: a Hercules and other bronzes by Adriaen de Vries (c. 1560-1626), and paintings by Bartholomäus Spranger of Antwerp (1546-1611) and Hans von Aachen.

The circuit continues through **Baroque and Rococo to the beginnings of Neo-classicism** around 1780. Painters featured here include: Karel Škréta (1610-74), Bohemia's most important early Baroque painter, who was influenced by the Venetian colorists and the classical elements of Poussin's Roman work; Michael Willmann (1630-1706), a Rembrandt epigone born in Königsberg; Willmann's stepson and pupil Jan Kryštof Liška (c. 1650-1712); Johann Peter Brandl (1668-1735), an excellent portraitist born in Prague; Jan Kupecký (1667-1740), also a painter of portraits;

Wenzel Lorenz Reiner (1689-1743), alongside Škréta and Brandl the leading light of Bohemian Baroque, especially noted for his fresco work; Franz Anton Maulpertsch, who has left us a sketch for the ceiling-fresco at Strahov (see p. 66); Franz Xaver Palko (1724-67) from Silesia, who studied at the Vienna Academy; and Norbert Grund (1717-67), Bohemia's foremost Rococo artist, who painted charming landscapes and genre scenes under the influence of such Venetians as Tiepolo and Guardi.

Sculptors: Johann Georg Bendl (c. 1630-80), the Italian-trained son of an Upper Swabian family of woodcarvers, who was one of the pioneers of Baroque sculpture in Bohemia and founded the Prague guild of sculptors. High Baroque is represented by the Tyrolean Matthias Bernhard Braun (1684-1738), who was trained in Salzburg in the Italian style and produced works full of drama and passion, Ferdinand Maximilian Brokoff (1688-1731), from a German family of sculptors settled in Slovakia, an exponent of the serene, epic style, and – not quite in the same league – the Lusatian Matthias Wenzel Jäckel (1655-1738). The most successful exponent of the Neoclassical tendency of Prague Rococo was Ignaz Franz Platzer (1717-87) from Plzeň, who studied at the Vienna Academy and had assistants working for him throughout Bohemia.

I I Golden Lane
Zlatá ulička

Picturesque alley immortalized in fable and literature, and a sinister tower of operatic fame, the Daliborka.

Parallel to the castle rampart, above the ditch on the north side, runs the famous goldsmiths' alley with its string of tiny, brightly painted cottages. Here, by royal privilege, lived the twenty-four members of the castle watch, who in their red uniforms guarded the gates; later, goldsmiths set up their workshops here. Popular tradition tells of mysterious figures bent over bubbling retorts, of flickering flames, and strange vapors issuing into the night; but Rudolf II's alchemists (p. 29) conducted their arcane experiments in the Powder Tower. From the eighteenth century onward, up to the 1930s, the "dolls' houses" were occupied by craftsmen, minstrels, fortune-tellers, and the like. This picturesque milieu has been the inspiration for artists and writers: in 1917, Franz Kafka lived for a time at No. 22; in his novel *The

The fabled Golden Lane in Prague Castle

Golem, Gustav Meyrink describes a house in "Alchemists' Alley" that could only be seen on a foggy day, by a Sunday's child. Since its restoration in the 1950s, Golden Lane has been a magnet for tourists.

The western end of the alley is marked by the **White Tower** (Bílá Věž), once a jail, where many a noble debtor languished. The last house at the other end abuts on the **Daliborka**, the most famous of the castle towers, built by Benedikt Ried in 1496. Its first inmate was Dalibor, baron of Kozojed, who had given sanctuary to rebellious serfs on his estate near Litoměřice. During his incarceration, so the legend goes, he learned to sing and play the violin; in fact he was tortured on an instrument known as the "violin," and executed in 1498. Smetana immortalized the tragic knight in his romantic opera *Dalibor.*

12 Lobkowicz Palace (Historical Museum)

Lobkovický palác

Jiřská 1

The history of Bohemia and Moravia – an interesting section of the National Museum.

In 1570, the powerful lords of Pernštejn built a Renaissance mansion on the site; part of its sgraffito decoration can still be seen in the courtyard. The Popels of Lobkovice acquired the property through the dowry of Polyxena of Pernštejn. In 1651 it was rebuilt in the early Baroque style by Carlo Lurago. The **gala rooms** on the first floor are decorated with imposing stuccowork by Domenico Galli and frescoes by Fabián (Sebastian) Harovník: in the foyer the Triumph of Caesar and the Allegory of Strength, in the main hall the Gods on Parnassus, the Seasons, and the Continents, and in the former chapel the Legend of St. Wenceslas. Later stucco decoration (strings of foliage, rocailles) dates from the first half of the eighteenth century. The Chinese Cabinet has been converted into a music-room.

The palace now houses the **Historical Museum**, where the chronological sequence begins on the second floor with the section on the archaeology of Bohemia and Moravia (head of a Celt from the second century B.C., objects brought by Roman traders), and proceeds through the Dark Ages (migrations of Germanic and Slavic peoples, the Greater Moravian Empire, the advent of Christianity in the ninth century) to the Middle Ages (jewelry from the tomb of Ottokar II, copies of the Bohemian coronation insignia, casts of some of the triforium busts in St. Vitus's). The exhibits on the first floor take us through the Hussite revolution and down to the nineteenth century.

The **Burgrave's Chancery** (Jiřská 4, House of Czechoslovak Children) was the residence and office of the lord lieutenant of the castle, the king's right-hand man; only members of the noblest families were appointed to this, the highest office of state. The gateway is adorned with the coats of arms of the Fürstenberg, Martinic, Valdštejn (Wallenstein), and Vrtba families. Originating in the thirteenth century, the complex was rebuilt several times over the years, most recently in the mid-sixteenth century in Renaissance style; in some rooms, painted wooden ceilings have survived from this period.

The mighty **Black Tower** (Černá Věž), which guards the eastern gate of the castle, is the best-preserved remnant of the Romanesque fortifications from the time of Prince Soběslav I, around 1135. The name probably derives from its function as a debtors' prison; during the reign of Charles IV it was known as the Golden Tower, on account of its gilt roof. The **Cannon Bastion**, built around 1570, offers a majestic panorama over the city. The Staré zámecké schody, or **Old Castle Steps**, lead down to Klárov and the Malostranská metro station by the river.

13 Royal Garden, Belvedere

Královská zahrada, Belvedér

Mariánské hradby/U Prašného mostu

Location of the first pure Renaissance building in Prague, one of the finest north of the Alps.

The **Royal Garden**, which runs parallel to Prague Castle on the other side of Jelení Příkop ("Stag Moat"), was laid out around 1534 for Emperor Ferdinand I, and was the first Italian *giardinetto* in Bohemia. There were greenhouses, in which Dutch gardeners cultivated limes, pomegranates, tulips, and other botanical novelties, and Rudolf II kept exotic animals in an enclosure. This "enchanted garden" in the Mannerist mode is a thing of the past – today it is more like a landscape garden, dotted here and there with Baroque sculptures: the *Hercules Fountain* by J. G. Bendl (1670), *Night* (1734) and other works by M. B. Braun and his assistants.

The large **Real-Tennis Court** (Míčovna) in the middle of the garden was designed by Bonifaz Wolmut and built between 1567 and 1569, no doubt commissioned by Maximilian II. It was originally conceived as an open loggia-type structure, on the model of Palladio's villas in northern Italy, but weather considerations led to solid walls, being substituted. The facade is articulated by attached Ionic columns and niches, and decorated with sgraffito grotesques and representations of the elements, virtues, arts, and sciences. The Real-Tennis Court was restored after being ravaged by fire during World War II; it is not usually open.

The **Royal Summerhouse**, or **Belvedere** (Mariánské hradby 1), was a present from Ferdinand I, the first Habsburg to rule over Bohemia, to his wife Anna Jagiello. The emperor, whose youth had been spent in Spain and the Netherlands, no doubt found the medieval castle in Prague rather inhospitable, and looked to Italian architects to bring something of the elegance and comfort of the Renaissance to these northern latitudes. The Belvedere is obviously modeled on Brunelleschi's orphanage in Florence, built well over a century before. Although several architects were

The undulating roof of the Belvedere was an inspiration to Prague architects until to the nineteenth century

The Real-Tennis Court is today used for exhibitions

involved in the project, the result was a masterpiece of harmony and beauty. The core structure, with its graceful arcade, was begun in 1538 by Hans von Spatio (Giovanni Spazio) in collaboration with the sculptor Paolo della Stella (Paul de la Stella de Mileto); the squat aspect of the building was something quite new, for the vertical emphasis of Gothic still endured in

The Singing Fountain in front of the Belvedere

Bohemia. The copious figural and vegetable ornamentation on the spandrels, from Stella's workshop, depicts mythological and historical hunting and genre scenes.

Construction had been going on for a good thirty years – interrupted by the great castle fire – when the court architect Bonifaz Wolmut (from Überlingen, on Lake Constance) completed the work in 1563. He set the ballroom on the upper floor a fair way back from the balustrade, and designed a huge curvilinear copper roof to top off the whole, no doubt inspired by the town mansions of northern Italy, such as the Salone in Padua. The elegant flow of the Belvedere roof was copied in Prague several times, down to the National Theater of the nineteenth century. Following restoration, the Belvedere is now used as an exhibition venue.

The celebrated **Singing Fountain** in front of the Belvedere, a typical example of the Italian basin type, takes its name from the tinkling of the water on the metal. It was cast by Bohemian craftsmen under the leadership of Tomáš Jaroš in 1564. The base is adorned with naturalistic scenes from Greek and Roman mythology – Pan with shepherds, goats' heads, masks, festoons, naked cupids – and the fountain is crowned by a bagpiper.

To the west of the Royal Garden lies the **Riding School**, an extensive complex designed around 1694 by Jean Baptiste Mathey to the order of Leopold I, now used for exhibition purposes.

Northeast of the Belvedere, at Mickiewiczova 1, is **Villa Bílek**, a pseudo-Egyptian structure of 1912 with sculptural decoration by František Bílek (1872-1941), the central figure of Czech Symbolism. In the garden stands his statue of Jan Ámos Komenský (1592-1670), better known as Comenius, bishop of the Bohemian Brethren and a pioneer of modern educational theory.

14 Castle Square
Hradčanské náměstí

Distinguished square in front of the castle gates, lined by aristocratic mansions.

The collection of courtiers' dwellings that had grown up around the present square was given town status in 1320 and placed under the jurisdiction of the burgrave. It expanded westward along Pohořelec as far as Strahov Monastery, and in 1360 had its boundary fixed at the Hunger Wall (p. 83). The Hussite wars and the great fire of 1541 took their toll, but toward the end of the sixteenth century a new building boom began, giving rise to mansions for the nobility and the clergy, merchants' houses, churches, and monasteries. In 1598 Hradčany became a royal city, and in 1784 one of the united townships of Prague. Even today, it still forms a distinct urban unit together with the castle.

A statue of Mary Immaculate crowns the Madonna column on Hradčanské náměstí

Late Renaissance sgraffito on the wall of Martinitz Palace

St. Mary's Column, or the Plague Column (1736), is surrounded by vigorous and lifelike statues by F. M. Brokoff and his workshop, representing SS. John of Nepomuk, Elizabeth, Peter, Norbert, Florian, Charles Borromeo (plague intercessor), and the Bohemian patron saints Wenceslas, Vitus, and Adalbert, with the figure of Mary Immaculate towering above all. Like all such columns, it is modeled on the one erected on Marienplatz in Munich in 1638 to commemorate the victory of the Catholic League at Bílá hora; the first Madonna column in Prague was set up on Staroměstské náměstí in 1650 (later destroyed).

The **Archbishop's Palace** at No. 16 derives from the Renaissance mansion of the counts of Gryspek. In 1675 Archbishop Count Johann Friedrich of Waldstein commissioned Jean Baptiste Mathey to rebuild it in the early Baroque style; the late Baroque facade with Rococo ornamentation stems from the last remodeling in 1764 by Johann Joseph Wirch, and the sculptural decoration is by Ignaz Platzer.

Hradčanské náměstí, the noble square fronting the castle, with the Archbishop's Palace (left)

Further along the north side of the square at No. 8, after a row of former canon's lodges, comes the **Martinitz Palace**, which is decorated with some impressive late Renaissance sgraffito scenes from the Old Testament and Greek mythology, executed between 1580 and 1630 and based in part on German woodcuts: on the facade Joseph in Egypt, in the courtyard Samson and the Labors of Hercules. In some of the rooms, painted wooden ceilings have survived, and in the chapel there are Baroque murals from the period around 1700, when Georg Adam of Martinice was imperial envoy and viceroy of Naples. The palace is open during exhibitions and other cultural events. Just to confuse matters, there is another Martinitz Palace around the corner (Loretánská 4); this Baroque mansion is now the headquarters of the castle guard.

15 Sternberg Palace (National Gallery)

Šternberský palác

Hradčanské náměstí 15 (passage on the left of the Archbishop's Palace)

Important collections of European art: icons from the fifteenth to the eighteenth centuries, nineteenth- and twentieth-century painting and sculpture, and an outstanding collection of Picasso paintings.

This large rectangular complex built around a central court, with its west wing bisected by a transverse oval that projects both horizontally and vertically, was commenced in 1698 by Wenzel Adalbert, Count Sternberg; Giovanni Battista Alliprandi probably based his design on plans by Domenico Martinelli, the personal architect of the Liechtensteins in Vienna. The gala rooms boast painted ceilings by Michael Wenzel Halbax and Johann Rudolf Byss depicting the Suicide of Dido, the Grieving Artemis, and Esther before Ahasuerus. The Chinese Cabinet is closed for restoration.

The collection of **early European art** be-

gins on the second floor with German painters of the Late Gothic period and the Danube School: Holbein, Cranach, Altdorfer, Grien, etc. The pièce de résistance is undoubtedly Dürer's **Feast of the Rosary** (in Room 4), the major work of his Venice period, painted in 1506 for San Bartolomeo, the church of the German merchants' guild, and later owned by Rudolf II. The Madonna and Child constitute the focal point of what is the first group portrait in German art; on the left are the representatives of the church, with a kneeling Pope Julius II and, standing behind him, St. Dominic, who places the rosary on the head of Cardinal Grimani, patriarch of Aquileia; on the right, Emperor Maximilian I receives the rosary, while behind him kneels Jakob (or Ulrich) Fugger, head of the Augsburg banking family. The artist has not forgotten to include himself, standing next to the tree.

Other rooms feature the works of most European painters of note, including Tintoretto *(St. Jerome), Goya (Don Miguel de Lardizábal)*, El Greco, Canaletto, Guardi, Pieter Bruegel the Elder *(The Hay Harvest)*, Rubens, and Rembrandt. The nineteenth and twentieth centuries are represented by Caspar David Friedrich, Max Liebermann, Edvard Munch, Gustav Klimt, Egon Schiele, Lovis Corinth, Gior-

Albrecht Dürer: The Feast of the Rosary, *in Sternberg Palace*

gio de Chirico, Joan Miró, and Oskar Kokoschka (particularly his views of Prague).

The excellent **collection of French art** of the nineteenth and twentieth centuries (access from the courtyard) comprises works by the Romantics, the Realists, the Impressionists, and the modern era, including Delacroix, Corot, Daumier, Courbet, Rousseau, Cézanne, Gauguin, Van Gogh, Toulouse-Lautrec, Monet, Pissarro, Sisley, Renoir, Utrillo, Degas, Matisse, Braque, and Chagall, and includes fourteen paintings by Picasso. Sculptures by Rodin can be seen in the garden.

16 Schwarzenberg Palace
Schwarzenberský palác
Hradčanské náměstí 2

One of the earliest and most important examples of Prague Renaissance architecture, housing a museum of military history from the Hussite wars to the end of World War I.

The imposing T-shaped structure was built by August Vlach between 1545 and 1563 for Count Johann of Lobkowicz. The palace was bought in 1600 by the Rosenbergs of southern Bohemia, and was subsequently inherited by the Eggenbergs of Styria and, in 1719, by the princely family of the Schwarzenbergs. On the facade, "nordic" features, such as the intricately contoured gables, harmonize happily with Lombard and Florentine elements, such as the pronounced concave overhang at the roofline and above the window lunettes; the sgraffito finishing has a Venetian air in its imitation of diamond-pointed rustication. Some of the rooms still have their ceiling paintings (tempera on canvas) with scenes from Homer's *Iliad* and Roman mythology.

In 1811 the Schwarzenbergs acquired the **Salm Palace**, the Empire-style mansion next door at No. 1.

17 Tuscany Palace
Toskánský palác
Hradčanské náměstí 5

Impressive early Baroque edifice commanding the west side of the square.

The palace was designed by Jean Baptiste Mathey for Count Michael Oswald of Thun-Hohenstein and built between 1689 and 1691. In honor of the Archangel Mi-

Facade of Schwarzenberg Palace; the sgraffito technique, an Italian invention, was very popular during the Renaissance era in Bohemia and Moravia

Principal facade of Tuscany Palace

Sculpture on Tuscany Palace: the Archangel Michael with flaming sword

chael, the count commissioned the dramatic sculptural group (1693) that adorns the corner of Loretánská; its sculptor, Ottavio Mosto of Padua, had come to Prague via Salzburg. Mathey, on the other hand, was a Frenchman, but had studied in Rome; it is not surprising, therefore, to find typically Roman features on the facade, such as the broad perspective and the two roof pavilions with a connecting balustrade. The statues of gods and the arts on the latter and the armorial cartouches above the two columned portals were added in 1718 by the new owners, the dukes of Tuscany.

Diagonally opposite at No. 3, stands the former Carmelite convent, which previously belonged to the Barnabite order and is now a hotel for state visitors. The Baroque church of St. Benedict developed from the old parish church of the castle quarter.

A picturesque descent to Malá Strana leads down the **Radnické schody** ("Town Hall Steps"). The old Hradčany town hall (Loretánská 1) has sgraffito decoration from the end of the sixteenth century and a mural on Justice. Let into the wall next to the Renaissance doorway is the Bohemian cubit, an old measure of length corresponding to about two feet.

18 Church of St. John of Nepomuk

Svatý Jan Nepomucký
Kanovnická 5

First church building in Prague by Kilian Ignaz Dientzenhofer, the foremost architect of the Bohemian High Baroque.

57

The former Ursuline convent and Church of St. John of Nepomuk, with Schwarzenberg Palace in the background

Dientzenhofer completed this church for the Ursuline order in 1729, and the convent buildings a few years later. After the dissolution of the convent (1784) under Joseph II, St. John's became the regimental chapel to the garrison that was quartered in the complex.

The portal, central window, and tower (shortened in 1815) lead the eye upward, creating a well-defined vertical axis. The decorative forms are reminiscent of the work of Johann Lukas von Hildebrandt, Dientzenhofer's mentor, in Vienna. The facade fronts a centrally planned, cruciform structure. Reiner's ceiling frescoes of scenes from the life of St. John of Nepomuk date from 1727, which was in fact two years before the martyr's canonization. The fine altarpieces by Michael Willmann and Jan Kryštof Liška were originally located in St. Adalbert's near the Powder Tower in Staré Město, which was demolished in 1904.

19   Černin Palace

Černínský palác

Loretánské náměstí 5

The largest stately home in Prague, and the most important example of (delayed) Palladian Mannerism.

The massive, rectangular pile, arranged around two courtyards, stands at the highest point of Hradčany; it was conceived as a pendant to Prague Castle, which at the time (before the construction of intervening buildings) lay in full view. The 492-foot long principal facade bears eloquent testimony to the aspirations of the Bohemian count to assert himself in the face of king and emperor – and in fact, Humprecht Johann Černin of Chudenice bit off more than he could chew, driving himself and his heirs to the verge of bankruptcy with this mammoth undertaking. Černin decided to build a magnificent family seat on his return from Venice, where he had been imperial ambassador, and after marrying a daughter of the margrave of Mantua. Work commenced in 1669, under the direction of Francesco Caratti, who was already known for his design for the Palais Nostitz in Malá Strana; after his death in 1677 other Italians supervised the further stages of construction until 1697.

The **facade** is modeled as a relief landscape, and is articulated by thirty columns with heavy mascaron capitals. The giant, or colossal, order, in which the columns rise through two or more stories, had been introduced by Andrea Palladio in Vicenza over a hundred years earlier. The high base in diamond-pointed rustication is indebted to palaces in Verona and Venice by Michele Sanmicheli, a pupil of Bramante. For all its severity (there are no projecting bays or pavilions), the facade is clearly infused with the Baroque spirit in the upward thrust of its columns. The portico and the curving balcony, designed by Anselmo

Garden facade of Černin Palace

Lurago, were only added in 1747, in the course of repair work necessitated by the ravages of the War of the Austrian Succession.

The **interior**, completed around 1720 under the direction of František Maximilián Kaňka, features stucco by Italian craftsmen and frescoes by Reiner. For all its extravagant decoration, the palace was seldom used as a residence, and only occasionally for festive events. From the mid-nineteenth century onward, it served as barracks, and it was only in the 1930s that President Masaryk ordered a complete restoration following Caratti's original plans.

20 Loreto Sanctuary

Loreta

Loretánské náměstí 7

Prague's most famous Marian sanctuary, a typically Bohemian complex with a quadrangular processional cloister.

After the victory of the Catholic armies at Bílá hora in 1620, which was ascribed to the intervention of the Virgin Mary, a wave of Mariolatry spread throughout Bohemia. Centers of pilgrimage to "Sancta Maria de Victoria" and newly founded monasteries and convents soon became cornerstones of the Counter-Reformation. Many of these institutions were founded on land confiscated from the Protestant nobility. The Loreto in Hradčany was en-

dowed by Countess Benigna Katharina of Lobkowicz in 1626, and placed in charge of the neighboring Capuchin monastery. The growing stream of pilgrims made additions and enlargements necessary over the years, until by 1750 the sanctuary had virtually found its present form; the principal architects were Christoph Dientzenhofer and his son Kilian Ignaz, the two members of the extensive Upper Bavarian family who left a lasting impression on Bohemian High Baroque.

The Dientzenhofers devised an original scheme for the **west facade**, which incorporates an older octagonal belfry and was erected between 1721 and 1724. Johann Friedrich Kohl contributed some of the statues: on the far left, the Capuchin monk Felix of Cantalice kneeling before the Virgin, on the far right St. John of Nepomuk; left and right of the entrance the best-known Franciscan saints, Francis of Assisi and Anthony of Padua. The forecourt is enclosed by a low balustrade with putti by Andreas Philipp Quittainer, which add an attractive Rococo touch. On holidays the facade used to be hung with banners and other decorations, creating a highly festive air. The carillon in the tower was made in Amsterdam, and installed by the Prague clockmaker Peter Neumann; in 1695, before the assembled dignitaries of the church and the nobility, he pulled the lever for the first rendition of the Czech Marian hymn that to this day can be heard every hour on the hour.

The Loreto sanctuary

Focus of the whole complex is the **Casa Santa**, or Holy House, a replica of the original in Loreto, Italy. The legend relates that in 1291 four angels carried the tiny house of the Virgin Mary, in which the archangel Gabriel had brought her the glad tidings, from Nazareth through the air to a laurel grove *(lauretum)* near Ancona. Loreto became world famous as a place of pilgrimage, and no less an architect than Bramante designed a "reliquary" for the house, a windowless, boxlike enclosure in the style of the High Renaissance. Prague's Casa Santa was built by Giovanni Orsi of Como and his successor, Andrea Allio. In 1664 Giovanni Batista Cometa and Jacopo Agosto covered the walls of the shrine with stucco reliefs, depicting prophets and

The Casa Santa in the courtyard of the Loreto, with the Church of the Nativity in the background

sibyls, the Life of the Virgin, and (on the east end) the Loreto legend. The **interior**, an intimate, twilight space, houses the brick reconstruction of the Holy House and the miracle-working Madonna statue in a silver frame; beneath it is the vault of the Lobkowicz family, the donors.

Two **Baroque fountains** add a theatrical note to the courtyard with their vigorous statuary by Johann Michael Biderle (or Biederle, Brüderle) depicting the Resurrection and the Assumption.

The **arcade** surrounding the courtyard served as an ambulatory for the pilgrims, who proceeded singing and praying from one altar to the next. The most popular chant was the Lauretanian Litany, whose Marian symbolism served as inspiration for the frescoes in the vaulting, by Felix Anton Scheffler (c. 1750, later overpainted); most of the laudations of the Virgin are derived from the Psalms and the Song of Solomon. The most interesting altarpiece is the *Stigmatization of St. Francis* by Peter Brandl, in the **chapel of St. Francis** in the north wing; the ancillary figures were sculpted by Matthäus Wenzel Jäckel in 1718. In the **chapel of the Virgin of Sorrows**, in the southwest corner of the ambulatory, a curious image is venerated – that of a bearded maiden hanging on a cross. Linked with the "Volto Santo" legend of the "true likeness of Christ" in Lucca, the legend of St. Wilgefortis (the name means "troubles") originated in South Tyrol and spread throughout the Catholic world: she is supposed to have been the daughter of a Sicilian (or Portuguese) king, to have lived in the second century, and to have refused to marry a heathen; to protect her virginity, she prayed for visible signs of manhood, whereupon her irate father had her crucified; in her death-throes she preached and converted many, including finally her own father.

The **Church of the Nativity** in the east wing, by the Dientzenhofers, is a jewel of Prague Baroque with its sumptuous, high-quality decoration. It is adorned with a theatrical array of angels, putti, prophets, apostles, and saints, most of them carved by the Tyrolean Matthias Schönherr. The eastern bay of the vault has a fresco of the Presentation in the Temple by Wenzel Lorenz Reiner (1736), Prague's leading Baroque fresco painter; the other two frescoes, of the Adorations of the Magi and of the Shepherds, are by Johann Adam Schöpf, a pupil of Asam. The oldest work of art, from before 1700, is the unpretentious painting on the high altar, by Johann

The Loreto Madonna in the Casa Santa

Georg Heintsch from Silesia. The soft tones of Venetian Rococo characterize the charming representations of SS. Agatha and Apollonia on the side altars, by Anton Kern, a native of northern Bohemia who studied in Dresden. The two side altars in the presbytery hold the relics of the Spanish martyrs Felicissimus and Marcia, whose figures are dressed in the Spanish court attire of the period. The walls of the church are dressed with artificial marble, by Johann Hennevogel, and the organ is by Josef Helwig.

21 Loreto Treasury

Loretánská klenotnice

West wing, first floor

The most important collection of Baroque craftsmanship in Bohemia.

Despite having been plundered several times to help finance the campaigns against the Turks and against Napoleon, the treasury, founded in 1636, still holds about three hundred liturgical objects and vestments, most of them of incalculable value. The oldest item is a Late Gothic chalice dating from 1510. In the Baroque era the Bohemian aristocrats vied with one another in the donation of precious monstrances: the Lobkowicz Monstrance (1673), studded with coral and Bohemian garnet; the Waldstein Monstrance (1721), with the Root of Jesse on the shaft; the Ring Monstrance, and the Greater and the Lesser Pearl Monstrances. The pride of the collection is the celebrated **Diamond Monstrance**, or "Prague Sun," the bequest of Countess Ludmila Eva of Kolovrat: nearly three feet tall and weighing 26½ pounds, the silver gilt artifact is studded with 6,222 diamonds; it was crafted in 1699 by Johann Baptist Känischbauer and Matthias Stegner, jewelers to the Viennese court, to a design by Johann Bernhard Fischer von Erlach inspired by creations of Giovanni Lorenz Bernini. The iconography is derived from the vision of light in the Revelation of St. John (12:1). A dragon, symbol of darkness and evil, winds itself around the base. Mary the Immaculate, Queen of Heaven, stands on a crescent moon, her halo formed by twelve stars and her eyes lifted toward the radiant disk of the sun, symbol of God, the Light of the World.

22 Capuchin Monastery

Kapucínský klášter

Loretánské náměstí 6

The humbler side of Hradčany.

In sharp contrast to the sacred and secular splendors that border the square, the Ca-

An idyllic corner of Prague

puchin monastery marks the beginning of quite a different world. In accordance with the order's vow of poverty, the **Church of St. Mary Angelic** is a simple early Baroque building with modest furnishings. A fine, almost lifesize crib is on view in the side chapel from Christmas Eve to the end of January. This, the oldest Capuchin settlement in Bohemia, was founded in 1602 on land donated by Margareta of Lobkowicz.

Černínská leads steeply down to the **New World** (Nový Svět), a picturesque corner of the castle ward where poor families made their homes as early as the fourteenth century. Among these cottages with their tiny yards and gardens, Franz Werfel set some of the scenes of his novel *Heaven Betrayed*. Restored in recent years, Nový Svět is now the haunt of artists: some of the houses have names and emblems that make the mouth water – the Blue Grape at No. 5, or the Golden Pear restaurant at No. 3.

23 Pohořelec, Úvoz

Picturesque square at the western end of Hradčany, with a link to Malá Strana.

The first houses were built in this corner of Hradčany in 1375; fire devastated the area three times, hence the name Pohořelec ("Place of Fire"). Both sides of the long square are lined with fine late Renaissance houses from the end of the sixteenth century, most of them with Baroque or Rococo facades. The statue of St. John of Nepomuk by Johann Anton Quittainer is an impressive example of early Rococo from 1752; it used to stand on Hradčanské náměstí.

The street leading down to Malá Strana is called Úvoz, or "Sunken Way," because it was originally hemmed in by the high wall of the Imperial Zoological Garden. Today it is lined with interesting old houses on the one side, and on the other offers a fine view, all the more enchanting in springtime when the trees are in blossom. A carved Calvary at No. 15 reminds us that this was once St. Elizabeth's Hospice, a dependency of Strahov Monastery. Around 1706, the Stone Column House at No. 24 belonged to the painter Christian Luna, which explains the busts of Luna (the moon) and Sol (the sun); neighbors used to speculate on the arcane practices of the Freemasons' lodge that met here, and there was a rumor that the house was linked by a tunnel to the castle. Several

Strahov Monastery; the tall building on the left is the library

houses on the street have quaint emblems, e.g., the Three Red Hearts, No. 14, or the Three Red Roses, No. 4.

24 Strahov Monastery

Strahovský klášter

Strahovskè nádvoří (access from Dlabačov or by the passage from Pohořelec 8)

One of Bohemia's major cultural sites, a center of religion, science, and the arts.

The Baroque **gateway** to the monastery precinct is crowned by a statue of Norbert of Xanten, founder of the Premonstratensian order, a work by Johann Anton Quittainer from 1755. On the left stands the old **parish church of St. Rochus**, which was founded by Emperor Rudolf II in 1599 in gratitude for the end of the plague. It is an interesting example of the "post-Gothic" style that made a brief showing at the end of the sixteenth century, combining Late Gothic forms with elements of the budding Renaissance (today used for exhibitions).

Strahov was founded in 1140 by Prince Vladislav II on the initiative of the bishop of Olomouc, Jindřich Zdík. The first canons came from Steinfeld in the Eifel, Germany. Medieval chronicles speak of a "monastery on Mount Zion," symbolically linking Prague with Jerusalem. The Czech name comes from the verb *strahovati*, "to guard," and relates to the site on the edge of Petřín Hill where the castle sentries stood watch.

Few traces are left of the fortified Romanesque monastery. Rebuilding in the Gothic style was under way when the Hussite wars brought work to a standstill, and during the Thirty Years' War the Swedish troops wrought havoc. Around the middle of the seventeenth century the fortunes of the monastery took a turn for the better, and over a period of years the whole complex was renovated and extended in the current Baroque fashion. Even during the reign of Joseph II, the "enlightened" emperor who dissolved so many religious institutions, Strahov was spared because of its fame in the field of learning, and with the opening of the library to scholars a period of fertile activity set in.

The **facade of the library** (on the right

The Church of St. Rochus in the grounds of Strahov Monastery

before the abbey church), the work of Ignazio Palliardi (1782-84), is considered the best example of early Neoclassicism in Prague. Ignaz Platzer was responsible for the sculptural ornamentation: the medallion of Joseph II, putti and allegorical figures in the segmental pediment, and garlands of leaves, a typical feature of Louis-Seize Neoclassicism.

The Baroque remodeling of the **Church of the Assumption** was completed around 1750, when Anselmo Lurago gave the two eastern towers and the west facade their present aspect. The niche above the main door contains an unusually graceful statue of Mary Immaculate by J. A. Quittainer. **Inside**, the basic structure of the Romanesque basilica is still evident. The space is uncramped: the vault springs from broad pilasters that only rise as far as the baseline of the tall lunettes, and the altars on the piers draw the eye forward. A host of artists were involved in the **late Baroque decoration and furnishings**: the vault was stuccoed by Michael Ignaz Palliardi, the frescoes are by Josef Kramolín (Life of the Virgin in the main panels of the vault), Ignaz Raab (Marian symbols in the pendentives), and Wilhelm Josef Neunherz (Life of St. Norbert above the arcades); Johann Lauermann fashioned the marble altars and the pulpit, Ignaz Platzer the sculptures on the high altar (SS. Augustine, Norbert, Gottfried, and Hermann Joseph), and J. A. Quittainer most of the figures on the side altars; the oldest altarpieces (Nativity, patron saints of Bohemia, Visitation – pre-1706) are by the Rembrandt pupil Michael Lukas Willmann; the other paintings are by Jan Kryštof Liška (Willmann's stepson) and Franz Xaver Palko; Franz Ryckel carved the early Baroque choirstalls (1544); F. Fassmann built the organ, on which Mozart played.

The **chapel of St. Ursula**, off the north aisle, harbors relics of SS. Ursula and Norbert. It was the latter who in 1120, in Prémontré near Laon, founded the Premonstratensian order on the basis of the Augustinian rule. Later appointed archbishop of Magdeburg, he died in 1134. When Magdeburg became Protestant in the sixteenth century, Norbert's remains were brought to Doksany Abbey, northwest of Prague, and then in 1627 to Strahov; from their former resting-place in the nave they were moved to an Empire-style tomb in the chapel in 1811.

In the **chapel of the Virgin of Passau** (also known as the "Pappenheim" chapel) in the south aisle we find the epitaph for Count Gottfried Heinrich of Pappenheim, who was killed at Lützen in 1632, in the battle that also saw the death of King Gustavus Adolphus on the opposing side. The murals, by Brother Siardus (František Nosecký), depict scenes from the Thirty Years' War.

The abbey church at Strahov: nave with pier altars

The Theology Hall in Strahov library

25 Strahov Library

Strahovska knihovna

Repository of a million books, exquisitely decorated historic halls, and the museum of Czech literature.

An attractive **gateway** with a statue of St. Norbert by J. A. Quittainer leads to the inner court of the monastery. The former **prelate's lodge**, built by Mathey in 1682, is now a restaurant with a panoramic terrace (open in summer). The **chapterhouse**, through which we enter the museum, has a ceiling fresco by Siardus depicting the Healing of the Sick Man as recorded in the gospel of St. John ("Take up thy bed and walk"). A statue commemorates Božena Němcová (1820-62), who with her novel *Grandmama (Babička)* became the most famous Czech authoress of the nineteenth century.

The **cloister** has been remodeled in the Baroque style, but still incorporates a considerable amount of the original Romanesque fabric. The first section of the exhibition presents documentation on the ancient Slavs, the Greater Moravian Empire, and the missionary work of the brothers SS. Cyril and Methodius in the ninth century, who were instrumental in the development of Old Church Slavonic and the Glagolitic script, the precursor of the Cyrillic alphabet today used in many Slavonic languages. **Three Romanesque rooms** in the west wing are devoted to the Přemyslid era, the Luxemburg kings (Charles IV), and the Hussite movement. The refectories (adjacent to the library stairs) are used for cultural events; the summer refectory has a painting of the Celestial Banquet by Siardus, and the winter refectory a stucco ceiling from 1730.

Since 1953, Strahov has been the home of the **Museum of National Literature**. The original Premonstratensian library was progressively enlarged through donations and purchases, including the library of Milevsko Abbey in southern Bohemia and other institutions. The present inventory numbers some nine hundred thousand volumes, five thousand priceless manuscripts and other rarities, two thousand five hundred incunabula, and a unique collection of Hussite literature (Utraquists, Bohemian Brethren, Comenius) – not to mention the literary archives of the National Museum, with some five million items. Understandably, only a tiny fraction of the treasures are on display.

The **Theology Hall** on the first floor is a powerful example of early Baroque, designed by Giovanni Domenico Orsi de Orsini, a member of a family of architects from the Lake Como region. The vaulted ceiling is adorned with intricate stucco work from around 1670 – scrolls, shells, foliage, angels' heads. In 1720 the room was extended by the addition of two bays in the same style, and frescoes were painted by Siardus (the artist-monk's self-portrait hangs in one of the window arches). The cycle of paintings, inspired by the philosophical treatises of Abbot Hieronymus Hirnheim and the Book of Proverbs, is a glorification of the "House of Wisdom," a homage to literature and learning. A number of Baroque cabinets, reading-desks, and magnificent seventeenth-century globes are also worthy of note.

In the corridor leading to the Philosophy Hall stands a copy of the **Strahov Gospels**, the oldest and most valuable manuscript in the monastery's possession. The Latin codex, which consists of 218 parchment folios in uncial script, was probably produced in Tours at the beginning of the ninth century; the pictures of the evangelists, on purple ground, were probably done in Trier at the end of the tenth century. The binding dates from the seventeenth century and comprises elements from previous centuries, including four enamel disks from St. Pantaleon's workshop in Cologne (1180), Romanesque statuettes, and crystals.

In the **Philosophy Hall**, designed by Ignaz Palliardi (1782-84), Prague Baroque bows out in style to make way for the noble restraint of Neoclassicism. The fine walnut bookcases are in full harmony with the room, even though they were made in 1770 by Johann Lachhofer for the Premonstratensian monastery in Louka, near Znojmo, and transported to Strahov after its dissolution. A niche cabinet contains books presented by Empress Marie Louise of France on the occasion of her visit in 1812; on top of the cabinet is a bust of her father, Emperor Franz I of Austria, by Franz Xaver Lederer.

The **painting** that covers the entire barrel vault of the ceiling was conceived and commissioned by the enlightened Abbot Wenzel Mayer, a member of the masonic lodge of the Three Crowned Columns – his portrait appears twice in the monumental fresco. It is a brilliant late work by Franz Anton Maulpertsch, Austria's foremost frescoist of the second half of the eighteenth century. Together with his assistant, Martin Michl, the seventy-year-old artist executed the work in the space of only six months, in 1794. Two years later he died in Vienna, where his career had begun in 1752 with the dome fresco for the Piarist church of Maria Treu. If the early Maulpertsch was influenced by the vigorous brushwork of a Rubens and the chiaroscuro of a Rembrandt, here in Strahov it is the light atmospheric coloring of Venetian Rococo. The subject of the fresco is humanity's striving for wisdom, depicted in four epochs – the Old Testament, mythological times, pagan antiquity, and the Christian era. Among others, it shows Alexander the Great with his steed Bucephalus, Diogenes in the barrel, the Ark of the Covenant contrasted with the apostle Paul preaching in Athens. Bohemia is included in the form of her patron saints, the Premonstratensian order and Strahov Monastery are naturally shown in a flattering light, while contemporary French Enlightenment philosophers are cast into the abyss. In the center, Divine Wisdom triumphs when the final page is turned; she is surrounded by allegories of religion and the virtues. The artist has left his autograph in the northeast corner (next to King David with his harp): "Anton Maulbertsch Pinxit Ano 1794," along with his symbol, the thistle.

Fresco by Franz Anton Maulpertsch in the Philosophy Hall ▷

Malá Strana
Lesser Town

Despite the encroachments of modern traffic, Malá Strana (literally "Little Side") has preserved much of its idyllic, old-world atmosphere. A maze of narrow lanes leads to secluded squares and gardens, pompous mansions of the nobility and dignified merchants' houses, picturesque arcades and courtyards, and again and again provides glimpses of the unique landscape of roofs and gables that is dominated by the majestic dome of St. Nicholas.

The district was inhabited as early as the ninth century. Thanks to its fortunate site at the confluence of trade routes from Regensburg, Nuremburg, and Leipzig, a bustling, prosperous community soon grew up. In 1257 King Ottokar II granted a charter to the "New Town below Prague Castle" (Nova civitas sub castro Pragensi), which came to be known as the "Lesser Town of Prague" ("Kleinseite" in German). The area of the township, which centered upon the present Malostranské náměstí, the main square, was considerably enlarged around 1360, during the reign of Charles IV, by the incorporation of existing settlements beyond the Hunger Wall (see p. 83). The Hussite wars and periodic fires took their toll of many an old building, and with the advent of the Habsburgs in the sixteenth century, the aristocracy began to build their residences in the quarter. The Catholic victory at Bílá hora heralded the triumphant era of the Baroque, which to this day remains the keynote of the Malá Strana townscape.

26 Lesser Town Square
Malostranské náměstí

A marketplace since the tenth century and hub of Malá Strana.

The square has always consisted of an upper and a lower section. The Gothic parish church and the tower are long since gone; today it is the former Jesuit college and the Baroque church of St. Nicholas that form the center of attention. In front of the east end of St. Nicholas at No. 28 looms the massive **Grömling Palace**, where in 1874 the Café Radetzky opened (in the 1920s, under the name of Malostranská kavárna, a popular resort of writers and artists).

Behind nearly all of the Renaissance, Baroque, and Empire facades there is a medieval core; the typical arcades and passageways are still to be seen, particularly on the south side. The dominant feature on the east side is the **Kaiserstein Palace,** No. 23, with a Baroque facade by Giovanni Alliprandi and statues of the four seasons by Ottavio Mosto; a bust commemorates the residence here of the soprano Emmy Destinn (Ema Destinnová), who partnered Enrico Caruso on the world's operatic stages. At the corner of Letenská stands the former **Malá Strana Town Hall**. Along the north side at Nos. 19 and 18 are the **Renaissance palaces** of the Sternberg and Smiřický families; it was in the latter

that on 22 May 1618 the leaders of the Bohemian estates met to consider their course of action, which culminated in the Second Defenestration of Prague the following day. The east facade of the former **Jesuit college**, No. 25, has a notable Baroque portal.

Detail of the facade of Malá Strana Town Hall

West facade of St. Nicholas, Malá Strana, an example of Baroque illusionism in the Roman manner

The upper part of the square used to be known as the Italian Square. The mansion on the west side at No. 13 is the **Liechtenstein Palace,** a Renaissance structure with a Neoclassical facade; this was once the residence of the royal governor Karl von Liechtenstein, notorious for ordering the execution of the rebels on Staroměstské náměstí in 1621. On the south side at No. 12, the Baroque **Hartig Palace** is followed by interesting Neoclassical facades by Palliardi, Nos. 9, 8 and 6. The Baroque **Trinity Column** sets an important accent in front of the facade of St. Nicholas. Designed by Alliprandi, it was erected in 1715 to mark the passing of the plague; the statues of the patron saints are by Ulrich Mayer and Ferdinand Geiger.

27 St. Nicholas
Svatý Mikuláš
Malostranské náměstí

Prague's most notable High Baroque church, with dome and bell-tower by Dientzenhofer.

The huge, 262-foot high dome, with its companion tower of equal height, is a landmark for miles around, testimony in stone to the triumph of the Counter-Reformation. The site was allocated to the Jesuits of Malá Strana soon after the Catholic victory of 1620, and the Waldstein and Kolovrat-Liebštejnský families made generous donations. The foundation stone was laid by Emperor Leopold I in 1673, but initially only the Jesuit institute was built (closed down in 1773). The church

69

was erected in two main phases: Christoph Dientzenhofer designed the nave and west facade (1702-11), and his son Kilian Ignaz Dientzenhofer, the chancel (1737-51), with the bell-tower being completed by Anselmo Lurago in 1756.

The Dientzenhofers made effective use of the spatial illusionism of high and late Baroque, as pioneered by Borromini and Guarini in their intricately curved designs in Rome and Turin. The concave modulations of the **facade** and the vertical thrust of the gable are best appreciated from an oblique angle. The **nave**, which virtually "sways" up to the vault, is a sequence of overlapping transverse ovals between diagonally set piers; typical for a Jesuit church are the galleries that run above the side chapels, a scheme introduced by Vignola at Il Gesù in Rome, the mother church of the order. Kilian Ignaz designed the **chancel** on a grandiose trefoil plan with semicircular apses and a soaring circular dome on a high drum.

On the younger Dientzenhofer's death in 1751, the architectural impact of the interior was as yet little modified by the presence of color; most of the **decoration** came subsequently, in the late Baroque or Rococo style. Franz Xaver Palko, the Silesian fresco painter who was later to become artist to the court of Saxony, painted the representation of the Celestial Glory in the dome; in the north apse he depicted the worldwide missionary work of the Jesuits, as far afield as Japan. Johann Lukas Kracker, a pupil of Paul Tröger, who was mainly active in Moravia and Hungary, contributed the two paintings on the side altars: the Visitation (left, signed), and the Death of St. Joseph (right). But Kracker's chef-d'œuvre, which clearly reveals the influence of the Venetians Piazzetta and Tiepolo, is the vast painting on the ceiling of the nave, at over 16,000 square feet one of the largest in Europe; it is dated by a chronogram on the chancel arch (1760). Depicted are scenes from the life of St. Nicholas, fourth-century bishop of Myra in Asia Minor – his good deeds toward prisoners, merchants, and seafarers, his ascension to heaven, and the miracles that occurred at his tomb (framed by a monumental triumphal arch). Kracker left a self-portrait as a cavalier leaning nonchalantly against the side of the steps.

Of more interest for their subject-matter than for their artistic quality are the huge statues by Ignaz Platzer: in the chancel four Eastern church fathers, on the entablatures above the double columns the four

Pulpit in St. Nicholas, by Richard Georg Prachner and his son Peter

cardinal virtues (fortitude, prudence, justice, temperance), and in the nave the Persian King Cyrus with a broken fetter (in allusion to the freeing of the Jews from their Babylonian captivity), the Roman emperors Constantine the Great and Theodosius, and a Jesuit saint. Richard Georg Prachner and his son Peter were responsible for the splendid Rococo pulpit, with its gilded wood carvings of Faith, Hope, and Charity and the Beheading of John the Baptist.

28 Neruda Street
Nerudova

Malá Strana's most attractive thoroughfare, with typical house emblems.

This is the last and steepest section of the old Royal Way, along which the kings of

◁ *Dome and north apse of St. Nicholas*

Bohemia rode to the castle on coronation day; in the fourteenth and fifteenth centuries they had their palace in the Old Town, and the later monarchs who resided in the castle continued the tradition.

Many of the quaint **emblems** that served to identify houses before the introduction of numbering can still be seen today: for example, the Three Violins at No. 12, which belonged to a family of violinmakers named Edlinger; the Golden Goblet, No. 16, once a goldsmith's workshop; and St. John of Nepomuk, No. 18.

Diagonally opposite each other stand two of the finest secular creations of Baroque Prague, in the dignified tradition of the Viennese High Baroque of Fischer von Erlach and Hildebrandt: **Morzin Palace** at No. 5 and **Thun-Hohenstein Palace** at No. 20. They are both the work of Johann Blasius Santin-Aichel, an architect of Italian origin also known as Santini, and date from 1713-14 and 1726, respectively. There are buildings by Santin-Aichel, both sacred and secular, throughout Bohemia; they are diverse and imaginative in design, and in some cases show idiosyncrasies of formal idiom that create an impression of "Baroque Gothic." The artistic effect of the two facades is enhanced by sympathetic sculptural works. The Morzin Palace, which is now the Romanian embassy, is buttressed by Brokoff's powerful black atlantes, the coat of arms of the Morzin ("Moor") family; above the portal the laughing bust of Day (sun) contrasts with

The Golden Goblet, emblem of a house on Nerudova

slumbering Night (moon). On the portal of the Thun-Hohenstein Palace (the Italian embassy), M. B. Braun – the other paragon of Bohemian High Baroque – has introduced the drama of untamed nature in the shape of two eagles with splayed talons, the heraldic emblems of the Kolovrats, for whom the mansion was originally built; the entablatures bear the reclining figures of Jupiter and Juno.

Before the introduction of numbering, houses were identified by fanciful emblems

On the site of the old Strahov, or Black, Gate stands the **Theatine Church** of SS. Cajetan and Mary of Perpetual Succor. Santin-Aichel is thought to have collaborated on the building, which was erected between 1691 and 1717. A project by the Turin architect Guarino Guarini, which was not realized, provided inspiration for the Dientzenhofers [see No. 27]. Of interest are the high altar sculptures by Jäckel (1724) and the painting of St. Thecla on the side altar by Palko.

The upper stretch of Nerudova also has its share of imposing **aristocratic and bourgeois residences**, most of which have Baroque or Rococo facades. The Golden Lion at No. 32 houses an apothecaries' museum. Mozart and Casanova were two of the guests who stayed at the Bretfeld Palace, No. 33, whose emblem is Spring and Summer. The twin gables of the Two Suns, No. 47, mark the home of writer Jan Neruda (1834-91), whose "Malá Strana Stories" conjure up a delightful picture of life in the quarter. At the corner of Úvoz, No. 48, where the castle approach bends sharply to the right (see p. 62), stands the Golden Star, also known as the Three Kings.

29 New Castle Steps, Slavata Palace

Zámecké schody, Slavatský palác

Thunovská 25 (access from Nerudova, between the Theatine Church and Thun-Hohenstein Palace)

The shortest route between Malá Strana and the castle.

The site fronting on a steep and narrow lane was not ideally suited to a display of pomp, but the New Castle Steps were a much-traveled thoroughfare, and the lords of Jindřichův Hradec made sure their status would be properly appreciated by crowning their mansion (erected 1540-60) with magnificent Renaissance gables. The owners were a branch of the powerful southern Bohemian house of Rosenberg (whose legendary ancestor Witiko is the hero of Adalbert Stifter's eponymous novel); when the male line of the Rosenbergs died out in 1602, the palace passed to the Slavatas, of whom Vilém was soon to have the dubious honor of being thrown out of a window of the castle. The building is actually part of Thun-Hohenstein Palace (p. 72), which was later extended as far as Nerudova.

Zámecké schody (New Castle Steps) used to be lined with craftsmen's workshops – No. 2, with its display window, is a good example of the type. Downhill, bridged by arches, runs Thunovská street. **Leslie-Thun Palace** (No. 14, the British embassy), a Renaissance structure in its

Zámecké schody, with the Renaissance gables of Slavata Palace

Street musicians on Zámecké schody

Kolovrat Palace, on Valdštejnská

core, was remodeled in the Baroque style when it was owned by Guidobald Thun-Hohenstein, archbishop of Salzburg; the neo-Gothic battlements were added around 1850. In 1787 Mozart and his wife Konstanze were guests here.

30 The Golden Well
U zlaté studně

A picturesque corner of old Prague.

The east side of Sněmovní is occupied by the Neoclassical Parliament House, where on 14 November 1918 the Bohemian assembly formally severed the centuries-old ties with Habsburg Austria and elected Tomáš Masaryk president of the new republic; today it is the seat of the **Czech parliament**. Two fine Baroque portals, perhaps by Fischer von Erlach, are the sole relics of the magnificent Thun Palace that once occupied the site before it was destroyed by fire. **Stately homes** still line the west side of the street: the palaces of the Lažanský, Černin, and Harbuval-Chamaré families at Nos. 5, 7 and 13.

The **Golden Swan** on the corner at No. 6, with its impressive Renaissance gables, marks the beginning of **U zlaté studně**, a cul-de-sac named after the cast-iron relief

from the Biedermeier era that adorns the little late Baroque house at No. 4: Jesus with the Woman of Samaria at Jacob's Well, which was popularly known as the "Golden Well." Zigzagging up steps and across courtyards, the alley leads to an open-air restaurant with a marvelous view (open summer only).

31 Waldstein Street
Valdštejnská

The surroundings of the Waldstein Palace, with fine mansions and gardens.

Behind the stately homes that line the north side of Valdštejnská run the famous terraced gardens, carved into the southeast slopes of the castle ridge. In the eighteenth century architects and sculptors – most of them Italians – converted what had once been vineyards into truly "enchanted gardens," a wonderland of fountains, loggias, pavilions, flights of steps, balustrades, and statues. Behind **Palais Ledebur**, Santin-Aichel designed a graceful *sala terrena* (open-sided hall facing the garden) for the then owner, the countess of Trautmannsdorf. The real jewel of the chain is the **Kolovrat Garden**, laid out in 1784 by Palliardi for Countess Maria Barbara of Černin. After years of restoration work, the Ledebur, Palffy, Kolovrat, and Fürstenberg gardens are now linked with one another, and offer delightful venues for summer concerts and theater performances (not usually open at other times).

The mansions that front these gardens are generally rather sober in appearance, but **Kolovrat Palace** at No. 10 has an elegant late Baroque facade by Palliardi (c. 1780) that foreshadows Neoclassicism.

32 Waldstein Palace
Valdštejnský palác
Valdštejnské náměstí 4

The first secular monument of Prague Baroque.

Until 1945 the palace still belonged to the descendants of the famous commander-in-chief of the imperial armies, Prince Albrecht of Waldstein (Wallenstein), duke of Friedland, Sagan, and Mecklenburg (1583-1634). A series of advantageous marriages, remuneration from the imperial purse for services in the Thirty Years'

The Waldstein Garden with sala terrena; *in the background the spires of St. George peep from behind the Institute of Noblewomen, with the cathedral to the left*

War, and the purchase of property confiscated from Protestant nobles laid the foundation of the family's wealth. In 1623 Waldstein secured the demolition of thirty houses and the leveling of several gardens to make room for his new residence in Malá Strana, a monumental complex ordered around five courtyards with an extensive garden and *sala terrena*, one of the finest palaces in Europe. Schiller's trilogy records Wallenstein's rise and fall, his unauthorized peace negotiations with Saxony

Early Baroque stuccoed and painted ceiling in the Waldstein sala terrena

Bronze statue of Apollo by Adriaen de Vries, in the Waldstein Garden

and Sweden, and his deposal and murder in Cheb by the imperial officers Aldringen, Gallas, and Piccolomini. Waldstein's property was confiscated; the palace and garden were ravaged by the Swedes, and remodeled several times in later years.

The palace was completed in 1630 to a design by Andrea Spezza that provided for a private domain shielded from the public eye, splendor being reserved for the inner precinct and the garden. Thus, the facade is relatively plain, almost bourgeois, with dormer windows of the northern European type; new at the time, however, was the broad perspective of nineteen bays, in contrast with the tall and narrow end elevation. The interior (some of the rooms are now occupied by the Komenský Pedagogical Museum) was decorated in the Italian early Baroque style by Baccio del Bianco of Florence. The ceiling fresco in the Grand Hall depicts Waldstein as Mars, the god of war.

33 Waldstein Garden
Valdštejnská zahrada
Letenská, open May to September

One of Prague's memorable views: statue-lined walks culminating in a grand loggia, with the castle as a backdrop.

The summer concerts held here today are only a dim reflection of the glittering spectacles of yesteryear, when the Waldstein Garden was a paradise of rare plants and exotic animals, of grottoes, ponds, and fountains; but still as compelling as ever is the focal point of the entire scheme, the majestic three-bay *sala terrena*, or **garden loggia**. A basically Renaissance architectural element, the loggia is decorated in the Mannerist spirit, while its monumental conception already reflects Baroque aspirations to grandeur. The architects Andrea Spezza and Giovanni Peroni took their inspiration from Tuscan and Roman models. The mighty barrel vault is decorated with vigorous stuccowork and paintings (Zeus, the Trojan War) by Baccio del Bianco (1629-30).

The bronze statues of mythological figures – Apollo, Bacchus, Neptune, Laocoön, Venus and Adonis, Hercules, horses – are for the most part casts of the originals by Adriaen de Vries. The Dutch sculptor was born in The Hague in 1560 and served his apprenticeship in Florence with Giovanni da Bologna, who was mentor to a number of notable sculptors during the transitional period between Mannerism and Baroque. De Vries first made his name with the Mercury and Hercules fountains in Augsburg (c. 1600), and subsequently worked in Prague for Emperor Rudolf II and later for Waldstein; these bronze figures are his last work, cast between 1622 and 1626, probably for a grand fountain. At the end of the Thirty Years' War, Count Königsmarck (who had served under Waldstein as a young officer and later went over to the Swedish camp) had the originals transported to Sweden, where they were set up in Drottningholm Palace.

The garden is bounded at the Klárov end by the **Riding School**, where Waldstein kept three hundred horses; it is now an exhibition hall for the National Gallery.

34 St. Thomas's Church and Monastery
Svatý Tomáš
Letenská

Fine Baroque facade by Dientzenhofer, notable decoration and furnishings.

In 1285 King Wenceslas II founded the church and monastery of the Augustinian Hermits. After a fire in the Hussite period it was rebuilt, and served as the main church of the Catholics during the heyday of the Utraquists in Prague. Rudolf II had it refurbished to serve as court church, and in the seventeenth century the monastery buildings were given an early Baroque mantle.

Between 1725 and 1731 the church was sympathetically remodeled in the Baroque style by Kilian Ignaz Dientzenhofer. For two of the elevations he designed dynamically articulated **facades** in the tradition of Roman illusionism. Above the portals stand early Baroque statues by Hieronymus Kohl (1684) – St. Augustine (west) and St. Thomas of Villanova (south). In the **interior**, the original early Gothic basilica plan (nave and two aisles, long monks' choir) was not altered, but Dientzenhofer introduced festive, palatial features: a dome, molded pilasters and engaged columns, and galleries. The frescoes were painted by Wenzel Lorenz Reiner in 1728: they depict the life of St. Augustine, Doctor of the Church, and the founding of the various orders that adopted his rule, the legend of St. Thomas (in the choir), and allegories of the four continents (in the cupola pendentives). The two paintings on the high altar, the Torturing of the Apostle

Panorama of Malá Strana, with the dome of St. Nicholas (left), the spire of St. Thomas (center), and Sancta Maria de Victoria (right foreground)

St. Thomas's Church: statue of St. Vitus

77

High altar in St. Thomas's Church, with copies of paintings by Rubens

Thomas and St. Augustine, were commissioned by the prior in 1637 from Rubens; the originals are in Sternberg Palace. The large statues of saints are by J. A. Quittainer, the smaller ones by F. M. Brokoff. Early Baroque, dating from 1671, are Karel Škréta's paintings for the side altars: the Holy Trinity, the Assumption, and St. Thomas of Villanova. The whitish figures in the north aisle are models for silver statues by Andreas Philipp Quittainer; particularly attractive are St. Vitus with the rooster and St. Wenceslas with the flag.

From 1352 until well into the twentieth century the monastery had its own brewery, which produced a celebrated dark beer. The old beer hall, with its Gothic vaulting, still serves a powerful brew, which can also be enjoyed in the garden (**U svatého Tomáše,** Letenská 12).

35 The Golden Stag
U zlatého jelena
Tomášská 4

Prague's most attractive house emblem.

This, one of the finest merchant houses in Prague, was designed by Kilian Ignaz Dientzenhofer in 1725. F. M. Brokoff sculpted the **emblem**, a delightfully natural and adroit representation of the key scene from the legend of St. Hubert, who in his passion for hunting failed to observe Sunday as the Lord's Day until he was finally converted by the apparition of a stag with a crucifix between its antlers. The historical Hubert died in 727, and was the first bishop of Tongeren (Belgium), instrumental in the evangelization of the Ardennes. In the fifteenth century his biography became entwined with legends about the early Christian martyr Eustachius (Placidus), hunter and chief of staff to Emperor Trajan.

Next door at No. 2 is a famous beer hall, **U Schnellů**.

House emblem: the Golden Stag

36 St. Joseph
Svatý Josef
Josefská

A jewel of Flemish Baroque in Prague.

In 1656 Emperor Ferdinand III founded the convent of the Discalced Carmelites.

West facade of St. Joseph

After the suppression of the institution in 1782, the buildings were transformed into a girls' school that was run by the Englische Fräulein, until in 1920 the Ministry of Finance moved in.

The two-story **facade** of this impressive church was built between 1687 and 1692 in the Flemish Baroque tradition, which in turn derives from the Mannerism of northern Italy. The design is attributed to Ignatius of Jesus (Johann Raas), architect of the Carmelite order at this time, though J. B. Fischer von Erlach in his *Sketch of a Historical Architecture* names Abraham Parigi.

The statues by Jäckel depict the church's patron in the central niche and, on the lateral volutes, Teresa of Avila and John of the Cross, the most famous mystics of the order. The interior is remarkable for its strictly central plan – a longitudinal oval with lateral niches.

The sculptures here are also by Jäckel, who was assisted in some works by Marcus Nonnenmacher, a cabinetmaker from Malá Strana. Peter Brandl, a leading light in Bohemian High Baroque, painted the altarpieces of the Holy Family and St. Teresa; the third altarpiece depicts St. Thecla.

Kaunitz Palace, on Mostecká

37 Kaunitz Palace

Palác Kauniců

Mostecká 15

A Rococo mansion on an important thoroughfare.

"Bridge Street" was where the old trade routes from Regensburg, Nuremberg, and Leipzig led down to the river and from there onward to the east. It is lined with well-preserved Baroque houses, but architecturally the most interesting building is Kaunitz Palace, the embassy of former Yugoslavia, a Rococo design with Neoclassical features by Anton Karl Schmidt (1773-75). The graceful stuccowork – mainly festoons of foliage and flowers – and the statues on the attic story are from Ignaz Platzer's workshop.

38 Vrtba Palace

Palác Vrtbovský

Karmelitská 25

Fronts Prague's finest Baroque garden, with a magnificent view.

The unpretentious Renaissance facade of the mansion bears a plaque commemorating Mikoláš Aleš, the leading Czech painter of the late nineteenth century, who for a time had his studio here. A Baroque gateway leads from the courtyard to the Italian terraced garden, which was laid out to the order of Jan Josef Vrtba, the chief burgrave, by František Maximilián Kaňka between 1720 and 1730. The statues are by M. B. Braun, the frescoes in the *sala terrena* by Reiner. Some of the mythological and allegorical figures (Atlas, Ceres/Summer, Bacchus/Autumn) are thematically related to Balthasar Permoser's statues in the Zwinger at Dresden.

39 Schönborn Palace

Palác Schönbornský

Tržiště 15

An imposing Baroque mansion among historic merchants' houses.

Tržiště, which used to be the "new market-place," is linked by passageways to Malostranskè náměstí. Schönborn Palace (now the American embassy) was built for the count of Colloredo-Wallsee in the mid-seventeenth century, and received its present High Baroque exterior around 1715 from Alliprandi or Santin-Aichel. Interesting historic buildings are also to be seen in the winding side alleys: Břetislavova, Jánský Vršek (steps leading to Nerudova), and Šporkova, where Sporck Palace is at No. 12 (earlier owners were the Martinic and Piccolomini families); originally the "Two Golden Lions," a late Renaissance house, it was remodeled in the Baroque style in the mid-eighteenth century.

A "walking Trabant" recalls the dramatic scenes at the German embassy in autumn 1989

40 Lobkowicz Palace

Lobkovický palác

Vlašská 19

A noble mansion and garden, also with a "proletarian" claim to fame.

Vlašská gets its name from the "Welsch" (i.e., foreign, in this case Italian) colony that began to establish itself hereabouts in the second half of the sixteenth century. Along with the merchants there was a steady flow of artists and craftsmen from Italy, who were instrumental in shaping the face of Baroque Prague. In 1602 leading members of the Italian community founded the **Italian Hospital** at No. 34, an early Baroque complex grouped around an arcaded courtyard, which today is the Italian Cultural Institute (Casa d'Italia).

Lobkowicz Palace, seen from the garden

Church of St. Lawrence on Petřín Hill, with a view over Nové Město

Lobkowicz Palace (the German embassy) grew out of a mansion built by Alliprandi in 1702 for the Přehořovský family. After 1769 it was radically rebuilt with an additional story for the Lobkowicz princes, to a plan by Palliardi. A striking feature of the garden elevation is the concave oval incorporating a three-bay *sala terrena*, reminiscent of Fischer von Erlach's mansions in Vienna. The ceiling fresco of the *Fall of Icarus*, by Hans Jakob Steinfels, is bordered with stucco reliefs by Tomaso Soldati. The unknown sculptor of the **garden gate** also took inspiration from Viennese models (Lorenzo Mattielli) for his versions of the Rape of Proserpine and that of Oreithya, daughter of an Athenian king, who was abducted by Boreas, the Thracian wind-god. Lobkowicz Palace hit the headlines in the fall of 1989, when thousands of East German citizens took refuge in the embassy before being granted transit visas to West Germany.

4I Petřín Hill *Petřín*
U lanové dráhy (funicular station)

Viewpoint with pleasant walks to Strahov Monastery, Malá Strana, and the Kinský Garden.

At Újezd 40, not far from the lower station of the funicular, the former **Michna Palace** is worth a visit, and not just for the Museum of Physical Education and Sport that is now housed there. The street elevation goes back to the unpretentious Renaissance mansion of the Kinský counts. The garden wing is altogether more imposing, being part of a pompous late Renaissance villa built between 1640 and 1650 for the Michnas, counts of Vacínov; Santino Bossi was in charge of the project, and Domenico Galli was responsible for the early Baroque stucco decoration. The Michna family had made their fortune as supporters of Waldstein and as army suppliers during the Thirty Years' War.

Whether we walk up **Petřín Hill** or take the hundred-year-old funicular, ever-changing views are presented that are particularly attractive in the springtime when the palace gardens below are covered in a mantle of blossoms. The summit is crowned by a 196-foot high **outlook tower**, which – like the funicular – was built for the National Fair of 1891 and, like the Eiffel Tower on which it is modeled, symbolizes the industrial developments of the period. On a clear day the view reaches as far as Bohemia's borders. The wooden pavilion nearby houses a mirror maze and a **diorama** depicting the students of Prague fighting Swedish troops in 1648.

Cosmas of Prague, the first chronicler of Bohemia, derives the name Petřín from the Latin word for "rock" *(petra)*; the German population knew the hill as Laurenziberg, from the Roman martyr St. Lawrence, whose church stands on the site of a pagan altar of the ancient Slavs and a tenth-century chapel of St. Adalbert. The original structure of 1140 was rebuilt several times before being given its present form, with dome and twin towers, by Palliardi between 1735 and 1770.

Interesting remnants of the Gothic **Hunger Wall** can be seen at several points on the Petřín Hill. Charles IV ordered the building of the wall, which formed part of the perimeter fortifications of the Prague townships (Old Town, Lesser Town, and Castle Ward with Strahov), during the great famine of 1360, to provide the people with work and bread.

42 Sancta Maria de Victoria

Panna Marie Vítězná

Karmelitská 9

Prague's oldest Baroque church, with a wax figure of the Infant Jesus that is known and loved the world over.

The city's oldest Baroque church was built between 1611 and 1613 for the German Lutherans to a design by Giovanni M. Filippi. Only a few years later, after the defeat of the Protestants at Bílá hora in 1620, it was assigned to the order of the Discalced Carmelites and renamed in honor of the Virgin, whose image, carried by a monk in the van of the Catholic troops, was believed to have brought them victory. A 1622 copy of the picture, which came from Strakonice in southern Bohemia, is displayed in the church. In 1628 the Carmelites received another miraculous image: Polyxena, wife of the chancellor

Facade of the Carmelite church of Sancta Maria de Victoria

Zdeněk Popel of Lobkovice and first lady of the Kingdom of Bohemia, presented the monks with an eighteen-inch high wax figure of the infant Jesus, which her mother, the Spanish princess Maria Magdalena Manriquez de Lara, had brought as part of her dowry when she married Vratislav of Pernštejn. In the climate of the Counter-Reformation, miraculous healings and other wonders were attributed to the image and it soon became a magnet for pilgrims. In 1648 it is supposed to have driven the Swedes out of Prague with silver bullets. To this day the "Jezulátko," "Bambino di Praga," or "Niño Jesús de Praga" is venerated by Catholics throughout the world, especially in southern Europe and Latin America. The exquisitely attired figure of the **Infant Jesus** stands in a silver-ornamented glass Rococo shrine on the right-hand side altar. The many gifts dedicated to it over the years include gold crowns, precious stones, ermine cloaks, and robes of velvet with gold embroidery, one of them made by Empress Maria Theresa personally.

The **facade** of the west-oriented church is modeled on the Roman two-stories-and-pediment scheme, and dates from 1636-40 (architect unknown). Above the portal stands a statue of the Virgin Victorious,

83

The world-famous "Infant Jesus of Prague" in its ermine mantle

the first of its kind in Prague. The barrel-vaulted **interior**, without aisles, is based on the style introduced by Vignola for Jesuit churches in Rome. Next to the pulpit is a fine altarpiece by Peter Brandl, which is also of interest for its subject: the Virgin appears to St. Simon Stock, General of the Carmelite order, in Cambridge in 1251. The painting on the first altar on the left, by Johann Georg Dietrich of Dresden, depicts St. Teresa of Avila, the great mystic and reformer of the Carmelite order. The ceiling is adorned with the imperial coat of arms, those of Bohemia and Hungary, and the Maltese cross (the church was taken over by the Knights of Malta in 1784).

Rohan Palace (Karmelitská 8) sports an elegant late Empire facade. The octagonal dome at the south end of the street at No. 2 belongs to the former **Mary Magdalen Church** of the Dominican monastery, which is now the Central Archive.

43 St. Procopius Street, Maltese Square

Prokopská, Maltézské náměstí

The alley is named after the medieval church of St. Procopius, the apse of which still juts out of the Baroque house at No. 3.

The quaint **sculpture** by Ignaz Platzer on the facade of No. 3 shows St. Procopius's triumph over the Devil. According to legend, the abbot (died c. 1053) of the Slavonic Benedictine monastery of Sázava harnessed the Devil to his plow; he later became one of the patron saints of Bohemia, and "Procopius with the Devil" was one of the most popular house emblems in Prague.

John the Baptist, patron saint of the Knights of Malta, presides over the Maltese square (Maltézské náměstí); the statue was sculpted for a fountain by F. M. Brokoff in 1715. The finest building on the square is **Turba Palace** at No. 6, the Japanese embassy, which – along with the **Muscon House** next door at No. 5 – was remodeled on Rococo lines by the Tyrolean architect Joseph Jäger in 1767. Parts of the walls of **Straka Palace** at No. 14 date back to Gothic times. The south end of the square is occupied by **Nostitz Palace** at No. 1, the embassy of the Netherlands, one of the earliest secular examples of Baroque in Prague, designed around 1650 by Francesco Caratti. During the eighteenth century the facade was variously adapted in line with prevailing trends: balustrade statues from the Brokoff workshop, a Rococo portal by Anton Haffenecker, window-moldings of a Neoclassical stamp, and balconies in the Empire style.

The main facade of Nostitz Palace

44 St. Mary under the Chain

Panna Marie pod řetězem

Lázeňská

Center of the "Maltese" district south of Karlův Most, which in the Middle Ages had an independent legal system.

In 1169, King Vladislav I founded the first commandery, or chapter, of the order of St. John of Jerusalem in Bohemia. The Knights Hospitalers, as its members were also known, are a military religious brotherhood founded in 1099 in Jerusalem, where they maintained a hospice for pilgrims; they defended Christianity against Islam in the Holy Land, and later from their headquarters on the islands of Rhodes and Malta. The martial character of the order is well evoked by the massive, squat towers of the early Gothic **Church of St. Mary under the Chain**. The name apparently alludes to the chain used to raise and lower the gate of the former house of the order.

Construction work was interrupted by the troubles of the Hussite period, and the church was never finished. The towers and the narthex give an idea of the imposing proportions of the original plan; where the nave should have been there is just a courtyard (a Romanesque church once stood on the site). The chancel was rebuilt by Carlo Lurago between 1640 and 1660 to create an early Baroque church, whose three altarpieces are by Karel Škréta, the best early Baroque painter in Bohemia: the Assumption, St. Barbara, and the Battle of Lepanto (1571).

To the left of the church, at Lázeňská No. 4, the **Baroque house** is the old commandery of the order. No. 6 used to be the **Malá Strana bathhouse** before it was converted into a high-class inn, which in 1698 accommodated Czar Peter I. The picturesque character of the quarter is rounded off by two mansions, **Sternegg Palace** at No. 9 and **Wolkenstein Palace** at No. 11, the "Golden Unicorn." A plaque notes that Beethoven slept here in 1796.

45 Grand Prior's Palace and Square

Velkopřevorské náměstí

Malá Strana's most idyllic square.

In 1725 Count Gundaker Poppo of Dietrichstein, grand prior of the Knights Hospitalers (who were now known as the Knights of Malta), commissioned Bartolomeo Scotti to design a mansion for him at No. 4, one of the finest examples of High Baroque in Prague. M. B. Braun and his workshop provided the sculptural decoration for the staircase. The stuccoed rooms on the upper floor now house the **musical instrument collection** of the National Museum. The Maltese Garden is in the summer months the venue of concerts and theatrical performances.

The peaceful, tree-lined square slopes gently down toward Kampa island. The High Baroque **Buquoy Palace** at No. 2, the French embassy, was designed around 1735 by Kaňka. The **Lesser Buquoy Palace** at No. 3 has preserved its Renaissance character; in the same style, though with some Baroque modifications, is **Hrzán Palace** at No. 1 which overlooks the Čertovka ("Devil's Channel"), a branch of the Vltava. The waterwheel still to be seen is a relic of the grand priory's mill.

The last surviving waterwheel on "Devil's Channel"

46 Kampa Island

Kampa

A riverside retreat below the busy Charles Bridge.

Of the various bridges linking Malá Strana with this longish island, that from Velkopřevorské náměstí offers the most attractive approach. The island's name comes from the Latin *campus*, "field." There were

The High Baroque palace of the grand prior of the Knights of Malta

once vegetable gardens and vineyards here, and it was only in the sixteenth century that the first houses were built on the northern part. Since the Middle Ages it has been the venue of a potters' market. **Na Kampě**, the "main street," is with its trees and grassy patches more like a village green. The most attractive house emblem graces the **Blue Fox** at No. 1, built in 1605 by Libeth Stewardt of Liège, armorer and gilder at the court of Rudolf II. On the bank of the Vltava (U Sovových mlýnů 4) stands **Liechtenstein Palace** (formerly Kaiserstein), an imposing early Baroque mansion with later Empire features, today used for official receptions. Not far from here stood the hut of the ferryman who maintained the link with the Old Town.

The stone steps to Karlův most are relatively recent, dating from the nineteenth century. One of the bridge piers (below statue No. 20, on p. 91) has a pillar with the so-called **Bruncvík statue** (copy). The armored knight brandishing his sword is, like the Roland figure in German cities, a symbol of authority – in this case of the jurisdiction of Staré Město over Kampa, which was a lucrative storage and market area for all the wares that passed through Prague.

The name of the figure suggests associations with the German city of Brunswick, and he has variously been identified with Henry the Lion or Duke Ernest, but also with the fabled Roland from the court of

Allegorical figure on Dětský ostrov (Children's Island)

The emblem of the Blue Fox, with a picture of the "Infant Jesus" above

Charlemagne, and with kings of the house of Přemysl. The most popular legend tells of a Czech knight who from his adventures in far-off lands brought back a tame lion; he incorporated this faithful companion into his coat of arms, engendering the Bohemian emblem of a white lion on a red ground. It is also said that Bruncvík's miraculous sword is immured in the masonry of the bridge, and will emerge to save the land in its hour of need.

47 The Three Ostriches
U tří pštrosů
Dražického náměstí 12
Prague's first coffeehouse.

Below Karlův Most on the other side is a corner house with early Baroque gables. The ostrich motifs were painted at the behest of Jan Fux, supplier of feather accessories to the imperial court around 1600, who made his fortune cashing in on the new craze for ostrich plumes. In 1714 the Armenian Deodatus Damajan opened Prague's first coffeehouse here; today the building, the core of which is Gothic, is a high-class hotel and restaurant.

Descending along Míšeňská, the walker should not miss the pretty house at No. 10, the **White Lamb**. The next street, **U Lužického Semináře**, is named after the Lusatian Seminary at No. 13 for students from the area of eastern Germany where many people today still speak Sorbian, a Slavonic language (the building now houses the Sorbian Library of the National Museum). No. 2 is the first of a picturesque row of houses along the Čertovka channel, known as "Prague's Venice."

48 Lesser Town Bridge Towers
Malostranské mostecké věže
Mostecká/Karlův most
Double pendant of the Old Town Bridge Tower.

The lower of the two towers has survived from the Romanesque twelfth-century bridge known as the Judith Bridge; the wedge-shaped roof and Renaissance gable were added in 1591. In the old customs house, adjacent, a Romanesque stone relief can still be seen that was once affixed to the outer wall of the tower. The taller, Late Gothic tower was erected in 1464 on the orders of King George of Poděbrady, who

The Lesser Town Bridge Towers and Church of St. Nicholas, seen from Charles Bridge

wanted a weightier counterpart to the tower at the other end of the bridge. It bears the arms not only of Malá Strana, but also of Staré Město, under whose jurisdiction the entire bridge, along with Kampa Island, belonged. The crenelated Gothic gate between the two towers probably replaced a Romanesque predecessor.

49 Charles Bridge
Karlův most

One of the oldest stone bridges in Europe, and surely the most beautiful – a unique open-air gallery of Baroque sculpture.

Prague owed its rise to become a major center of international trade to the existence of a bridge over the Vltava. The first stone bridge, replacing a wood construction, was built between 1158 and 1172 on the orders of King Vladislav I, who named it after his wife, Judith of Thuringia. The Judith Bridge collapsed in 1342, and in 1357 Charles IV laid the foundation stone of the present, Gothic bridge. The emperor entrusted the planning and supervision of the project to the cathedral architect, Peter Parler, who was twenty-seven years old when building began; the bridge was not completed until some years after his death in 1399. Until the nineteenth century the "Stone Bridge" was the only permanent link between the Prague townships on each side of the river.

St. John of Nepomuk on Charles Bridge

With its width of 33 feet, Charles Bridge could accommodate four carriages abreast; its 1706-foot span rests on sixteen arches. It is slightly angled to incorporate the bridgeheads of the old Judith Bridge. For a long time the only work of art here was the bridge itself, with its noble proportions and fine stonework; apart from a crucifix, there was no sculptural embellishment until the end of the seventeenth century. It was probably the three hundredth anniversary of the death of John of Nepomuk, in 1693, that gave rise to the idea that the bridge, with Prague Castle as a backdrop, might serve as the perfect setting for a statue of the saint. Other statues soon followed: religious institutions, high-ranking officials, faculties, and other donors vied with each other to commemorate their favorite saints, and there are some curious combinations of figures that have chronologically and thematically very little in common. In the course of some two hundred and fifty years the number of individual or group sculptures reached a total of thirty. Almost all are in Bohemian sandstone, and due to the effects of atmospheric pollution, they are gradually being replaced by copies. The originals are held at the Lapidarium (see p. 160), which also

Plinth relief below the statues of SS. Vincent Ferrer and Procopius

The Vision of St. Luitgard, *by Matthias Bernhard Braun*

contains F. M. Brokoff's statue of St. Igna-tius of Loyola, which stood at position No. 9 on the plan opposite until it was washed away during a flood.

The best of the sculptures in artistic terms is the **Vision of St. Luitgard [24]**, a Cistercian nun from Brabant, whom Christ reaches down from the cross to embrace; it was sculpted by the Tyrolean Matthias Bernhard Braun, who here displays a theatrical expressiveness equal to that of Bernini's Rome sculpture of St. Teresa in mystic rapture. In quite another spirit – more of this world – are the less dramatic and more composed works of Ferdinand

Maximilian Brokoff, son of the sculptor Johann Brokoff [**15**] and foremost repre-sentative of Bohemian High Baroque. He contributed the statue of **St. Cajetan of Tiene [23]**, donated by the Theatine congregation of Malá Strana, and the **Trinitarian group [28]**: SS. John of Matha and Felix of Valois, founders of the Trini-tarian order for the redemption of Chris-tians from Muslim captivity, are helping a galley slave to his feet, while a nonchalant Turk guards a dungeon; the stag that fig-ures in the legend of the saints is also included. Less obviously relevant is the fig-ure of St. Ivan, a princeling's son from Dal-

Statues on Karlův most
Malá Strana

St. Wenceslas, Bohemian martyr and [30]
patron saint, d. 935
Josef Kamil Böhm, 1858

[29] SS. Cosmas and Damian, patrons of
physicians and apothecaries
Johann Ulrich Mayer, 1709

SS. John of Matha and Felix of Valois, [28]
Trinitarians, and Ivan,
a Bohemian hermit (c. 900)
Ferdinand Maximilian Brokoff, 1714

[27] St. Vitus, patron saint of Charles Bridge
Ferdinand Maximilian Brokoff, 1714

St. Adalbert, Bishop of Prague and [26]
patron saint of Bohemia, founder of the
Benedictine monastery at Břevnov
Josef Michael Brokoff, 1709

[25] St. Philip Benitius,
founder of the Servite Order
Michael Bernhard Mandl, 1714

St. Luitgard, a Cistercian nun, [24]
before the Cross
Matthias Bernhard Braun, 1710

[23] St. Cajetan of Tiene,
founder of the Theatine Order
Ferdinand Maximilian Brokoff, 1709

St. Nicholas of Tolentino, [22]
an Augustinian hermit
Johann Friedrich Kohl, 1708

[21] St. Augustine, Doctor of the Church
Johann Friedrich Kohl, 1708 (copy)

St. Vincent Ferrer, Dominican, [20]
and St. Procopius, Benedictine and
patron saint of Bohemia
Ferdinand Maximilian Brokoff, 1712

[19] St. Jude the Apostle and
"Brother of the Lord"
Johann Ulrich Mayer, 1708

On the bridge pier below:
the "Roland" or Bruncvík statue

St. Franciscus Seraphicus [18]
(Francis of Assisi),
founder of the Franciscan Order
Emanuel Max, 1855

[17] St. Anthony of Padua, a Franciscan
Johann Ulrich Mayer, 1707

St. Ludmila, first Christian princess and [16]
patron saint of Bohemia
Workshop of Matthias Braun, 1720/30

[15] St. John of Nepomuk, vicar-general of
the archbishopric of Prague, drowned in
the Vltava in 1393
*Johann Brokoff and Matthias
Rauchmüller (models), 1683; Wolf W.
Herold, Nuremberg (bronze cast)*

St. Francis of Borja, a Spanish Jesuit [14]
Ferdinand Maximilian Brokoff, 1710

[13] St. Wenceslas, St. Norbert, founder
of the Premonstratensians, and
St. Sigismund, 5th-c. King of Burgundy
Josef Max, 1853

St. Christopher, patron saint of travelers [12]
Emanuel Max, 1857

[11] St. John the Baptist, patron saint of the
Knights of Malta
Josef Max, 1853

St. Francis Xavier, Jesuit missionary [10]
*Ferdinand Maximilian Brokoff, 1711
(copy)*

[9] SS. Cyril and Methodius,
Apostles to the Slavs
Karel Dvořák, 1938
Originally: St. Ignatius Loyola by
Ferdinand Maximilian Brokoff

St. Joseph [8]
Josef Max, 1854

[7] St. Anne with the Virgin and Child
Matthäus Wenzel Jäckel, 1707

Pietà [6]
Emanuel Max, 1859

[5] Crucifixion
*Hans Hillger, 1629 (bronze Christ),
Emanuel Max, 1861 (Mary and John)*

SS. Barbara, Margaret, and Elizabeth [4]
Ferdinand Maximilian Brokoff, 1707

[3] Virgin with St. Dominic and St. Thomas
Aquinas, Dominicans
Matthäus Wenzel Jäckel, 1708 (copy)

St. Ivo, patron saint of the [2]
legal profession
Matthias Bernhard Braun, 1711 (copy)

[1] Virgin with St. Bernard of Clairvaux,
Cistercian
Matthäus Wenzel Jäckel, 1709

Staré Město

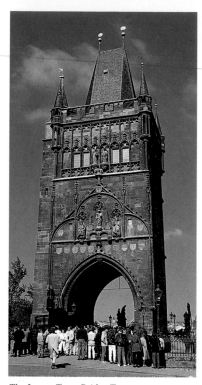

The Lesser Town Bridge Tower

the archbishop of Prague. His championing of ecclesiastical rights, and perhaps also his influence on the queen, aroused the ire of King Wenceslas IV, who in 1393 ordered him to be tortured and, when this failed to achieve the desired effect, thrown from the Stone Bridge into the Vltava. According to legend the corpse rose to the surface in a ring of shining stars; the people flocked to see the miracle, and buried the martyr. During the Counter-Reformation the Jesuits exhumed the body and reputedly found the tongue undecayed. The Jesuits campaigned for the canonization of John of Nepomuk, which was finally granted in 1729.

50 Old Town Bridge Tower
Staroměstská mostecká věž
Křižovnické náměstí

One of Central Europe's finest Gothic towers, with sculptural decoration from Peter Parler's workshop.

The genius of Peter Parler is again seen in this, the last work definitely attributable to him, which was commenced around 1370 and not completed until around 1400. The defensive tower was originally approached by a ramp, before the present plateau was banked up in the nineteenth century. The **statues**, by Parler and his assistants, are masterpieces of Bohemian High Gothic, and already display marked naturalistic traits. Portrayed in the upper blind arcade are St. Adalbert, bishop of Prague, and St. Sigismund of Burgundy, patron of the house of Luxemburg. Below, elegant baldachin tracery frames St. Vitus, standing on two arches of Charles Bridge (of which he is the patron), to the left the enthroned figure of Emperor Charles IV with the insignia and eagle coat of arms of the Holy Roman Empire, and to the right his son and successor Wenceslas IV with the lion, the emblem of Bohemia; at the apex of the ensemble is the Přemyslid eagle. The abutting arches on the left and right contain the arms of Staré Město and the Moravian eagle. The shields above the gateway represent the hereditary domains of the Luxemburgs. The emblem of Wenceslas IV appears several times: the kingfisher within a knotted sash, or towel, was popularly associated with the king's liaison with a pretty bathhouse attendant. The sculptural decoration on the river side of the tower was destroyed in 1648 by artillery fire from the Swedish troops who had occupied the other side of the river.

matia, who lived in a cave near Karlštejn and worked miracles around the year 900, some three hundred years before the other two subjects. Nor does there appear to be any iconographic link between St. Procopius and St. Vincent Ferrer [20]: Procopius, abbot of Sázava and one of the patron saints of Bohemia, died c. 1053, while Vincent, a Spanish Dominican and fanatical converter of Jews and Saracens, lived in the fourteenth century. Also notable are the works of the Lusatian sculptor Matthäus Wenzel Jäckel, who like Braun was receptive to Italian influences: a particularly interesting group is the Institution of the Rosary [3] with the Virgin, St. Thomas Aquinas, and St. Dominic, a gift of the Dominicans at St. Aegidius in Staré Město.

Most appropriate for this site is of course St. John of Nepomuk [15], since Baroque times the patron saint of bridges and of the secret of the confessional. Johann Welfflin, born in Nepomuk (near Plzeň) in 1340, doctor of theology and of law, was a compelling preacher and vicar-general to

Staré Město
Old Town

Of the various settlements that sprang up on both sides of the river between Hradčany and the fortified hill of Vyšehrad, the one around Staroměstské náměstí had become a focal point of international trade as early as the eleventh century. King Wenceslas I ordered the erection of a defensive wall (its course is marked by the present-day streets Revoluční, Na příkopě, and Národní), and in 1235 granted the "Alte Stadt Prag" (Old Town of Prague) a municipal charter on the German model. By the late fourteenth century, thanks not least to the patronage of Charles IV, the Old Town was one of the grandest cities in Central Europe. By decree of Emperor Joseph II, in 1784, it became part of the new unified Prague, along with Hradčany, Malá Strana, Josefov, and Nové Město.

Most of the superb medieval structure of the city has been preserved. The only marked alterations were caused by the redevelopment of the ghetto in the northern part toward the end of the nineteenth century, where late Historicism and Art Nouveau buildings dominate the streets. Pedestrian zones around Staroměstské náměstí (Old Town Square) make sightseeing a pleasure.

51 St. Francis

Svatý František

Křižovnické náměstí

The church's majestic dome is one of the most imposing features of the Old Town skyline.

The complex that extends north of the square along the river bank is the erstwhile

home of the Order of the Cross (Red Star), the only military religious order to be founded in Bohemia (in 1237). The grand masters of the order were the archbishops of Prague over a considerable period of time, from 1561 to 1694 – a state of affairs that generated not a little friction with the Jesuits. And the latter may well have seen it as a slight to their own church of St.

Křižovnické náměstí, with the dome of St. Francis (left), the facade of St. Savior (center), and the Old Town Bridge Tower

93

St. Francis, church of the Knights of the Cross: high altar and pulpit

The cupola of St. Francis

Savior when the Red Star knights across the way crowned their church with a grand dome.

The **church** was built between 1678 and 1687 to a design by the French painter and architect Jean Baptiste Mathey, who had spent twenty years in Rome. Of Roman inspiration is the early Baroque central plan,

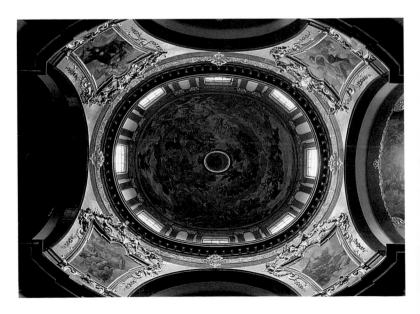

with an oval dome on a high drum – the first in Prague. The broad facade, on the other hand, is more on the coolly classical lines of French Baroque. The formality of the elevation is modulated by the late Baroque and Rococo statues that were added later: above the portal St. Francis of Assisi, to whom the church is dedicated, on the left St. Agnes (the Order of the Cross was originally a brotherhood that maintained a hospice at the convent of St. Agnes) and St. Ludmila, on the right SS. Wenceslas and Vitus (Anton Philipp Quittainer, 1723), on the attic story angels from the workshop of Matthäus Wenzel Jäckel, and flanking the steps a Mary Immaculate and St. John of Nepomuk by Richard Prachner. At the corner of Křižovnická stands a vine-clad early Baroque **Wenceslas column** by Johann Georg Bendl (1676), which used to adorn the old customs house by the bridge tower.

The **interior** is decorated with Bohemian marble, stucco by Tomaso Soldati, and frescoes of the Last Judgment by Wenzel Lorenz Reiner. Wall niches house monumental stucco figures by the Süssner brothers from Dresden (1690-91): Jeremias Süssner fashioned the "composed" statues of SS. Joachim and Anne, Konrad Max Süssner the "dramatic" renditions of SS. Martin, George, and Catherine (inspired by Bernini). The other sculptures are by Matthäus Wenzel Jäckel: on the high altar God the Father amid a host of angels, and SS. Helen and Augustine. Jan Kryštof Liška painted the Stigmatization of St. Francis in the sanctuary cupola, and Michael Lukas Willmann the altarpieces in the lateral arms.

On the river side of Křižovnické náměstí stands a neo-Gothic **statue of Charles IV**, cast in Nuremberg from a model by Ernst Hähnel of Dresden, to mark the five-hundredth anniversary of the university founded by the emperor.

Monument to Emperor Charles IV

in the mid-sixteenth century. The **portico and facade** on the east side of the square are adorned with vigorous stuccowork by Giovanni Battista Cometa and statues by Bendl dating from 1659: at the apex Christ as Savior of the World flanked by the four evangelists, in the gable niche the Virgin Mary with the Jesuit saints Ignatius of Loyola and Francis Xavier on the lateral plinths, and on the balustrade the four Western church fathers between SS. Clement and Adalbert. An early Baroque wrought-iron gate lead into the **interior**. Worthy of attention here are the stucco angels in the pendentives of the lantern and the figures of apostles on the confessionals by Bendl (1648). The paintings of SS. Ignatius and Francis Xavier on the side altars are by Johann Georg Heintsch (c. 1700).

52   St. Savior

Svatý Salvátor
Křižovnické náměstí

An impressive early Baroque facade with a three-bay triumphal arch – symbol of the Counter-Reformation.

The first Jesuit church in Bohemia, founded in 1578, was a Renaissance-Gothic basilica; it was still unfinished when the Thirty Years' War interrupted construction work. Carlo Lurago and Francesco Caratti completed the edifice in the Baroque style

53   Clementinum

Klementinum
Křižovnická-Platnéřská-Seminářská-Karlova

The most extensive complex of buildings in Prague after the castle; formerly the Jesuit institute, now university and state library.

View across the roofs of the Clementinum; the most prominent tower is that of the observatory, topped by a statue of Atlas

In 1556 the Habsburgs handed over the Dominican monastery, which had been laid waste in the Hussite wars, to the Jesuits, who proceeded to transform it into a college that would be a bulwark of the Counter-Reformation: some thirty thousand Utraquist books were burnt in the courtyard, and after the Catholic victory at Bílá hora the Jesuits also took over Charles University, which had been a stronghold of Protestantism. After the order was disbanded in 1773 the premises were used as archiepiscopal seminary, university, and library.

One hundred forty years of building resulted in a wide-ranging complex with five courtyards, three churches (the Czech St. Savior, the German St. Clement, and the Italian Chapel), living-quarters, school, library, observatory, printing-shop, and theater. The oldest part is the **main facade** on Křižovnická, a late Mannerist design by Carlo Lurago dating from circa 1636; it is articulated by pilasters of rough-

Plan of the Clementinum
1 St. Savior (p. 89) **2** Chapel of the Assumption (p. 92) **3** St. Clement (p. 93)

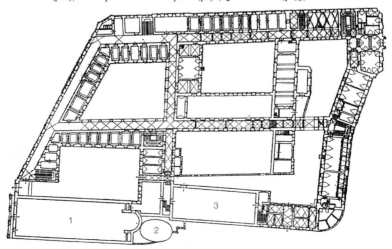

Stuccoed hall in the Clementinum, today a reading-room of the library

Main facade of the Clementinum

hewn blocks of stone with assertive capitals. Bartholomäus Cometa contributed heads of emperors in stucco, and the gables give a "Netherlandish" touch. Between 1720 and 1727 František Maximilián Kaňka was in charge of major rebuilding and extensions in the High Baroque style, which produced the east wing, the observatory tower (surmounted by Atlas supporting the globe), the Mirror Chapel, the mathematics hall, and the **Grand Library Hall**, which is one of the finest High Baroque interiors in Prague. A ceiling fresco by the Swabian painter Johann Hiebl, a pupil and faithful epigone of Andrea Pozzo, affords an illusionistic vision of the "Temple of Wisdom." The **Rococo chapel** of St. Eligius (now Mozart Hall) on Platnéřska was once used by the goldsmiths of Prague.

97

Interior of the Chapel of the Assumption, with frescoes illustrating the life of the Virgin Mary

The Chapel of the Assumption, with tower of St. Savior behind; on the left the Golden Snake café

Some of the rooms in the Clementinum may be viewed on request; the Mirror Chapel is only accessible during concerts.

54 Chapel of the Assumption
Kaple Nanebevzetí Panny Marie
Karlova

Prague's first centrally planned church in the style of Roman Mannerism.

Picturesquely nestling between the east end of St. Savior's and the portico of St. Clement's, with its attractive wrought-iron gate, is the domed oval of the chapel, built around 1590 for the Italian congregation by itinerant artists from Italy. The **interior** is articulated by eight double pilasters and round arches, which generate a ring of chapels with galleries above. Murals depict scenes from the life of the Virgin Mary.

55 St. Clement *Svatý Kliment*
Karlova 1 (access from the chapel of the Assumption or the Clementinum court)

Major examples of Bohemian Baroque sculpture.

Interior of St. Clement, with sumptuous Baroque decoration

In place of a medieval Dominican church, Christoph Dientzenhofer planned a High Baroque edifice around 1712. Building was probably carried out under the supervision of Antonio Lurago or František Maximilián Kaňka (the latter designed the portico on Karlova in 1715). The ceiling frescoes by Johann Hiebl relate the legend of Pope Clement, who was subsequently canonized. The altar wall is an illusionistic painting by Josef Kramolín, with a portrayal of St. Leonard by Peter Brandl. The most valuable works of art in the church are the **sandstone and limewood carvings** by Matthias Bernhard Braun (1715), which are masterpieces of High Baroque expressiveness in the style of Bernini: in the wall niches, evangelists and church fathers, on the altars saints – especially noteworthy is the Ecstasy of St. Aloysius of Gonzaga. The church is today used by the Greek Catholic congregation.

56 Charles Street
Karlova

One of the most picturesque lanes in the Old Town, part of the Royal Way that led from the Powder Tower to Prague Castle.

At the river end, the corner with Smetanovo Nábřeží is dominated by **Colloredo-Mansfeld Palace** (Karlova 2), which was remodeled as a Baroque mansion around 1735 for Prince Vinzenz Paul of Mansfeld-Fondi; the coats of arms, the putti, and the Neptune fountain in the courtyard are by Anton Braun and his workshop. The French Crown at No. 4, a Renaissance house, was from 1607 to 1612 the studio of the German astronomer **Johannes Kepler**. Pötting-Persing Palace at No. 8 has been a Unitarian meetinghouse since 1924. House No. 14 has a Gothic emblem, the Stone Maiden. At the beginning of the eighteenth century, the **Golden Snake** at No. 18 was the residence of the Armenian Deodatus Damajan of Damascus, who opened Prague's first coffeehouse. The finest building in the street is the **Golden Well** at No. 3, a Renaissance house with a magnificent Baroque facade stuccoed by

The Golden Well

Johann Ulrich Mayer: depicted are the Madonna of Mladá Boleslav between SS. Wenceslas and John of Nepomuk, the plague intercessors SS. Rochus, Sebastian, Francis Xavier, and Charles Borromeo (cardinal archbishop of Milan, died 1584), and at the top Rosalia of Palermo reclining in her grotto in Monte Pellegrino.

57 Clam-Gallas Palace

Clam-Gallasův palác
Husova 20

The most important secular example of High Baroque in Prague, an echo of imperial Vienna.

Count Johann Wenzel of Gallas, whose line later amalgamated with that of the counts of Clam in Upper Austria, was a high-ranking officer of the realm (among other postings he was viceroy of Naples); as such he was able to afford the services of Johann Bernhard Fischer von Erlach, the celebrated architect to the Habsburg court, for the planning of his Prague mansion. Fischer's design was executed by Domenico Canevale and Thomas Haffenecker between 1713 and 1725. The facade, whose pristine grandeur can no longer be properly appreciated due to the encroachments of later buildings, still shows a pleasing interplay of architecture and sculpture. M. B. Braun contributed the splendid pairs of giants that flank the two portals, with reliefs of the Labors of Hercules on the plinths. Of the thirteen statues of gods on the attic story only fragments have survived (in the Lapidarium); the present figures of Jupiter, Mercury, and Venus are copies. The main gateway opens onto a courtyard with a **triton fountain**, a favorite motif in Prague mansions since early Baroque times. The magnificent **staircase** is

Art Nouveau house on Karlova

Pairs of giants flank the main portal of Clam-Gallas Palace

adorned with sculptures by Braun and a ceiling fresco depicting the Triumph of Apollo, by Carlo Carlone, member of an Austro-Italian family that produced several notable artists. Clam-Gallas Palace today houses the municipal archive.

In the garden wall on the south side of Mariánské náměstí is an interesting fountain with a **figure representing the Vltava**; popularly known as "Terezka," it is a replica of the original by Václav Prachner (1812), which is now in the National Museum. The square is dominated by the **New City Hall** (1908-11), with sculptures by Stanislav Sucharda, Josef Mařatka, and Ladislav Šaloun (Iron Knight and Rabbi Löw at the corners).

58 Kunstatt-Podiebrad Palace

Dům pánů Kunštátu a z Poděbrad
Řetězová 3

Staré Město's most notable Romanesque patrician house, now used for exhibitions.

The neighborhood of St. Giles is one of the oldest inhabited areas of Prague, where since the High Middle Ages an important trade route led from Vyšehrad to the north. Below street level there are still some eighty Romanesque chambers (e.g., Husova 19-21, Karlova 44) that once, before the construction of the Vltava weirs entailed the raising of the adjacent land, were the entrance-halls of noble patrician residences. Kunstatt-Podiebrad Palace boasts three Romanesque chambers from the late twelfth century, of which the central one is divided into two bays. George of Poděbrady, who was later (1458) to be elected king of Bohemia, had the house rebuilt in the Late Gothic style.

59 St. Giles

Svatý Jiljí
Husova/Zlatá

An interesting Gothic structure with fine furnishings and decoration in a Baroque style already turning toward the Rococo.

The bold mass of the church of St. Giles, with its rudimentary towers of unequal height, asserts itself within the urban context. Commissioned as a collegiate church by the bishop of Prague, it was erected between 1340 and 1370; in the fifteenth century it served the Utraquist faction of the Hussite movement, and in 1626 it was taken over by the Dominicans. The hall-type nave, with its rudimentary chan-

Romanesque cellar in Kunstatt-Podiebrad Palace

cel, was transformed into a sumptuous celebration of High Baroque around 1730, by František Špaček (probably following a plan by Kilian Ignaz Dientzenhofer). The stucco decoration is by Bernardo Spinetti, the frescoes are by Wenzel Lorenz Reiner.

Dominican church of St. Giles: vault frescoes by Wenzel Lorenz Reiner

High altar of St. Giles: the painting depicts the institution of the Dominican order

The main field of the vault is given over to a representation of the triumph of the Dominicans over the heretics (in Prague, as elsewhere, the order was in charge of the Inquisition, especially against the Albigensians and the Waldensians); the lives of SS. Dominic and Thomas Aquinas are illustrated in the aisles. The altarpiece of St. Wenceslas in the left aisle is also by Reiner, who was buried here in 1743. A relic of the early Baroque inventory is the painting on the high altar, the Institution of the Do-

minican Order, by Johann Friedrich Hess (1668). The sculptures and wood carvings are the work of Franz Ignaz Weiss, Johann Anton Quittainer, Matthias Schönherr, and Richard Prachner (note Prachner's versions of the Four Last Things on the confessionals).

The cloister and monastery buildings (Husova 8), whose early Baroque appearance is the work of Carlo Lurago, have now been restored to the Dominican order. In the **refectory** there are anonymous frescoes of the Wedding of Cana and Dominican saints in stucco cartouches by Spinetti.

60 Bethlehem Chapel

Betlémská kaple

Betlémské náměstí

National cultural shrine, cradle of the Hussite movement.

In 1391 a number of Czech patricians endowed a chapel in which sermons were to be preached only in the Czech language. It has its place in the history books thanks to one of the occupants of its pulpit: **John Huss** (Jan Hus), rector of the university from 1402 onward, inveighed in words of fire against the abuses of the established church and called for a return to true Christian humility. When he was excommunicated and subsequently burnt at the stake during the Council of Constance in 1415, his followers saw this as a direct attack on the Bohemian nation – the Bethlehem Chapel became a national shrine. Other reformers preached from its pulpit, among them Thomas Müntzer, leader of the German peasant movement, in 1521. After the Thirty Years' War the Hussite movement became taboo, and the Jesuits sought to erase all memory of the reformers; the chapel and preacher's house were torn down in 1786. Remains of the original structure were unearthed in 1919, and in the 1950s the chapel was reconstructed under the supervision of Jaroslav Fragner.

Between Konviktská and Bartolo-

Bethlehem Chapel, where John Huss preached to the people in Czech

mějská stands the old **Jesuit college**, once a residential school for the sons of the nobility. After 1773 it became a college of organists, numbering among its students Antonín Dvořák; Beethoven and Wagner performed in its concert hall. The Baroque church of St. Bartholomew was designed by K. I. Dientzenhofer and features murals by Reiner; it is awaiting restoration.

61 Holy Cross Rotunda

Rotunda Svatého Kříže

Karolíny Světlé/Konviktská

Romanesque round churches once lined the route from Prague Castle to Vyšehrad and on to southern Bohemia.

The castle had a St. Vitus rotunda (no longer extant) as early as the beginning of the tenth century. Holy Cross would appear to be the second oldest of the three churches of this type that have survived in Prague, and was built around 1150 as a cemetery chapel or parish church of a small community. In the nineteenth century it was saved from demolition by the efforts of an artists' association. During subsequent restoration, fragments of Gothic murals from the fourteenth century were discovered.

62 Smetana Embankment

Smetanovo nábřeží

A riverside promenade with a magnificent view.

The 174-foot high Late Gothic **water tower** to the south of the Old Town Bridge Tower used to be fed from the river via a waterwheel. The former waterworks building (Novotného Lávka 1), planned by Antonín Wiehl, the "pioneer of the Czech neo-Renaissance," is decorated with sgraffito work depicting the defense of Charles Bridge against the Swedes in 1648; the design stems from František Zeníšek and Mikoláš Aleš. Since 1936 it has been the home of the **Bedřich Smetana Museum**. Smetana (1824-84), along with Dvořák the founder of a Czech national musical idiom, immortalized the Vltava in his famous cycle of symphonic poems *Má Vlast* ("My Country"). The **Smetana monument** on the quayside is by J. Malejovský (1984).

Smetanovo nábřeží, the oldest of Prague's riverside promenades, was designed by Bernhard Grueber around 1840. The neo-Gothic Francis Monument in the small park was a gift of the Bohemian es-

The Bedřich Smetana monument

of the art and theater world housed in the neo-Renaissance Lažanský Mansion, where Smetana composed his operas *Prodaná Nevěsta (The Bartered Bride,* 1866) and *Dalibor* (1868).

63 St. Martin in the Wall

Svatý Martin ve zdi
Martinská

Notable for its connections with the Hussite movement.

The Romanesque parish church of the old Újezd quarter did indeed once form part of the city wall; it underwent various stages of gothicization, and was partially remodeled in the Baroque style after a fire. On the outer wall of the chancel is a relief portrait commemorating Ferdinand Maximilian Brokoff (1688-1731), the most important member of the family of sculptors who shaped the face of Bohemian High Baroque; he and his kinsmen were buried in the old St. Martin's Cemetery.

In October 1414 the church was the scene of a historic event: for the first time the congregation received communion in both kinds *(sub utraque specie)*, the bread and the wine. The chalice – which had hitherto been reserved for the priest – became the symbol of the Hussite revolution, and St. Martin's remained a Calixtine, or Utraquist, church until the Counter-Reformation; mass was said here in Czech. Today it is again a Protestant house of worship, belonging to the Bohemian Brethren.

tates: the allegorical figures are by Josef Max and Kamil Böhm; the equestrian **statue of Emperor Franz I** of Austria was removed to the Lapidarium in 1918. The panorama of Hradčany, Malá Strana, and Karlův Most was captured by Oskar Kokoschka in some of his paintings. It can be enjoyed in style from the **Café Slavia**, (Národní 1), the traditional rendezvous

The Slavia, a café with literary and theatrical associations

64 Coal Market

Uhelný trh

An irregular square at the confluence of seven lanes, in the Middle Ages site of a smithy that sold charcoal.

Here it was that you could pick up a sedan chair, before they were edged out by the horse-drawn cabs at the end of the eighteenth century. Nowadays it is not too savory a place at night, unless you want to pick up something quite different. The pretty **fountain in Empire style** (1797) used to stand in front of the mansion of the military supplier Jakob Wimmer in Národní; the sculptures by Franz Xaver Lederer – allegories of horticulture and viticulture – are an allusion to the estates his client owned on the outskirts of Prague. The **Three Golden Lions** at No. 1 belonged to the composer František Xaverský Dušek and his wife Josefina, a celebrated singer; they had Mozart as house-guest in 1787, on the occasion of the first performance of *Don Giovanni*. The librettist of the opera, Lorenzo da Ponte, lodged at the **Platýz House** at No. 11, which later had such illustrious guests as Paganini and Liszt.

65 Estates Theater

Stavovské divadlo

Ovocný trh 6

Prague's oldest Neoclassical building, with important associations for the cultural history of Europe.

The first permanent theater in Prague was built for the German-speaking population. The plans of Count Künigl, who had made a study of theater design, were executed by Anton Haffenecker (the designer of the fine Rococo portal of Nostitz Palace in Malá Strana). It was Count Franz Anton of Nostitz-Rieneck who provided the funding and gave his name to the theater, which opened in 1783 with a performance of Lessing's *Emilia Galotti*. As can be seen from old prints, the original structure had more of a "Baroque" touch, being more vertically orientated with windows in the full height of the four monumental columns; the present aspect derives from a Neoclassical refurbishing by Achill Wolf in 1881.

When the Bohemian estates purchased the building in 1798, the Nostitz Theater became known as the Estates Theater. After a spell under the name "Landestheater" (National Theater), it until recently bore the name of Josef Kajetán Tyl,

a Czech poet and playwright; his light opera *Fidlovačka* ("Cobblers' Fair"), with music by František Škroup and premiered in 1834, contains the song "Kde domov můj" ("Where is my home?"), which is now the Czech national anthem.

But the theater made musical history much earlier, with the triumphal premiere of *Don Giovanni* on 29 October 1787. Mozart returned on 6 September 1791 to conduct the first performance of *La Clemenza di Tito*, which had been commissioned by the Bohemian estates for the coronation of Emperor Leopold II as king of Bohemia. Further landmarks in the theater's history were Carl Maria von Weber's years as director of opera (1813-16) and 1854 performance of Wagner's *Tannhäuser* conducted by the composer.

The pediment of the main portal of the Estates Theater

66 St. Gallus

Svatý Havel

Havelská

A historic church with a stylistically significant Baroque facade, hub of an interesting old market-quarter.

The faithful had been flocking to St. Gallus's ever since Charles IV presented the church with the saint's skull, which he had acquired from the monastery of St. Gallen in Switzerland. Gifted and controversial preachers were invited to the pulpit: Konrad Waldhauser, from the Augustinian abbey of Waldhausen in Upper Austria, John of Nepomuk (who was later canonized), and John Huss. Czech hymns were sung here. The venerated relic of the patron saint was lost during the Hussite wars, but the Calced Carmelites, who took over the church after the battle of Bílá hora, brought a new attraction – bonemeal from the remains of St. Amathosius, which was reputed to drive out the Devil. In 1671, Emperor Leopold I granted funds for the

The twin Baroque towers of St. Gallus

building of a monastery (now the Russian Cultural Center, Rytířská 31). The culture of Mammon is opulently represented in the neo-Renaissance banking hall of the Česka Spořitelna, Rytířská 29.

At the end of the seventeenth century the first steps were taken to convert the Romanesque-Gothic basilica into a Baroque church. A new facade was erected on a convex plan, probably the first of its kind in Bohemia, and from 1723 onward the undulating cornice and statue-studded balustrade were added, to designs by Santin-Aichel; Paul Ignaz Bayer was in charge of the whole project. The **interior** boasts a number of noteworthy features: the Marian cycle on the nave arcades and

the high-altar painting of the Virgin with St. Gallus and Leopold I are the work of Liška (1696); the calvary in the left choir aisle and the wood carvings of the evangelists are by F.M. Brokoff (1726); Cometa contributed the stucco decoration. In the right choir aisle is the tomb of Karel Škréta (1610-74), Bohemia's foremost early Baroque painter.

The medieval **"Galli-Town"** (Nova civitas circa S. Gallum), which was founded around 1235 by Eberhard, master of the mint to King Wenceslas I, occupied the area between Železná, Uhelný trh, and Rytířská. An arcaded sidewalk has survived from Gothic times on Havelská, which boasts a number of fine merchants' houses. The street-name **V kotcích** reminds us that on either side once stood the stalls *(kotky)* of the cloth and wool merchants. A theater was later erected on the site, and the first performance of a play in Czech was given here in 1771; the "fleapit" was demolished when the Estates Theater was built.

67 Carolinum

Karolinum

Ovocný trh 3/Železná 9

The oldest part of Charles University and a national monument; a magnificent Gothic oriel by the Parler workshop.

In 1348 Emperor Charles IV founded the oldest university in central Europe, and the first one in the Holy Roman Empire. In 1383 his successor, Wenceslas IV, granted the "Collegium Carolinum" the use of the house that had belonged to the master

Gothic arcade on Havelská

of the mint, Johlin Rotlöw; to this day it is used for graduation ceremonies, as well as conferences and cultural events. The finest element of the original house is the **oriel chapel** (c. 1370) at the east end of the great hall; it is dedicated to SS. Cosmas and Damian, the patrons of physicians and apothecaries.

The **Gothic complex**, which was extended at the end of the fourteenth century, was remodeled on Baroque lines in 1718, and re-gothicized in the nineteenth century; an archeological study in 1934 eventually led to the restoration of the original form, a project led by Jaroslav Fragner.

John Huss, who became rector of the Carolinum in 1402, urged that the Czech professors and students be given more say in the running of the university. In 1409 King Wenceslas IV acceded to these demands, granting three votes to the *natio bohemica* and only one joint vote to the other three "nations" (Bavarian, Saxon, and Polish), whereupon the German contingent walked out and went to Leipzig, where they set up their own university. In 1622, when the tide had turned against the Protestants, the Jesuits were placed in charge. Emperor Ferdinand III injected new life into the university, which from 1654 onward bore the name Carolo-Ferdinandea. In 1882 it was split into a German and a Czech university.

68 The Two Golden Bears

U dvou zlatých medvědů

Kožná 1

Finest Renaissance house portal in Prague.

Melantrichova, with its wall-to-wall arches one of the most charming lanes in Staré Město, is named after the Czech printer Melantrich, who lived from 1511 to 1580. Many of the buildings have a medieval core behind their Renaissance or Baroque facades. The **Golden Pitcher** at No. 20 dispenses wine in Romanesque-Gothic vaulted cellars. The house on the corner of Kožná has a superbly carved late Renaissance portal (c. 1590); the relief sculptures of bears, once gilded, are the source of the name. A plaque commemorates the birthplace of the journalist Egon Erwin Kisch (1885-1948), who penned some fascinating pictures of everyday life (including its seamier side) in his native city. Along with Franz Kafka, Franz Werfel, Max Brod, and other German-language writers, Kisch helped to build Prague's reputation as an exciting literary center.

The Gothic oriel of the Carolinum, on the old fruit market

Other interesting **old buildings** are the former Servite monastery of St. Michael (Melantrichova 17), a house with a Rococo facade and a late Renaissance arcaded courtyard at No. 15, the Green Tree at No. 12, and the late Renaissance Five Crowns at No. 11. At Michalská 19 the Iron Door (tavern) has a Gothic doorway in the passage leading to Jilská.

69 Little Square

Malé náměstí

Triangular space lined with ancient buildings.

Here, too, many of the houses have Romanesque or Gothic vaulted chambers, and here and there facade details bear witness to a venerable age. In the twelfth century French merchants had a depot on the square; later it was the venue of the fruit

Late Renaissance portal of the Two Golden Bears

market. The **fountain** is guarded by a magnificent Renaissance grille (1560). The Golden Lily gallery at No. 12 is installed in the vaulted Gothic hall of a fourteenth-

Sgraffito decoration on the house known as the "Minute"

century pharmacy. The Golden Crown at No. 13 was the residence of Christoph Dientzenhofer around 1700. Mikoláš Aleš designed the historicizing murals on the Rott House at No. 3, which extol the virtues of the tiller of the field and the industrious tradesman.

70 Staré Město Town Hall
Staroměstská radnice
Staroměstske náměstí 3

Its Gothic tower affords a fine view over the city; the astronomical clock is a magnet for tourists.

In 1338 King John of Luxemburg accorded the citizens of "Prague Old Town" the privilege of building their own town hall, which they financed by levying a duty on wine. The 230-foot high tower was completed in 1364, and the complex evolved with the incorporation of adjacent houses and building of extensions down to the nineteenth century. The neo-Gothic east and north wings came under fire from German tanks in the Prague Uprising of May 1945 and burnt down, leaving an unfilled void in the configuration of the square.

The **Gothic oriel choir** of the upper-floor chapel is a masterly creation of the Parler lodge; it was consecrated in 1381. Also of great artistic interest is the Madonna statue on the corner (original in the city museum),

Fountain on Malé náměstí, before the Rott House

The animal symbols are derived from the *Physiologus*, an old book of popular science compiled from classical and oriental sources. The calendar-disk, with signs of the zodiac and representations of the months, is a replica of that painted in 1865 by Josef Mánes, the foremost Czech artist of the nineteenth century (original in the city museum). The pointer at the top shows the day of the month and its saint. The upper clock-face has arabic figures for the twenty-four hours of the old Bohemian time system, in which the day began at sunset, and two sequences of roman figures for the time as we know it; both are indicated by the gilt hand. The sidereal time can be read from the roman numerals with the aid of the star-pointer. The position of the golden sun with reference to the arcs numbered 1 through 12 indicates the "planetary" or daylight time. (In the photograph it is approximately 11 a.m., or 17:30 Bohemian time, and sunset is at 5 p.m.; it is about 13:00 sidereal and 5:00 planetary time.) The smaller ring shows the positions of sun and moon in the zodiac.

The show begins just before the hour: the twelve apostles (half-figures newly carved by Vojtěch Sucharda in 1948) march past, grim Death turns over the sandglass and rings the knell, and the cock crows. The other allegorical figures on the left and right symbolize vanity (with the mirror), parsimony (with the moneybag), and heathenism (the Turk). Below, the archangel Michael with sword and shield reminds us of the Day of Judgment.

The core structure of the town hall, immediately to the west of the tower, is Late Gothic, and the **ogee portal** ornamented with crockets is by Matej Rejsek (c. 1475). To the left follows a **Renaissance facade**, whose fine tripartite window bears the inscription *Praga caput regni* ("Prague capital of the realm"), dating from the reign of Ferdinand I (1526-64), the first Habsburg to ascend the Bohemian throne. The next two sections have **Gothic vaults** on the ground floor; the facades were remodeled in the nineteenth century.

The projecting house known as the **Minute** (U minuty, Staroměstské náměstí 2) has also been incorporated into the town hall. Gothic at core, it was rebuilt in the Renaissance style at the end of the sixteenth century and decorated with sgraffito representations of classical, biblical, and allegorical themes; it has been restored several times over the years. The stone carving on the corner recalls that there was once a White Lion pharmacy here.

an early example of the French-influenced "Soft Style"; the other figures are neo-Gothic. A pillory and a scaffold were erected on the site in front of the east wall as early as the twelfth century; a plaque commemorates the Hussite preacher and agitator Jan Želivský, who was executed here in 1422. The twenty-seven crosses in the paving are for the ringleaders of an anti-Habsburg rebellion who were executed on 21 June 1621: the headsman's ax spared neither nobleman nor burgher, Czech nor German, young nor old. A few suffered the indignity of hanging, and before dispatching Dr. Jessenius – a notable scholar and rector of Charles University – the executioner cut out his tongue, "that fearsome weapon of the thinking nation" (Václav Havel).

The world-famous **astronomical clock** was probably built around 1410; it was given a more sophisticated mechanism by Magister Hanuš, the university astronomer, around 1490. The carving around the lower stone ring features some superb specimens of ramose and cartilaginous ornamentation from the waning Gothic era.

In the town hall **vestibule,** mosaics designed by Mikoláš Aleš (restored 1937) depict milestones in the history of the western Slavs: in one scene, Libuše, the fabled ancestress of the Přemyslid line, prophesies the glory of Prague. The most notable room is the **Late Gothic council chamber** with its beamed ceiling painted in Renaissance times, coat of arms of Staré Město, and forty or so guild insignia. The Late Gothic figure of the *Man of Sorrows* (1405) is interesting as the antecedent of the Ecce Homo statue in the town hall of Nové Město. A late Renaissance portal of red marble leads to the **New Council Chamber**, built in 1879-80, with historical paintings by Václav Brožík: John Huss before the Council of Constance, and the election of the Hussite king Georg of Poděbrady, which took place here in the town hall in 1458.

71 Old Town Square
Staroměstské náměstí

The heart of Staré Město, a magnificent architectural ensemble.

The generously proportioned square originated at a crossroads of major international traffic routes. Since the High Middle Ages it has been the scene of spectacles both pompous and piteous – glittering coronation processions, knightly tournaments and popular pageants, political and religious gatherings, executions and massacres.

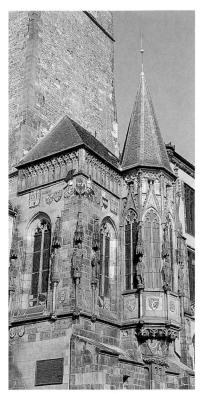

Gothic oriel chapel in Staré Město Town Hall

Mosaic vault in the Staré Město Town Hall vestibule

◁ *The astronomical clock of Staré Město Town hall*

The square is still a feast for the eyes today, with its handsome **merchants' houses** and elegant **mansions of the aristocracy**. The vicissitudes of more recent times have however left lacunae, particularly in the northwestern part: the Pařížská boulevard cuts a merciless swathe through the old Jewish quarter, the Krenn House was demolished at the beginning of the century, the St. Mary column was removed in 1918, and the north and east wings of the town hall were destroyed at the end of World War II.

The **Huss Monument** was erected in 1915, to mark the five-hundredth anniversary of the reformer's death at the stake. The foundation-stone for this "national symbol" had been laid in 1903, and the Habsburgs did not view the project with great enthusiasm – John Huss (1369-1415) had, after all, been a staunch advocate of the rights of the Czechs during his rectorship of Charles University. It may be debated whether the siting of the monument is aesthetically ideal, but there is no denying the artistic quality of the sculpture. Ladislav Šaloun, the leading representative of Czech Impressionism, was inspired by the work of the French sculptor Auguste Rodin, particularly the ensemble of the *Burghers of Calais*. In vivid images he evokes the persecution, eclipse, and re-emergence of the Czech nationalist movement; highly idealized is the gaunt, ascetic figure of Huss, whose message to posterity is inscribed on the base of the monument: "Love each other; let each partake of the truth."

A number of houses around the square still have the **vaulted basements** that in Romanesque and Gothic times were the entrance-halls; some of these now provide pleasant surroundings for wining and dining. On the corner of Železná, the Golden Unicorn at No. 20 was built by Matěj Rejsek, the architect of the Powder Tower, in 1496, and is notable for the fragments of Late Gothic lily ornaments and the net vault in the passage; the facade is Baroque (Smetana opened his first music school here in 1848). The Stork House at No. 16 is also Gothic at core; it has a neo-Renaissance facade with a picture of St. Wenceslas by Aleš. In front of the Týn Church, Gothic arcades testify to the venerable age of two particularly interesting buildings. The White Unicorn at No. 15 is of Romanesque origin, with a late Baroque facade. The old Týn School at No. 14 spans the centuries from Romanesque (vaulted basement) to Renaissance (Venetian-type gables). It was attached to the Týn Church, whose facade towers in the background; Rejsek was rector here at the end of the fifteenth century.

Staré Město Town Hall, with a corner of St. Nicholas at the far right

View from Staré Město Town Hall to St. Mary before Týn, with the Týn School in front and the Gothic house of the Stone Bell on its left; the Kinský Palace protrudes into the square at the center, and on the extreme left the Pařížská boulevard cuts through the old Jewish quarter to the river

Tourists rub shoulders with locals at the Huss monument, erected in 1915 to commemorate the Czech reformer

72 Kinský Palace

Palác Kinských

Staroměstské náměstí 12

Behind the finest Rococo facade in Prague is housed the print collection of the National Gallery.

The late Baroque edifice, which juts markedly into the square, was built for Count Johann Arnold Goltz between 1755 and 1765 by A. Lurago on the basis of an older project by K. I. Dientzenhofer. The stucco ornamentation is by Giuseppe Bossi, the statues of gods on the attic story are by Ignaz Platzer and his workshop.

The Countess Kinský, who was born here in 1843, became famous as Berta von Suttner, winner of the Nobel Peace Prize in 1905 for her pacifist appeal *Die Waffen nieder* ("Down Arms!"). Later, the building housed the Imperial German High School of the Old Town, from which Franz Kafka graduated in 1901; for a time his father had a textile shop on the ground floor.

A late Gothic net vault in the Golden Unicorn passage

73 The Stone Bell

U kamenného zvonu
Staroměstské náměstí 13

A beautiful example of early Gothic architecture, and an ideal venue for concerts and exhibitions.

In the 1980s the imposing **tower-like house** was stripped of its neo-Baroque mantle and reconstructed on the basis of what had survived of the original fabric. The house takes its name from the stone bell emblem on the corner toward Týn School, no doubt a memento of the entry into Prague of King John of Luxemburg in 1310. A mansion on such a prime site could only have been built for a very high-ranking person, perhaps the king's wife Elizabeth, the last of the Přemyslids. The ground floor is relatively plain, with early Gothic features, while the upper stories (c. 1330) display magnificent High Gothic window tracery and finely molded statue niches; the fragments of knightly figures that were discovered suggest a homage to the united royal house of Luxemburg and Přemysl. Remains of the original murals (Ecce Homo) were discovered in the **chapel** off the entrance-hall; the other chapel (first floor) was probably the repository for a precious relic, perhaps a fragment from the Crown of Thorns.

Section of the facade of Kinský Palace

The Stone Bell

74 St. Nicholas

Svatý Mikuláš
Staroměstské náměstí/Pařížská

A theatrically Baroque church by Kilian Ignaz Dientzenhofer.

The first early Gothic church was founded by German merchants; in 1634 it was assigned to the Slavonic Benedictines from Emmaus Abbey in Nové Město. K.I. Dientzenhofer designed the new High Baroque edifice, which was built between 1732 and 1737. The site on the poultry market was very cramped (it was only in 1901 that the demolition of the Krenn House enabled the noble south facade to assert itself toward Staroměstské náměstí). It is understandable, therefore, that the architect paid special attention to the modeling of the twin towers and the drum of the dome. Anton Braun sculpted the statues: patron saints of Bohemia at the corners of the towers, SS. Benedict and Scholastica on the segmental arches above the central bay, and SS. Adalbert and Procopius on either side of the portal.

St. Nicholas from the southeast

Asam the Elder the frescoes: in the cupola the legend of the church's patron, in the chancel St. Benedict, and in the panels below the baseline of the drum evangelists (heavily overpainted in 1914). From 1870 to 1914 the church was used by the Russian Orthodox congregation, and a relic of this period is the chandelier, made at the glass works in Harrachov. Since 1920 the church of St. Nicholas has been the central house of worship of the Czechoslovak Hussite Church.

The **monastery** was dissolved in 1785 and its buildings converted for residential use. Franz Kafka was born in the house on the corner (U Radnice 5/Maiselova) on 3 July 1883.

Plaque commemorating Franz Kafka near St. Nicholas

The **interior** plan and articulation of the walls are inspired by Jules Hardouin-Mansart's Chapel of St. Louis-des-Invalides in Paris and Filippo Juvarra's work in Turin. The octagonal dome is supported by perforated piers with balconies on the upper level. Bernardo Spinetti executed the delicate stucco decoration, Peter

The Green Frog (U Radnice 8) is a Gothic tavern where they have been serving wine from the Labe (Elbe) valley since 1404.

The drum and cupola of St. Nicholas

75 St. Mary before Týn

Panna Marie před Týnem
Týnská

The most notable Gothic church in Prague after St. Vitus's Cathedral; the furnishings include fine works of art from the pre-Hussite period.

A Romanesque/early Gothic church with a hospital and cemetery had stood on the site in front of Týn Court (the name comes from the old word for "fence" or "enclosure"). In 1365 German merchants provided funds for the building of a new basilica to serve as their main church. Peter Parler and his cathedral masons took charge of the work in 1390, and from this period dates the splendid **portal**, worthy of a cathedral, in the north wall (opposite Týnská ulička); the tympanum relief with scenes from the Passion is now in the National Gallery in St. George's Convent.

The **west front** was not erected until after the Hussite wars, and the south tower was completed in 1511. From 1419 to 1620 the church was the headquarters of the Utraquists: the gable of the west front was adorned with a statue of the "Hussite King" George of Poděbrady and a gilt chalice, the symbol of communion in both kinds. After the defeat of the Protestants at Bílá hora the Jesuits replaced these with a statue of the Virgin, whose golden gloriole was fashioned from the metal of the chalice.

The church is entered from Staroměstské náměstí via the arcade of the **Týn School**. Halfway down the nave on the left a stately Late Gothic stone baldachin (Matěj Rejsek, 1493) shelters the tomb of the Italian bishop Augustinus Lucianus of Mirandola, who consecrated Utraquist priests (despite their breach with Rome the reformers attached great importance to the apostolic succession). Before a pillar on the opposite side of the nave stands a carved altar in the tradition of the Danube School (early sixteenth century), depicting

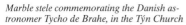

Marble stele commemorating the Danish astronomer Tycho de Brahe, in the Týn Church

Týn Church, with the Týn School and the Golden Unicorn, seen from the tower of Staré Město Town Hall

the Baptism of Christ. The limewood carving of the Virgin Enthroned in the south aisle is the Týn Madonna, dating from c. 1400. The stone pulpit has been reworked with neo-Gothic elements.

Let into the first chancel pier on the right is the red marble memorial slab for Tycho de Brahe (1546-1601), the Danish

Nave of St. Mary before Týn, with pier altars

St. Mary before Týn: detail of the carved altarpiece depicting the baptism of Christ

astronomer at the court of Emperor Rudolph II. The baptismal chapel in the south choir aisle contains a bench recess with portrait busts of a monarch and his consort (Wenceslas IV and Sophia?) by the Parler lodge; the pewter font (1414) is decorated with reliefs of the Apostles. The representations of the Assumption and the Holy Trinity (1649) on the high altar are by Karel Škretá, who also painted the Annunciation, St. Joseph, and St. Adalbert on the pier altars. The Crucifixion group in the north choir aisle is a major work of Bohemian Gothic, dating from around 1410. The St. Wenceslas altar features a painting by Anton Stevens and statues by Johann Georg Bendl. The High Baroque oval relief of the Holy Family (1717), beneath the organ gallery, is believed to be the work of F. M. Brokoff.

76 Týn Court
Týn (Ungelt)
Týnská

Ancient customs yard of the princes of Bohemia.

The old Germanic word *ungelt* means "dues" – as early as the eleventh century these payments for customs, storage, and lodging were collected from all merchants who passed through Prague. It must have been a bustling place, with its money-changers' booths and workshops, where tin and wax were the most prized raw materials. The principal building, next to the Týnská gateway, is the Renaissance mansion of the chief customs inspector Jakub Granovský; the Tuscan arcade and the facades are adorned with chiaroscuro paintings of allegorical, biblical, mythological, and historical motifs, including a portrait of Emperor Ferdinand I. After a fire toward the end of the seventeenth century the whole complex was rebuilt as merchants' houses.

77 St. James
Svatý Jakub
Malá Štupartská/Jakubská

The awe-inspiring interior, with its Gothic architecture clothed in festive Baroque, makes an ideal venue for concerts.

King Wenceslas I founded a Minorite friary in 1232; the High Gothic monastery buildings and church were built between 1320 and 1370, under the patronage of King John of Luxemburg and his wife

Elizabeth. The **facade of the church** is decorated with three High Baroque stucco reliefs by Ottavio Mosto of Padua (c. 1695), dynamic compositions in the theatrical spirit of the Jesuits, inspired by Lorenzo Bernini's work in Rome: in the center we see the apostle James with pilgrims at his tomb in Santiago de Compostela in Spain, on the left St. Francis of Assisi (founder of the Minorite order), and on the right the glorification of the Franciscan saint, Anthony of Padua.

The longitudinal emphasis of the basilica (the longest church in Prague after St. Vitus's) is characteristic for mendicant orders. The **transformation to Baroque** was initiated by Jan Šimon Pánek after a fire in 1689; a positively palatial degree of High Baroque splendor was attained between 1736 and 1739 with the incorporation of gallery arcades with balustrades and vases and the decoration in stucco and fresco. Abbondio Bolla was the stuccoist, Franz Guido Voget painted the frescoes of the life of the Virgin and the Trinity. The high altar painting of the Martyrdom of the apostle James is by Wenzel Lorenz Reiner (1739), its carved frame by Matthias

Church of St. James: the monks' choir as remodeled in the Baroque period

High altar of St. James

Schönherr; the small Late Gothic *Pietà* in the Neoclassical retable was in Baroque times reputed to have miraculous powers. Some of the fine paintings on the side altars are the work of Peter Brandl.

The north aisle houses a masterpiece of Bohemian Baroque sculpture, the memorial to Count Jan Václav Vratislav of Mitrovice. Johann Bernhard Fischer von Erlach – whom the count knew as architect of the Bohemian Court Chancery in Vienna – provided a design inspired by works by Bernini in Rome, which was executed in marble, sandstone, and stucco by F. M. Brokoff. The moment of death is captured with typical Baroque realism. Chronos, the lord of time (signed and dated 1716), holds aloft a sandglass – an upward gesture continued in the wreath and the trumpet of the angel of victory and fame; only the allegory of the arts, grieving for her patron, sets a counternote.

To the north of the church lie the **friary buildings**, with a Gothic cloister and winter and summer refectories that were given their Baroque appearance at the same time as the church (stucco by Bolla, frescoes by Voget).

Memorial to Chancellor Count Vratislav of Mitrovice

Relief on the facade of St. James, featuring the church's patron

78 Celetná

One of the most attractive streets in Staré Město, the first stage of the Royal Way to Prague Castle.

The picturesque pedestrian thoroughfare wends its way between rows of fine **old houses**, most of them dating back to Romanesque or Gothic times. Behind the Baroque facade of the Sixt House at No. 2 Cola da Rienzi, people's tribune of Rome, was kept prisoner before he was taken to Raudnice, in the mid-fourteenth century. Under more agreeable conditions, Petrarch, the great poet and humanist, stayed here as guest of Emperor Charles IV. In

The Presentation of Jesus in the Temple, *a fresco in the vault of St. James*

View along Celetná to the Old Mint and Powder Tower

Middle Ages residence of the queen of Bohemia), with an early Neoclassical facade by Philipp Heger and atlantes by Ignaz Platzer.

The Black Madonna at No. 34 – the early Baroque statue was rescued from the previous building on the site – is an excellent example of how a modern building can blend into a historic precinct. Around 1910, progressive architects in Prague turned from the highly decorative Art Nouveau to a more strictly geometrical style with emphasis on the cube; facades were generously modulated to a high degree of plasticity, and contrasts of light and shadow – a revival of one of the predilections of High Baroque architects – were exploited to enhance the aesthetic quality of the materials used. The Black Madonna, designed by Josef Gočár in 1911, is the first major example of Czech cubism.

79   Powder Tower
Prašná brána
Celetná/Na příkopě

Monumental entrance to Staré Město.

The gate that stood here in the thirteenth century was named after the road that led to the silvermining town of Kutná Hora. In 1475 King Vladislav II laid the foundation stone for a "New Tower" that would more effectively mark the beginning of the Royal Way; Matěj Rejsek, rector of the Týn

the middle of the sixteenth century the house belonged to the Protestant chancelor Johann Sixt of Ottersdorf. Other notable buildings are: No. 6, the White Lion; No. 8, the Golden Sun; Nos. 10 and 11, with Rococo stuccowork; No. 12, Hrzán Palace, with sculpted masks and busts from the Brokoff workshop; No. 13, Millesimo Palace; No. 17, the Menhart House (originally Stubig Palace, later a Piarist college), with a Baroque statue of St. John of Nepomuk, Gothic alcove seats and a Baroque statue of Hercules in the passageway; No. 20, Buquoy Palace, with a Renaissance portal; No. 22, the Vulture (beerhall), with a Baroque portal and a Neoclassical facade; No. 23, with a statue of the Virgin from the Braun workshop; No. 27, "In the Temple," formerly St. Paul's Church and hospital; No. 31, Pachta Palace, remodeled in Baroque by Dientzenhofer, with stucco medallions of Emperor Francis I and Maria Theresa; No. 36, the Old Mint (in the late

The Late Gothic Powder Tower

The Black Madonna, from the house that once occupied the site, now adorns a later structure

School, was put in charge of the project. A wooden bridge connected the tower with the old royal palace, which stood on the site now occupied by the Civic Hall. Wenceslas II and George of Poděbrady had resided here, but after an attack on his life Vladislav II moved his court to the castle on Hradčany Hill, which offered better protection. The old residence subsequently served as a seminary and as a barracks, but soon fell into disrepair and was eventually demolished. The tower was at one time used for the storage of gunpowder, hence its present name. It suffered severe damage during the Prussian siege of Prague in 1757, and was restored in 1875 in a simplified version by Josef Mocker, the cathedral architect; the figures and ornaments are neo-Gothic.

80 St. Castulus
Svatý Haštal
Haštalské náměstí

Gothic church with an unusual format.

A homely little porch softens the gauntness of the church that presides over the square. The aisles date from the original fourteenth-century structure; a curious feature is the asymmetrical widening on the north side to create a double aisle. Traces of Gothic murals are visible in the sacristy. The Baroque Calvary sculpture is by a member of the Brokoff family, or one of their associates.

The Gothic church of St. Castulus

Cloister of the Poor Clares in St. Agnes's Convent

81 St. Agnes's Convent

Klášter svaté Anežky
U milosrdných 17

The most important complex of French-influenced early Gothic architecture in Bohemia; museum of nineteenth-century Czech painting and applied art.

The "Bohemian Assisi," as it was popularly known, once having been the home of Franciscan friars and nuns, lies not far from the Vltava. It was here, between 1231 and 1234, that Agnes, the daughter of King Ottokar I and sister of Wenceslas I, founded a Minorite friary and a convent of Poor Clares, of which she was the first abbess. Refusing all proposals of marriage, even the hand of Emperor Frederick II, Agnes had chosen the "crown of chastity." Her correspondence with St. Clare, the childhood friend of St. Francis of Assisi and "Mother of the Clares," has been pre-

served. During her lifetime Agnes was revered for her humility and asceticism, and after her death in 1285 the Bohemian monarchs led the campaign for her canonization; she was beatified by the church, but

St. Agnes's Convent: Gothic portrait heads on the chancel arch of St. Savior's Church

not until 1989 was she finally canonized as Agnes of Bohemia.

The friary did not survive the troubled years of the Hussite wars. The convent, which for a time was occupied by Dominican nuns, was finally dissolved in 1782, and the buildings soon fell into disrepair. At the end of the nineteenth century experts began to make a study of the ruins, and after World War II the complex was restored in an exemplary fashion to serve cultural purposes.

The noble High Gothic **cloister** of the convent of Clares is preserved in its original form from the mid-fourteenth century. The east wing abuts on the oldest parts, the chapter house and refectory dating from the time of Agnes. The "new" chapter house (in reality the nave of a church) leads to the small Mary Magdalen chapel and the **Church of St. Savior**, the most mature example of French-influenced early Gothic in Bohemia (1275-80).

The tombs of St. Agnes, Queen Kunigunde (Kunhuta of Hungary, consort of Ottokar II), and other Přemyslids were discovered during excavations in the church; the crowned heads carved into the imposts of the chancel arch are also

The High Gothic cloister of St. Agnes's Convent

believed to represent members of the dynasty. The hub of the Minorite friary was the **Church of St. Francis**, completed in 1240: King Wenceslas I is buried in the

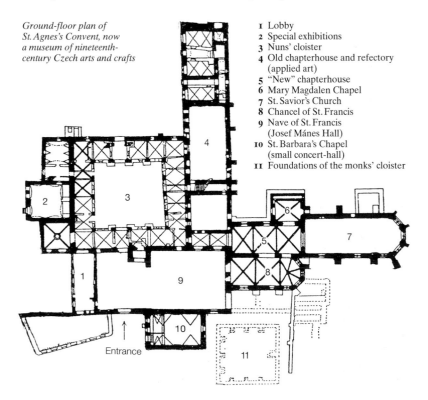

Ground-floor plan of St. Agnes's Convent, now a museum of nineteenth-century Czech arts and crafts

1 Lobby
2 Special exhibitions
3 Nuns' cloister
4 Old chapterhouse and refectory (applied art)
5 "New" chapterhouse
6 Mary Magdalen Chapel
7 St. Savior's Church
8 Chancel of St. Francis
9 Nave of St. Francis (Josef Mánes Hall)
10 St. Barbara's Chapel (small concert-hall)
11 Foundations of the monks' cloister

Entrance

St. Agnes's Convent: east end of St. Savior's Church

choir; the rebuilt nave is now used as a concert hall.

The **museum**, a department of the National Gallery, is devoted to painting and applied art of the nineteenth century. Represented are the Neoclassical, Romantic, Historicist, and Realist streams, and the artists of the "National Theater Generation," who reflect the resurgence of Czech

Institute of the Brethren of Mercy, south facade

nationalism. The foremost painter of his day was Josef Mánes (1820-71), who traveled to Dresden, Poland, Silesia, Munich, Moscow, and Rome; he is here represented by historical and genre scenes, portraits, and landscapes. Karel Purkyně (1834-68), who in Paris had come under the influence of Courbet and Manet, also painted still lifes in the Dutch spirit. Soběslav Pinkas (1827-1901) is the leading representative of Czech Realism. Mánes's successor as most celebrated painter and draughtsman was Mikoláš Aleš (1852-1913), who had studied in Prague and Italy; his favorite themes were historical and mythological, and he also illustrated folk songs.

82 Institute of the Brethren of Mercy

Klášter Milosrdných bratří

U milosrdných

Its very long facade is a pleasing example of late Baroque architecture.

There was a hospital on this site in the fourteenth century. In the early seventeenth century the Protestant congregation of the Bohemian Brethren built the **aisleless church**, but during the process of re-catholicization, the Brethren of Mercy took over. The altarpiece depicting the church's patrons, SS. Simon and Jude, was painted by Wenzel Lorenz Reiner in 1731; a painting by Johann Rudolf Byss shows the Portuguese saint, John of God, who founded the Brethren of Mercy.

Museum of Arts and Crafts: a seventeenth-century Bohemian glass and detail of an engraved glass goblet by C. Lehmann (1605)

83 St. Savior *Svatý Salvátor*
Salvátorská

An aisleless church in the "Renaissance-Gothic" style.

When Emperor Rudolf II granted freedom of religion in a charter of 1609, the Lutherans of Prague called in the Swiss architect Johann Christophel, from Graubünden, to build a church for them in which the pulpit would be the central feature. But the era of tolerance was short-lived: in 1620 the church was assigned to the Order of St. Francis of Paula. The monks were responsible for the building of the tower and the stucco and fresco decoration. The **Baroque facade** of the monastery building can still be seen on the north side of Staroměstské náměstí at No. 7; the statues of Christ, angels, and sainted monks are by Jäckel. The church reverted to the Protestants after Joseph II's promulgation of the Edict of Tolerance in 1781; since 1918 it has been the principal church of the Bohemian Brethren, a denomination formed by adherents of the Augsburg and Helvetian confessions.

84 Rudolfinum
Náměstí Jana Palacha 1

A major neo-Renaissance structure, named after Crown Prince Rudolf.

The "House of Artists," as it is also known, is the home of the Czech Philharmonia, whose concerts can be heard here in the Dvořák Hall. The building was designed by Josef Zítek and Josef Schulz, the architects of the National Theater and National Museum, and erected between 1876 and 1884. Flanking the steps are allegories of music and art by Anton Wagner, who also fashioned the statues of Czech composers and other artists on the attic story. On the south side of the square the College of Arts and Crafts, by Jan Kotěra, constitutes an architectural pendant.

The Vltava Bridge, built in 1911, was originally named for Crown Prince Franz Ferdinand. Its present name, **Mánesův most**, recalls the famous nineteenth century artist, whose monument by Bohumil Kafka stands on the embankment.

85 Museum of Arts and Crafts
Umělecko-průmyslové muzeum
Ulice 17. listopadu 2/4

The largest collection of glass in the world.

This neo-Renaissance building by Josef Schulz was erected between 1897 and 1900. The allegorical reliefs symbolize the various crafts. The collections provide a survey of European applied art since antiquity, with special emphasis on ceramics, textile design, metalwork, bookbinding, furniture, and glass. The museum also has an important library of specialist literature.

Josefov
The former Jewish quarter

There were Jewish merchants in Prague as early as the ninth or tenth century. They first settled in Malá Strana and at the foot of Vyšehrad Hill, but by the twelfth century a Jewish community had established itself in the vicinity of the international marketplace on "Broad Street" (Široká), around the Old School Synagogue. From the mid-thirteenth century onward the Old-New Synagogue was the spiritual and topographical center of what was at one time the largest Jewish quarter in Europe. Behind its high walls, the **ghetto** survived until well into the nineteenth century, by which time it was a maze of narrow alleys, so densely and haphazardly built up that the cramped and unsanitary living conditions were no longer tenable. Between 1893 and 1912 a slum clearance program razed and rebuilt the whole area, sparing only a few historic monuments.

Like their kinsmen throughout western Europe, the **Jews of Prague** experienced alternating periods of prosperity and persecution. For King Ottokar II they were a protected species, his *servi camerae* ("servants of the chamber"). After the Synod of Prague (1349) Charles IV disqualified them from engaging in trade, forcing many into the opprobrious business of money-lending; they had to wear yellow clothes and pointed hats. The ghetto, where they were now compelled to live, had to withstand the onslaught of plague, fire, and pogrom. The Jews were twice expelled from Prague, in 1541 under Ferdinand I and in 1744 under Maria Theresa, but they were allowed to return in due course.

The economic and cultural zenith of the Jewish community came toward the end of the sixteenth century, when Mordechai Maisel was its chief elder. Maisel, who was court banker to Rudolph II, had contributed valuably to the emperor's war effort against the Turks, and as a reward he was granted the privilege of free disposition of his own property. He funded the building of Talmud schools, synagogues, bathhouses, a town hall, and the paving of all public squares. Before the fire of 1689 the ghetto had three hundred houses and thirteen synagogues; at the beginning of the eighteenth century its population was about twelve thousand. Thanks to Joseph II's Edict of Tolerance (1781) the strict regulations of the ghetto were relaxed: Jews could now live in other parts of town, and Christians began to move into Josefov, as the quarter became known in honor of the enlightened emperor. The wall was not demolished until 1848, the year of revolution, when the Jews were also granted the rights of citizens. The demolition of the old quarter at the turn of the century made room for elaborate displays of bourgeois pride and prosperity, such as the late Historicist and Secessionist buildings that line the boulevard of Pařížská between Staroměstské náměstí and the Vltava.

As the Czech nationalist movement gained impetus, most of Prague's Jews felt more of an affinity with German culture, but in neither camp were they fully accepted. The German-language literature of Jewish writers began to evince an eery – perhaps premonitory – fascination with the darker side of the human soul, with the ghostly and the macabre. Franz Kafka succumbed to tuberculosis in 1924 at the age of forty, Ernst Weiss committed suicide, Max Brod emigrated to Israel, Franz Werfel and Johannes Urzidil went to the United States. In 1940 the National Socialists began to implement the systematic extermination of the Jewish people; of Prague's thirty-five thousand Jewish citizens only one-sixth survived the war. For their projected "Museum of an Extinct Race" the Nazis brought to Prague cult objects and documents from all over Europe; these now form the main corpus of the collections of the State Jewish Museum, which are installed in the old synagogues.

86 Old-New Synagogue

Staronová synagoga
Pařížská/Červená

The oldest synagogue in Europe.

The second synagogue in the Jewish quarter (after the Old School) was originally called the New, or Great, School. Its traditional appellation derives from the German "Alt-Neu," which in turn is thought to be a corruption of the Hebrew *al tnay*, which refers to the legend that stones from the Temple of Solomon were miraculously incorporated into the foundations, and

Bema *of the Old-New Synagogue*

these must be returned to Jerusalem on Judgment Day. The need for a new synagogue arose no doubt from the influx of German Jews from Worms, Speyer, and Regensburg; it was built around 1270 by the king's masons, who were working on the nearby convent of St. Agnes at the time. Stylistically, the venerable edifice recalls early Cistercian Gothic; but the steeply pitched roof with Late Gothic gables, which was added in the fifteenth century, is more reminiscent of brick buildings in northern Germany. The low peripheral structures served as a vestibule and women's hall.

The **south portal** is adorned with an early Gothic relief sculpture of a vine, the symbol of everlasting life. The **interior** is articulated by two octagonal pillars, from which springs five-rib vaulting – a quadripartite bay would have been avoided for its association with the Christian cross. In the center of the room stands the *bema (almemor)*, the podium from which the Torah (the five books of Moses) is read; the Torah scrolls are kept in the niche *(aron hakodesh)* in the east wall. The Jewish community of Prague was granted its *flag*, the "High Banner," by Charles IV in 1357; the present banner dates from the reign of Charles VI (1716). During the Easter Pogrom of 1389 the walls of the synagogue

Brick gable of the Old-New Synagogue

were splashed with blood; the event was commemorated by Rabbi Avigdor Kara in an elegy *(selicha)*, which is still sung on the Day of Atonement.

On the lawn outside the synagogue stands a statue of Moses by František Bílek (1872-1941), a leading Symbolist sculptor.

87 High Synagogue

Vysoká synagoga
Červená 5

The "town hall" synagogue, harboring a unique collection of ritual drapery.

In 1580, Mordechai Maisel financed the building of a **town hall** (Maiselova 18) for the Jewish quarter, with a synagogue accessible from the first floor. The present aspect of the town hall is late Baroque. Beneath the clock tower, facing the Old-New Synagogue, is a second clock with Hebrew digits and hands that rotate counterclockwise. The building houses a kosher restaurant (open to all).

The **High Synagogue** was sealed off from the town hall in the nineteenth century, and its entrance is now opposite the Old-New Synagogue. The magnificent Renaissance vault was designed by South Tyrolean architect Pankraz Roder; the stuccowork imitates Italian terracotta ornaments. Exhibited here are precious synagogue curtains and Torah mantles embroidered with gold and silver, from all parts of Europe. The world's oldest extant synagogue drape was fashioned in 1592 in the Prague workshop of Shelomo Shalit Perlsztiker, which also produced the drape for Maisel's private synagogue. A recurring motif in such fabrics are the pillars of the Temple of Solomon.

88 Maisel Synagogue

Maiselova synagoga

Maiselova 10

Collection of Jewish religious artifacts in metal.

Mordechai Maisel had his family synagogue built in 1592; the Renaissance edi-

The Maisel Synagogue

The former Jewish Town Hall with its two clocks

fice with its sumptuous furnishings was the showpiece of the Jewish quarter until the fire of 1689. It was rebuilt in its present neo-Gothic form at the end of the nineteenth century. The exhibition of ritual objects, mainly of silver, comprises candelabra, vessels, Torah crowns and rolls, and scepter-like "pointing hands" of wood, ivory, or metal as aids to following the Torah verses.

The High Synagogue: the oldest extant synagogue curtain (1592)

Tombstones in the Old Jewish Cemetery

89 Close, or Klausen, Synagogue

Klauzová synagoga

U starého hřbitova 4

Exhibition of Hebrew manuscripts and printed works, and insights into Jewish tradition.

At the end of the sixteenth century Morde-chai Maisel also founded a small temple with school and ritual bathhouse *(mikve)* – these three "enclosures" account for the name. One of the Talmud instructors here was the famous Rabbi Löw. The present building dates from 1694; the sober Baroque hall was altered in the nineteenth century.

90 Old Jewish Cemetery

Starý židovský hřbitov

U starého hřbitova

One of the world's most historic Jewish sites.

The neo-Romanesque entrance hall with its corner tower (1906) stands on the site of a structure used for the ceremonies of the funeral brotherhood since the sixteenth century. It now houses an exhibition of drawings and exercise-books of Jewish children from the concentration camp of Theresienstadt (Terezín).

Until the fifteenth century the **Jewish cemetery** was located on the edge of Nové Město. The present graveyard was used from the early fifteenth century until 1787, when Emperor Joseph II banned burials in residential areas. The site gradually grew until it covered over 13,000 square yards. When there was no more space, another layer of earth was laid – in some parts there are as many as twelve graves on top of each other; the number of extant **tombstones** (estimated at twelve thousand) thus bears no relation to the number of interments. The oldest stone dates from 1439 and commemorates Rabbi Avigdor Kara, the author of a famous elegy on the 1389 pogrom. The **tomb of Rabbi Löw** is world-famous: the lion on the pink late

Renaissance chest alludes to his descent from the tribe of Levi. Jehuda Liva ben Bezalel (1513-1609), known as Rabbi Löw, was a scholar, judge, preacher, and philosopher of high repute; he even had the ear of Emperor Rudolf II, whom he instructed in the secrets of the cabbala, the Jewish mystic tradition. The son of a rabbi of Worms, he had studied in Lubin, Poland. The name of Rabbi Löw is most popularly associated with the fabled Golem, a Frankenstein-like creature fashioned out of clay, who could be brought to life by the utterance of magic words and sent out on patrol to protect the ghetto from its enemies; until one day he got out of control... The legend – which in fact can only be traced back to the eighteenth century – has been a fertile source of inspiration for writers of both Czech and German tongue, among whom Gustav Meyrink should be mentioned for his novel *Golem* (1915) and Egon Erwin Kisch for his investigative piece *On the Trail of the Golem*; the German director Paul Wegener made two Golem films in the 1920s.

The Pinkas Synagogue, with bema *in the center*

91 Pinkas Synagogue

Pinkasova synagoga
Široká 3

Second only to the Old-New Synagogue in architectural interest; a memorial to the Jewish victims of Nazism.

There is evidence that a Talmud school existed on the site as early as the eleventh century. The present building was constructed with a donation from the Horowitz family in 1535. The interior is very impressive, with its blend of Late Gothic (ribbed vault) and Renaissance elements (fluted wall shafts, egg-and-tongue moldings, rosettes). The women's gallery, vestibule, and meeting room were added in the early seventeenth century. The *bema* is enclosed by an intricate Rococo screen. The synagogue was converted into a memorial in 1950: the death camps are listed on either side of the Torah niche, and the side walls commemorate in alphabetical order the names of the 77,297 Bohemian and Moravian Jews who were murdered.

92 Old School, or Spanish, Synagogue

Španělská synagoga
Dušní 12

The nineteenth-century building replaced Prague's oldest synagogue.

The "Old School" is documented as far back as the twelfth century, which makes it the first synagogue in Prague; no doubt Jews of eastern origin had been settled in the neighborhood for some time already. Up to the nineteenth century this was the heart of the ghetto of the Jews who followed the eastern rite (the west-oriented community established itself around the Old-New Synagogue). Over the centuries, the Old School burnt down several times and was rebuilt. The present building was designed in a historicizing style by Ignaz Ullmann and Josef Niklas after 1868; for its sumptuous decoration (stucco arabesques, wood carvings) it came to be known as the "Temple" or "Spanish" Synagogue, a reference to the once-flourishing Jewish culture of Spain.

Diagonally opposite stands the Gothic **Church of the Holy Spirit**, which before the Hussite wars had belonged to a convent of Benedictine nuns. The Baroque exterior stems from the eighteenth century: the statue of St. John of Nepomuk is by F. M. Brokoff, and the St. Joseph altarpiece is by Heintsch.

Nové Město

New Town

New only in a relative sense, the township was founded by Charles IV in 1348 – a very ambitious town-planning project for its time. It was the biggest of the Prague townships in terms of area, and was soon the most densely populated; from the early fifteenth century this district of artesans and other humbler social classes provided numerous recruits for the radical wing of the Hussite movement. Nové Město was a municipality in its own right until 1784, when it was amalgamated with the other inner-city townships. The present-day character of the quarter is largely colored by the monumental buildings in the Historicist and Art Nouveau styles that were a product of the industrial and commercial upswing of the second half of the nineteenth century.

93 Wenceslas Square
Václavské náměstí

Prague's central axis and principal shopping street, the heart of the Czech nation.

The former horse market, a long drawn-out square measuring 820 by 65 yards, has been the center of Nové Město, indeed of Prague as a whole, since the fourteenth century. It has often been the scene of major political events, most recently in the fall of 1989, when mass demonstrations heralded the downfall of the Communist regime.

Wenceslas Square (Václavské náměstí) and the National Museum

Old engravings show the square lined with two-to-three-story merchants' houses, overlooked by the tall, slender silhouette of St. Mary of the Snows; the late Baroque Hotel Adria at No. 26 is one of the few relics of a bygone age. The transformation into a modern, **cosmopolitan boulevard** began around 1848, when the square received its present name. The finest specimen of Historicist architecture is the Wiehl House at No. 34, named for Antonín Wiehl, the leading architect of Czech neo-Renaissance; Mikoláš Aleš and Josef Fanta designed the mural decoration. The most attractive Secessionist buildings are the Hotel Ambassador at No. 5, house No. 12, and particularly the Hotel Evropa at No. 25/27, designed in

Dome of the Koruna Building

Art Nouveau doorway of the Novák House, Vodičkova 30

1906 by Alois Dryak and F. Bendelmayer; golden floral motifs on smooth surfaces betray the influence of French Art Nouveau. The Koruna Building at No. 1, designed by Anton Pfeiffer in 1911, already bears a definitive Modernist imprint. The upper part of the square is dominated by the **equestrian statue of St. Wenceslas**, a masterpiece by the Prague sculptor Josef Václav Myslbek, who spent thirty years working on it; in 1912 it replaced a Baroque statue of the saintly prince by Johann Georg Bendl. The plinth is flanked by other patrons of Bohemia: Adalbert, bishop of Prague; Procopius, abbot of Sázava; Princess Ludmila, grandmother of St. Wenceslas; and Agnes, the daughter of King Ottokar I and foundress of the convent that bears her name. In front of the monument, flowers and candles keep alive the memory of the victims of the Communist regime, among them the student Jan Palach, who with his act of self-immolation in 1969 demonstrated against the violent crushing of the "Prague Spring."

In the old days the square, which slopes gently upward toward the Royal Vineyards, ended at the Horse Gate. Since 1890 it has been dominated by the 230-foot high central tower of the majestic National Museum, which was designed by Josef Schulz, a pupil and later associate of Josef Zítek. The **facade** seems to have been inspired by

Memorial to Jan Palach in front of the statue of St. Wenceslas

94 National Museum
Národní muzeum
Václavské náměstí 68

A major work of Czech neo-Renaissance architecture that dominates the square.

Staircase of the National Museum

The Pantheon of the National Museum

the east front of the Louvre in Paris. Anton Wagner, Josef Mauder, Bohuslav Schnirch, and others contributed the statuary: the enthroned figure Čechie (Bohemia) at the top of the ramp, flanked by the Vltava (girl), the Elbe (old man), Moravia, and Silesia; Čechie reappears in the tympanum as patroness of the arts and sciences. The bronze statues in the **vestibule and staircase** are by Ludwig Schwanthaler (Libuše, Přemysl the plowman, King Ottokar II, St. Wenceslas – on the landing Elizabeth, last of the Přemyslids, and King George of Poděbrady). The Pantheon on the first floor is decorated with murals by František Ženíšek and Václav Brožík depicting seminal events in Czech history: Libuše's envoys summon the peasant Přemysl to rule over the Czechs, St. Methodius completes his translation of the Bible into old church Slavonics, Charles IV founds the university of Prague in 1348, Comenius presents his writings on education to the city council of Amsterdam; the pendentives of the cupola feature allegorical paintings by Vojtěch Hynais.

Collections: the first floor of the museum houses exhibitions of prehistory, recent history from the Czech renascence in the nineteenth century to the present day, numismatics, and mineralogy; the second floor is primarily devoted to zoology and paleontology.

Adjacent to the National Museum, at the beginning of Wilsonova, stands the **House of the Federal Parliament**, designed in 1965 by Karel Prager. After the dissolution of that body on 31 December 1992, a new use for the building has yet to be found.

95 Sylva-Taroucca Palace (Savarin Palace)

Palác Sylva-Tarouccovský
Na příkopě 10

Delightful Rococo staircase.

The medieval moat separating Staré from Nové Město was filled in 1781; after a phase of life as a "green belt," Na příkopě is now a highly commercialized pedestrian thoroughfare. The finest building is **Sylva-Taroucca Palace**, which originally belonged to Piccolomini, commander in the

The late Baroque Sylva-Taroucca Palace ▷

Mosaics by Mikoláš Aleš
(Na príkopě 20)

Thirty Years' War and Waldstein's mortal enemy. It was remodeled as a late Baroque mansion around 1749, K.I. Dientzenhofer's plan being realized by A. Lurago; the sculptural work is by Platzer. Giuseppe Bossi decorated the staircase with stucco, and Wenzel Ambrozzi painted the frescoes of Helios the sun-god and the Four Seasons. One of Prague's most elegant casinos is now located on the premises.

At the corner of Panská stands the Neoclassical **Piarist Church** of the Holy Cross. The former **Nostitz Palace** at No. 20 was rebuilt in a neo-Renaissance style by Osvald Polívka, with mosaics and reliefs by Aleš; the only relic of the Baroque edifice is the side portal, by the Braun workshop. The bank building at No. 24 stands on the site of the Blue Star Inn, in which Emperor Wilhelm I and Prince Bismarck signed the Peace of Prague in 1866.

96 Civic Hall
Obecní dům
Náměstí republiky 5

The most important example of Secessionism (Prague's interpretation of French Art Nouveau), with an elegant café and other fine interiors.

Next to the Powder Tower, on the site of the medieval royal court, stands the extravagant showpiece of the municipality of Prague, which was erected between 1906 and 1912 to a design by Osvald Polívka and Antonín Balšánek. Generous use is made of cast iron and glass; relief medallions illustrating various types of Bohemian national dress strike a folksy note. The **mosaic** by Karel Špillar constitutes a Homage to Prague, and is flanked by Ladislav Šaloun's visions of the Yoke of Oppression and the People's Awakening. The latter also fashioned the allegorical statues in the **Smetana Hall**, concert venue of the Prague Symphony Orchestra. Among the other notable sculptors and artists who helped to shape the interior are Josef Václav Myslbek, Mikoláš Aleš, and Alfons Mucha. Nearby (U obecního domu 1), the **Hotel Paříž** is another interesting specimen of Art Nouveau (with a touch of the neo-Gothic).

St. Joseph's Church (Náměstí republiky 2) is an unpretentious Baroque structure of the Capuchin type, dating from 1630. Two altarpieces (St. Anthony of Padua and St. Felix of Cantalice) are attributed to the early Baroque master Karl Škréta. The statue of St. Francis by Franz Preiss (1708) originally stood on Charles Bridge; before

the church stands a statue of St.Jude from 1741.

The street name Na poříčí ("Beside the River") evokes the old German merchants' quarter Am Poritsch, which began to take shape in the eleventh century between Powder Tower and the river. Its center was the Romanesque **St. Peter's Church** (Petrská/Biskupská), which in 1215 passed into the hands of the Teutonic Knights and was later taken over by the Red Star order of the Knights of the Cross; after having been rebuilt several times over the years, it was given a neo-Gothic facelift by Josef Mocker.

The Romanesque predecessor of **St. Clement** (Klimentská/Nové mlýny) became the first Dominican church in Prague when the order established itself here in 1226. The present church is a late-nineteenth-century neo-Gothic restoration of a Gothic structure; it belongs today to the Bohemian Brethren.

The nearby Vávra House (Nové mlýny 2) originally belonged to a mill owner. The Biedermeier facade is decorated with delightful murals in the Romantic spirit by Josef Navrátil (1847). The building now houses the **Museum of Postage Stamps**, opened on the occasion of the world philatelic exhibition in 1988.

97 The Hibernians
U hybernů
Náměstí republiky 4

Exhibition hall with an elegant Empire facade.

In 1355, the Benedictine abbey of St. Ambrose of Milan was founded on the site. In the sixteenth century it became the home of Franciscan friars who had been expelled from Ireland, hence the name; the refugees brought with them the potato, which from the monastery garden soon spread to become a staple crop throughout the land. The church was secularized in 1790 and subsequently used as a customs office; the Empire-style facade was erected in 1808.

98 St. Henry
Svatý Jindřich
Jindřišská/Jeruza lémská

Its freestanding bell tower is a prominent landmark.

The sober Gothic structure was founded by Charles IV around 1350 as the parish church for the northern part of Nové Město around the old hay market

The Civic Hall, a fine specimen of Art Nouveau

The Gothic tower adjacent to St. Henry

The Jubilee Synagogue of 1905: neo-Moorish architecture infused with Art Nouveau

(Senovážné náměstí). The Baroque sandstone statues by the door, of SS. John of Nepomuk and Jude, are ascribed to Michael Josef Brokoff. For the high altar Johann Georg Heintsch painted the scene of the church's patron, Emperor Henry II, and the ordeal by fire of his wife, St. Kunigunde.

It is worth making a short detour down Jeruzalémská to see the **Jubilee Synagogue** at No. 7, which was designed on Moorish lines in 1905 by Wilhelm Stiassny.

Harrach Palace (Jindřišská 20) is a Rococo mansion by Ignaz Palliardi. Diagonally opposite at No. 19 is the birthplace of the poet Rainer Maria Rilke (1875-1926). The neo-Renaissance building of the **Central Post Office** at No. 14 stands on the site of the first botanical garden in central Europe, which was founded by Magister Angelus, court apothecary to Charles IV, in the fourteenth century.

99 State Opera

Státní opera

Wilsonova 4

Also known as the Smetana Theater, originally the New German Theater.

The charming neo-Rococo building was designed for the German Theater Association by Ferdinand Fellner (1847-1916) and Hermann Helmer (1849-1919), who won fame as architects of theaters throughout the Austro-Hungarian Empire and as far afield as Hamburg, Riga, Odessa, and Yashi in Moldavia. The curtain first rose in January 1888 on a performance of Wagner's *Meistersinger*. Many well-known actors and film stars of the German-speaking world began their careers on this stage.

In the hall of the main station

The main station: Art Nouveau meets the modern world

The **main station** (Wilson Station) now stands rather forlorn at the other side of an expressway, with trite glass bubbles impeding the view, but it is still a noble example of Art Nouveau in its Czech expression; Josef Fanta was the architect, the allegorical sculptures are by Stanislav Sucharda. On the lower levels we must find our way through vast and inhospitable modern concourses to discover on a wall at the left the plaque dedicated to Woodrow Wilson, the American president who was instrumental in the creation of the republic of Czechoslovakia. On the upper level the high circular hall is a lavishly decorated reminder of the days when a station was more than just a place to catch a train.

Longinus. The interior, with its basilican proportions, still exudes a Gothic atmosphere; from the original decoration fragments of Gothic frescoes (Life of the Virgin Mary) have survived, as well as the St. Stephen's Madonna, a Late Gothic (1472) panel painting of the type of the Raudnitz or Hohenfurt Madonnas, framed by a sequence of miniatures. The high altar is a huge construction of early Baroque craftsmanship with offertory doors, and is adorned with statues of Bohemian patron saints by Johann Georg Bendl and paintings by Matthias Zimprecht. Karel Škréta painted some of the other fine altarpieces (c. 1650): St. Rosalia, St. Wenceslas, the Baptism in the Jordan.

100 St. Stephen
Svatý Štěpán
Štěpánská/Na rybníčku

Imposing Gothic building with a modest Romanesque neighbor.

The old village of Rybníček (Fish Pond) has bequeathed to posterity its tiny parish church, the **rotunda of St. Longinus**, a Romanesque structure from the late twelfth century. The Gothic church of **St. Stephen** was founded by Charles IV in the mid-fourteenth century as the center of upper Nové Město. A number of interesting gravestones are let into the outer wall, coming from the old cemetery of St.

101 St. Mary of the Snows
Panna Marie Sněžná
Jungmannovo náměstí

Highest Gothic chancel in Prague, of overwhelming beauty.

The tall, slender church, which presents its most attractive side to **Františkánská zahrada** (Franciscan Garden), is in fact only the east end of what Charles IV, when he founded it in 1347, had planned as a huge coronation cathedral, larger even than St. Vitus's. The emperor summoned Discalced Carmelites from the Rhineland to take charge of the church. But the building remained a torso: work was stopped in

The soaring Gothic interior of St. Mary of the Snows

1397 for lack of funds. Jan Želivský, the Hussite leader, was pastor of St. Mary's; and it was here, on 30 July 1419, that he assembled his followers before leading them to Nové Město Town Hall (see p. 147).

After the Gothic vault collapsed at the beginning of the seventeenth century, the church was given a Renaissance barrel vault, at 115 feet only slightly lower than the original; the pseudo-Gothic rib structure is merely decorative. The Franciscans, who had replaced the Carmelites as cura-

tors of St. Mary's, commissioned the monumental high altar, which is the largest of its kind in Prague. Two generations of artists and craftsmen worked on the early Baroque structure, which is built up of superimposed aedicules; the statues of saints were installed in 1641. The painting on the left-hand side altar is an Annunciation by Wenzel Lorenz Reiner (1724).

To the north of the church, betwe Jungmannovo náměstí 13 and 14, the an interesting **cemetery gate**, a repli the pre-1346 original which is now in St. George's Convent: the tympanum relief depicts the coronation of the Virgin and the throne of grace, beneath which kneel the donors, King John of Luxemburg and his son Wenceslas, margrave of Moravia (eagle escutcheon), who styled himself Charles IV, in allusion to Charlemagne, when he became Holy Roman Emperor.

I02 National Street

Národní třída

A busy commercial thoroughfare, continuing the course of the medieval moat.

On Jungmannovo náměstí a statue by Ludvík Simek (1878) commemorates the philologist Josef Jungmann (1773-1847), the author of the first German-Czech dictionary. The Adria insurance company's building (Národní třída 40), an example of "Rondo-Cubism" by Pavel Janák, reminiscent of a Venetian Renaissance palace, and its name was allegorized by Jan Štursa in the bronze ensemble on the attic recess (1924). It formerly housed the **Laterna Magika** theater, which has now moved to the Nová Scéna (p. 145). The oldest building on the street is the Kaňka House at No. 16, c. 1735, by the Baroque architect of that name. Opposite St. Ursula's are two interesting **Art Nouveau buildings** de-

The high altar of St. Ursula

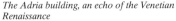

The Adria building, an echo of the Venetian Renaissance

signed by Osvald Polívka around 1910: No. 9, formerly the home of the Topič publishing house, and No. 7. One of the **oldest Historicist buildings** in Prague, begun around 1860 by Ignaz Ullmann, is now the Czech Academy of Sciences at Nos. 5/3, also built in a style evoking the Venetian Renaissance.

I03 St. Ursula

Svatá Voršila

Národní 8

A High Baroque aisleless church decorated and furnished to a consistent plan.

The church of the Ursuline convent was the first in Prague to have its piers incorporated into the walls; the Italian architect Marco Antonio Canevale, who built it between 1702 and 1704, probably followed a plan by Paul Ignaz Bayer. The facade statues of the virgin martyrs Agatha, Ursula, and Margaret are by Franz Preiss, the Rococo figure of St. John of Nepomuk is by Ignaz Platzer (1747). The **interior**, with its original decoration and furnishings,

presents an attractively consistent appearance. The ceiling frescoes of the Trinity are by Johann Jakob Steinfels (1707); Tomaso Soldati executed the stucco decoration, and Franz Preiss sculpted the statues of apostles and saints. Jan Kryštof Liška painted the Apotheosis of St. Ursula on the high altar, Peter Brandl the Assumption on a side altar.

The Neoclassical facade at Voršilská 8/10 is the **Schwarzenberg Palace**, designed by Ignaz Palliardi around 1780; the statues are by Ignaz Platzer.

104 National Theater

Národní divadlo

Národní 2

The "Golden Chapel on the Vltava" was financed by public contributions; only those who were not true Czechs would not willingly dig into their pockets for this embodiment of the national spirit. On 16 May 1868 the foundation stone was laid in the presence of Bedřich Smetana and the historian František Palacký, the "Father of the Nation." Josef Zítek designed the grandiose neo-Renaissance structure, whose curved, set-back roof is modeled on that of the Belvedere; the stone was quarried on the "sacred mountains" of Bohemia and Moravia. Smetana's patriotic opera *Libuše* was chosen for the opening night, on 15 June 1881. Only two months later, the theater was devastated by fire. Josef Schulz, a pupil of Zítek's, took charge of the rebuilding, which was accomplished in a remarkably short time: on 18 November 1883 the curtain again rose on *Libuše*.

The leading Czech artists of the day collaborated on the project. The sculptures on the north facade – Apollo and the Muses, three-horse chariots with the goddess of victory – are for the most part the work of Bohuslav Schnirch, those on the west facade (to the river) by Josef Václav Myslbek. In the lunettes of the loggia Josef Tulka painted allegories of the "Five Songs." The foyer is decorated with wall and ceiling frescoes by František Ženíšek (folk song, myth, and Decline, Renascence, and Golden Age of Art), a cycle on the theme of Homeland by Mikoláš Aleš, and sculptures by Myslbek. The Allegory of

◁ *The National Theater, with Slav Island on the left*

◁ *The three-horse chariot of Victory, sculpted by Bohuslav Schnirch*

the Arts in the auditorium was painted by Ženíšek, the Founding of the National Theater on the safety curtain by Vojtěch Hynais. In the proscenium arch Čechie personifies the nation, flanked by Apollo, Dionysos, Melpomene (muse of tragedy), and Thalia (comedy); the ensemble was sculpted by Schnirch.

The National Theater was renovated in the 1970s, and at the same time an annex was built, the **Nová Scéna** (Národní 4); the facade of Karel Prager's design is clad with panels of Cuban marble behind glass. The "New Stage" is now home to the **Laterna Magika**, one of the best-known and most original shows in town. The company was founded by the Prague theatrical producer Alfred Radok, who first presented it to the world at the Brussels World Fair in 1958, and produces multimedia shows involving drama, music, mime, slide projections, and film.

105 Slav Island

Slovanský ostrov

Opposite Masarykovo nábřeží

The product of silting, the island was made accessible and landscaped at the end of the eighteenth century.

The Sophia Hall that was erected here in the early nineteenth century (and gave rise to the old name "Sophia Island") was an important center of musical life in Prague: celebrities such as Franz Liszt, Hector Berlioz, Richard Wagner, and the violin virtuoso Jan Kubelík gave concerts here. In 1848, the year of revolution, the Slavic Congress was held here under the chairmanship of the historian František Palacký.

A prominent landmark is the Gothic water tower with its Baroque bonnet, also known as the Šítek Tower after the old mills on which it was built. The Mánes exhibition hall, headquarters of Prague's principal artists' association, is a Cubist structure dating from 1930. In the park stands a bronze monument to the authoress Božena Němcová (1820-62).

106 St. Adalbert

Svatý Vojtěch

Vojtěšská/Šítkova

Originally the church of the tanners' guild.

The Gothic structure once again bears a resemblance to its original form, after the removal of the Baroque trappings in

Church of SS. Cyril and Methodius

sculptures by Platzer. A **memorial room** has been installed here for the composer Josef Bohuslav Foerster (1859-1951), a friend of Gustav Mahler.

107 SS. Cyril and Methodius
Svatí Cyril a Metoděj
Prague 2, Resslova/Na Zderaze

Church of the Czechoslovak Orthodox congregation since 1935.

Paul Ignaz Bayer designed a modest aisleless chapel (originally dedicated to St. Charles Borromeo) for a home for retired priests. In 1733, probably to a design by K.I. Dientzenhofer, the High Baroque **west and south facades** were added, creating an interesting resolution of the corner situation. In 1942 the exile-Czech parachutists who had assassinated Heydrich, the deputy governor of the Nazi protectorate, barricaded themselves in the **crypt** of the church, and took their own lives to avoid capture by the Germans.

The **Church of St. Wenceslas**, diagonally opposite on Dittrichova, today belongs to the Hussite denomination. The original Romanesque and Gothic building underwent several transformations, and served as abbey church for the Discalced Augustinians; it was re-gothicized in 1926. Fragments of Gothic murals have survived in the chancel; late Baroque frescoes illustrate the legend of the patron saint.

which, like many other Prague churches, it was clad. The rectory (Pštrossova 17) is adorned with landscape and mythology murals by Josef Hoffmann (1778) and

The English alchemist Edward Kelley once lived in the Faust House

108 Charles Square

Karlovo náměstí

Prague 2

Prague's biggest marketplace was planned by Emperor Charles IV as part of his "New Town."

Every year, on the feast of Corpus Christi, the square was even more thronged with people than usual: the crown jewels and insignia of the Holy Roman Empire, which had been transferred from Nuremberg to Karlštejn, were then displayed to the public in Prague, and it was believed that they possessed miraculous powers of healing and the forgiveness of sins. The sale of devotional objects to pilgrims was just one of the pillars on which Charles Square soon established itself as a prime commercial center of the prospering imperial city of Prague; the cattle market was held here, and the calendar offered plenty of occasions for fairs of one kind or another. The influential "Brotherhood of the Hoop and the Hammer" sponsored a Corpus Christi chapel in the center of the square; from 1437 onward it was the repository of the stone tablets on which were recorded the Basel Compacts, the agreement between the moderate Hussites (Calixtines and Utraquists) and the Church of Rome. The chapel was demolished at the end of the eighteenth century; "cattle market" (as it was known until 1848) was for a time used as a fish market and subsequently landscaped with green spaces.

To the north of Spálená stands **Trinity Church**, a Baroque edifice from 1712 designed by Ottavio Broggio; the Trinitarian monastery to which it belonged was secularized in 1783. The Baroque statues flanking the facade are by F. M. Brokoff (St. John of Nepomuk) and the workshop of A. Braun (St. Jude). The Trinity painting of the high altar is by Maulpertsch.

The fine Renaissance gables of Nové Město Town Hall

Town scribe here from 1411 to 1414 was Johannes von Saaz, one of the first German-language writers in the land; he is famous for his polemic dialogue *The Tiller from Bohemia*. A bronze monument commemorates the Hussite preacher Jan Želivský, a former Premonstratensian monk, who marched to the town hall with his followers on 30 July 1419 to demand the release of fellow believers held in custody. When their request was dismissed none too politely, the enraged mob proceeded to throw the Catholic councillors out of the window. The consequence of this First Defenestration of Prague was fifteen years of war; the incident upset King Wenceslas IV so much, it is said, that he died of a stroke a few days later.

109 Nové Město Town Hall

Novoměstská radnice

Prague 2, Karlovo náměstí 23

Scene of the "First Defenestration of Prague" on 30 July 1419.

When the Prague townships were amalgamated in 1784, the administrative headquarters of Nové Město lost its raison d'être; subsequent alterations also spoiled its outward appearance. The original Gothic structure has been restored; the High Renaissance gables were added by the lodge of Benedikt Ried (1526).

110 St. Ignatius

Svatý Ignác

Prague 2, Karlovo náměstí/Ječná

An early Baroque Jesuit church of the type devised by Vignola in Rome.

The Jesuits built their second institute in Prague on the east side of Karlovo náměstí. Giovanni Domenico Orsi designed the church, which was completed in 1671 under the direction of Carlo Lurago. The facade is modeled on that of St. Savior's in the Clementinum. Tomaso Soldati carried out the stuccowork at the end

The Jesuit Church of St. Ignatius

of the seventeenth century; Paul Ignaz Bayer built the portico and the east tower. The **interior**, with its galleries and barrel

St. John of Nepomuk on the Cliff

vault, is on the pattern of Il Gesú in Rome. The walls and ceiling are covered with a wealth of stucco ornamentation from the time of the church's construction, with later elaborations in the Rococo style; the figural elements represent Jesuit saints and patron saints of Bohemia. The marbled stucco and gilding, and most of the furnishings, are in the spirit of late Baroque and Rococo (mid-eighteenth century). The high altar painting of the Apotheosis of St. Ignatius of Loyola, founder of the Jesuit order, by Johann Georg Heintsch, is rather older, dating from 1688.

III St. John of Nepomuk on the Cliff

Svatý Jan Nepomucký na skalce
Prague 2, Vyšehradská

Kilian Ignaz Dientzenhofer's masterpiece of High Baroque illusionism, inspired by Roman models.

When leaving Karlovo náměsti we should perhaps give a wide berth to the Faust House at No. 40 (see photograph on p. 140) on the corner of Vyšehradská. Back in the fourteenth century a duke of Opava is said to have dabbled in black magic in a building that once stood on this site. The Renaissance mansion of the barons Mladota of Solopysk now wears a Baroque mantle. Edward Kelley, the English alchemist in the service of Rudolf II, lived here around 1600. The name of Doctor Faustus was not associated with the house until the nineteenth century, by which time the blood-brother of Mephistopheles already had three residences in Prague, if we are to believe the legends.

A defiant repudiation of the Devil and all his works, St. John of Nepomuk germinates as it were by genial sleight of hand from the high garden wall of the Faust House. The theatrical effect of the **facade** (1731-38), with its obliquely set twin towers, is heightened by the double flight of steps, a later addition. The **interior** is a combination of rounded octagon with an oval cupola and two transverse ellipses (vestibule and choir); the ingenious blending of a longitudinal and a central plan was a specialty of K. I. Dientzenhofer's, as is evidenced, for example, by St. Mary Magdalen in Karlovy Vary (Karlsbad). The cupola fresco by Jan Karel Kovář (1748) depicts the Ascension of St. John of Nepomuk. Near the high altar stands Johann Brokoff's wood model (1682) for the statue of the saint on Charles Bridge.

112 Monastery of the Slavs (Emmaus)

Klášter Na Slovanech (Emauzy)
Prague 2, Vyšhradská/Na Slovanech (open 10 a.m.-5 p.m. except Mondays)

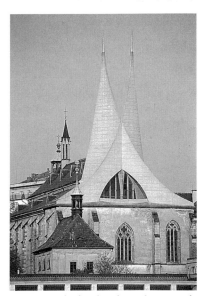

A prominent landmark in the southern part of Nové Město: the modern facade of the Gothic abbey church of Emmaus

The most eye-catching feature of the abbey church is an idiosyncratic piece of modern architecture: František M. Černý replaced the Baroque towers of the **west facade**, destroyed in an air raid in February 1945, with two interlocking concrete "wings," which are clearly inspired by Gothic roof forms, such as those of St. Barbara, Kutná hora.

The **monastery** was founded by Charles IV in 1347 as an institute for the cultiva-

Cloister of Emmaus monastery

Annunciation fresco in the cloister at Emmaus

tion of the Slavonic liturgy, and was entrusted to Benedictines from Bohemia, Croatia, Serbia, and Russia; the emperor hoped thus to gain advice and support for his policies in eastern and southeastern Europe. The abbey was consecrated on Easter Monday of 1372, and its alternative name derives from the gospel for the day, which tells of the disciples on the road to Emmaus. The scriptorium produced a number of precious manuscripts in Old Church Slavonic, in the Glagolitic script devised by the Apostles to the Slavs, SS. Cyril and Methodius; a particularly magnificent Gospel codex originated here (1395), passing by way of Constantinople to become part of the coronation regalia of the French kings in Rheims. After falling into decline during the Hussite period, the monastery was revitalized in 1636 by the arrival of Spanish Benedictines of the reformed Montserrat order. In 1880 it was taken over by monks from the Benedictine abbey of Beuron in Upper Swabia, who renovated the **hall church** and the monastery buildings in the neo-Gothic/Byzantine style that is the hallmark of the "Beuron school."

The **cloister** boasts a very fine Gothic fresco cycle (c. 1360), Italian in its formal structure but betraying stylistic influences from northern France. It is the work of three painters from the court of Charles IV, one of whom is known as the "Master of Emmaus." The frescoes were heavily over-painted in later years, and badly damaged during fire fighting operations in 1945; two

restorations have since managed to rescue parts of the Biblia Pauperum, the "poor man's Bible" in pictorial form for the benefit of the illiterate. The wall panels are divided into two parts, with episodes from the life of Christ being typologically paralleled by Old Testament scenes: in the south wing Adam and Eve and the birth of Christ, in the west Jesus's childhood, in the north his miracles, and in the east the Passion and Transfiguration.

The squat, Baroque tower in the hollow to the south of Emmaus belongs to the **Church of the Most Holy Trinity** (Trojická), a Gothic structure at core that was built by the masons who worked on the abbey.

113 Church of St. Mary of Sorrows
Panna Marie Bolestná
Prague 2, Na Slupi/Apolinářská

A Baroque convent church with an attractive Rococo chapel.

The convent, hospital and church of the Elizabethine nuns were designed by K. I. Dientzenhofer around 1725. The **Rococo chapel of St. Thecla**, by an unknown hand, has a particularly charming interior, with fine frescoes by Johann Lukas Kracker (1762) and an altarpiece by Ignaz Raab depicting the early Christian martyr to whom the chapel is dedicated; the statues were fashioned in the Platzer workshop.

The **Church of the Annunciation** (St. Mary on the Column), a little further south (Na Slupi/Albertov), has its name from the single central pier of the square interior. The church was built around 1365 as part of a Servite monastery and has since been considerably remodeled; its present aspect is neo-Gothic.

114 Michna Pavilion (Villa Amerika)

Michnův letohrádek (Villa Amerika)

Prague 2, Ke Karlovu 20

Home of the Dvořák museum, and an attractive venue for chamber music concerts.

This delightful little **garden mansion** (the spacious park no longer exists, unfortunately) was built by K.I. Dientzenhofer between 1717 and 1720 for Count Jan Václav Michna of Vacinov. The statues are from the workshop of Anton Braun. The Innsbruck artist Johann Ferdinand Schor painted the frescoes in the Grand Hall (Apollo, Pegasus, gods). Antonín Dvořák did of course spend several years in America (1891-95) and composed a *New World* symphony, but the popular name of the villa is in fact derived from that of a local pub; the museum was installed here in 1932.

The octagonal Gothic tower that rises behind the walls of the nearby hospital (Kateřinská/Viničná) is the only survivor of the original **Church of St.Catherine**, which was built for a congregation of Au-

Church of St. Apollinaris, who brought Christianity to Ravenna

gustinian nuns in the fourteenth century. The present Baroque church was built between 1737 and 1741 to plans by Kaňka and K.I. Dientzenhofer; frescoes by Reiner illustrate the legend of the patron saint.

The **Church of St.Apollinaris** (Apoli-

The Michna Pavilion (Villa Amerika)

nářská/Studničkova) is a foundation of Charles IV from the mid-fourteenth century. The aisleless Gothic structure was reworked in the neo-Gothic idiom by Josef Mocker in 1897. Most of the altars are Baroque.

115 Karlov

Prague 2, Ke Karlovu, Karlov 1

A centrally planned High Gothic church modeled on the palace chapel in Aachen; converted into a pilgrimage church in the Baroque era.

In 1351, to commemorate his coronation as King of Rome in the octagonal chapel at Aachen, Charles IV founded a church and monastery for Augustinian (Lateran) canons. The church was dedicated to Our Lady and Charlemagne, the donor's "patron saint" (Charlemagne had been canonized by the antipope Paschal III in 1165, at the urging of Emperor Frederick Barbarossa, but this was never recognized by the official church – though in 1176 Rome did permit his veneration). After being destroyed in the Hussite wars the **stellar vault** was not reconstructed until 1575, and then without the central pier. At the beginning of the eighteenth century Karlov became a popular place of pilgrim-

The "holy steps" at the Karlov church

Stellar vault in the Karlov church

age, and the **"Holy Steps"** were built, a replica of the Scala Santa from the Lateran in Rome (these represent the steps that Jesus is supposed to have trod in Pilate's palace, and the faithful must ascend them on their knees).

116 Karlín

Prague 8

A heavily industrialized district, but not without its attractions.

After the Napoleonic wars the process of industrialization soon set in, and Prague began to grow outward from its ancient core; the outlying villages became the new suburbs. The Karlín district to the north-east was laid out after 1817, and most of its notable buildings date from the nineteenth century.

Prague Municipal Museum (Švermovy Sady/Křižíkova) is installed in a neo-Renaissance building (1898) by Antonín Balšánek and Antonín Wiehl, with sculptures by Ladislav Šaloun. It has an interesting collection of objects connected with the old guilds, and the face of the city in bygone days is graphically illustrated by a panorama in the round, based on a painting by Sachetti, and a colored model of the town by A. Langweil (1826).

The **Karlín Theater** (Křižíkova 10) is a

Prague Municipal Museum

neo-Baroque building from 1891, designed by the famous Vienna theater architects Fellner and Helmer. Operettas and musicals are now staged here.

The dominant feature of Karlínské náměstí is the neo-Romanesque **Church of SS. Cyril and Methodius**; designed by the Vienna architect Karl Rössner, it was erected under the supervision of Ignaz Ullmann of Prague between 1854 and 1863. Three portal reliefs by Václav Levý illustrate the legend of the Apostles to the Slavs. The interior is of interest especially for the murals by Peter Maixner at the ends of the aisles and two paintings on side altars by Josef Mánes and Antonín Lhota.

Hybešova has a monumental specimen of Art Nouveau dating from 1911, today used by the broadcasting corporation.

The **Invalidovna** (Kaizlovy Sady), originally a home for war invalids, takes us back to an age when hereabouts all was green; it was built between 1731 and 1737 by Kilian Ignaz Dientzenhofer to plans by Joseph Emanuel Fischer von Erlach, architect to the court in Vienna.

Following the curve of the Vltava toward the north we are soon in the neighboring district of Libeň. The local **park** became the property of Staré Město in 1662, and its **mansion** (U Libeňského Zámku), whose Rococo facade by Johann Prachner dates from 1770, is the summer residence of the mayor of Prague.

117 Royal Vineyards
Královské vinohrady

The "Upper New Town" evolved on the slopes above the Vltava Valley.

Virtually the whole area of what, to the east of the National Museum, is now the Vinohrady district was planted with vines at the behest of Charles IV. Today it presents some interesting examples of architecture from the last hundred years or so.

St. Ludmila's Church (Náměstí míru) is an imposing neo-Gothic edifice with twin spires; it was built between 1888 and 1893 by Josef Mocker, with the sculptor Josef Myslbek collaborating on the portal. The **Vinohrady Theater** on the same square (No. 7) was built by Alois Čenský between 1905 and 1907, graphically reflecting the transition from period imitations to Secessionism (Art Nouveau).

The **Church of the Sacred Heart** (Náměstí Jiřího z Poděbrad) is a work of the Slovenian architect Josip Plećnik (1928-32).

Further out, in Žižkov, the **Olšany cemeteries** constitute one of Europe's largest burial grounds. The oldest section was originally a plague cemetery, laid out in 1680; it centers on the early Baroque Chapel of St. Rochus, an elliptical structure attributed to Jean Baptiste Mathey. Many of the funerary monuments were sculpted by famous artists, such as Prachner, Lederer, Platzer, Max, Myslbek, Bílek, and B. Kafka. Since the beginning of the nineteenth century Olšany has been the main cemetery for the right bank of the Vltava, and it is the resting place of many notable personalities of the Czech national resurgence.

The entrance to the Russian cemetery is on Jana Želivského. On the opposite side of the road lies the Jewish cemetery, whose most famous grave is that of Franz Kafka, who died of tuberculosis in 1924. Those whose appetite for dust and ashes is not yet sated may walk a few yards on along Vinohradská to the Vinohrady cemetery, where many more national and folk heroes are laid to rest.

118 Vyšehrad

Prague 2

The legendary "cradle" of Prague.

The **rocky outcrop** that rises steeply from the right bank of the Vltava is for the Czechs a veritable shrine. As far back as the eighth century the ancient Slavs probably had a wooden fort here (the name means "high castle"). Here, the legend relates, was the court of **Libuše**, the youngest of the three daughters of the wise prince Krok, whom her people had elected to rule over them. Libuše chose as her husband and founder of a new dynasty the plowman Přemysl (the saga no doubt reflects how the matriarchy of the old Slavs gave way to a male-dominated system), and to him she prophesied the founding of Prague Castle on the spot where "near Strahov Wood a man fashions the threshold of his house." Thus, *prah* ("threshold") is reputedly the source of Praha, the name of a city whose glory should – in Libuše's words – "reach to the stars." Smetana devotes a whole movement of his symphonic poem *Ma Vlast* to Vyšehrad, and pays tribute to the ancestress of the Přemyslids in his opera *Libuše*. The subject matter also interested German composers and writers: the best-known work is Franz Grillparzer's drama *Libussa* (1872), which was only premiered in Prague as recently as 1991.

Turning from legend to history, we know that the first Romanesque stone castle was built, along with several churches, during the reign of Prince Vratislav II; on the occasion of his coronation as first king of Bohemia (Vratislav I) in 1085, the **Vyšehrad Codex** was written, one of Bohemia's most

Leopold's Gate commands the approach to Vyšehrad

View from the cemetery to the west facade of SS. Peter and Paul

precious manuscripts (now in the State Library). By the end of the twelfth century, when the House of Přemysl ruled from Prague Castle, Vyšehrad was no longer of political importance, but it continued to be a religious center. Emperor Charles IV ordained that every king, before his coronation, walk barefoot in pilgrimage to Vyšehrad and there don raffia shoes and a haversack to remind him of his descent from Přemysl the plowman. Over the years, war or fire did not spare the churches or the royal residence, the "most august of Bohemia's castles." Only **St. Martin** has survived, Prague's oldest round church, dating back to the end of the eleventh century.

In the middle of the seventeenth century Italian architects constructed brick fortifications on the hill, and on the south ap-

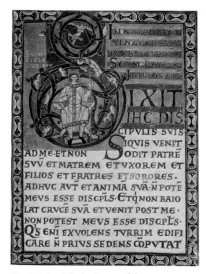

The Vyšehrad Codex is one of the most precious Bohemian manuscripts

St. Martin is the oldest of Prague's round churches

proach Carlo Lurago designed the early Baroque **Leopold's Gate** (1676), named after Emperor Leopold I. Since 1903 the site of the medieval collegiate church has been occupied by the neo-Gothic **Church of SS. Peter and Paul**, a work of the cathedral architect Josef Mocker. The Romanesque stone sarcophagus in a chapel in the south aisle may once have contained the bones of a Přemyslid prince. The Vyšehrad Madonna, or "Rain Madonna," is a fourteenth-century Gothic image to which the people prayed in times of drought. To the south of the church, where the old castle used to stand, is now an expanse of lawn with **monumental statues** of figures from Czech saga, sculpted by Josef Václav Myslbek around 1890 for Palacký Bridge: Lumír and the allegory of song, Ctirad and Šárka, Záboj and Slavoj; Přemysl and Libuše are replicas of the originals, which were destroyed in 1945.

The **cemetery** to the north of the church is the resting place of illustrious figures of Czech culture: the painter Mikoláš Aleš, the writers Božena Němcová, Jan Neruda, and Karel Čapek, the violin virtuoso Jan Kubelík, and many others. The centerpiece is the **"Slavín" memorial**, designed by Josef Mauder; to its right an obelisk marks the grave of Bedřich Smetana (1824-84). Antonín Dvořák (1841-1904) is buried under the arcade on the north side.

Southeast of Vyšehrad, on the main rolad to Brno (5. Května 65), can be seen the huge Palace of Culture, which was built by a team of architects in 1981. It comprises a three-thousand-seat hall for congresses and concerts, and several restaurants.

A mile or two to the east, in Vršovice, St. Wenceslas (Náměstí Svatopluka Čecha) is an interesting example of Cubist architecture, designed by Josef Gočár in 1930. The structure is accommodated to the sloping terrain by terracing, with the sanctuary as its culmination. Notable works of sculpture are the altar of Our Lady, by Karel Pokorný, and the Stations of the Cross, by Bedřich Stefan.

Prague Cubism: St. Wenceslas in Vršovice

Memories of Mozart in the Villa Bertramka

The tomb of Count Thun-Hohenstein in Malá Strana Cemetery

119   Villa Bertramka

Prague 5, Mozartova 2

Memories of Mozart.

Mozart stayed at the summer villa of his friends the Dušeks three times in all (1786, 1787, 1791). František Xaverský Dušek was himself a composer and pianist, and his wife Josefina was a celebrated concert singer. It was at Bertramka that Mozart completed *Don Giovanni*, shortly before the opera received its triumphal first performance at the Nostitz (Estates) Theater on 29 October 1787. Shortly before his death, in 1791, Mozart was again in Prague to conduct the premiere of his last opera, *La Clemenza di Tito*.

The spirit of the Mozart age lingers on in the tastefully appointed rooms, and makes itself felt during the regular evenings of chamber music. The most prized exhibits are the piano and the harpsichord on which the maestro played. The corner salon has a fine painted wooden ceiling.

120   Malá Strana Cemetery

Malostranský hřbitov

Prague 5, Plzeňská/Erbenova

An old plague cemetery opened in 1680, now a public park.

The funerary sculpture to be seen here includes some fine creations from the hands of Platzer, Prachner, Max, and Malinsky.

The most imposing work of art is the cast-iron memorial to Count Leopold of Thun-Hohenstein (1830), who was bishop of Passau until he was deposed by Napoleon.

121   Villa Portheim (Portheimka)

Prague 5, Štefánikova 12

A delightful Baroque mansion, now the home of the "Galerie D."

Kilian Ignaz Dientzenhofer, inspired by the work of Fischer von Erlach, designed this beautiful **Baroque villa** for his family in 1725. The principal salon, an oval room, is decorated with a Bacchus fresco by Wenzel Lorenz Reiner. Subsequent owners of the property were the counts of Buquoy and a factory owner by the name of Portheim.

The south wing of Villa Portheim was sacrificed around 1880 to make room for the Church of St. Wenceslas, an impressive **neo-Renaissance building** modeled on Sangallo's San Biagio in Montepulciano – the architect, Antonín Barvitius, had spent some years in Italy working as a restorer. The sculptural ornamentation is by Ludvík Šimek. The mosaic by Josef Trenkwald in the main apse depicts Christ and the patron saints of Bohemia.

The **Bear Fountain**, adjacent to St. Wenceslas, dates from 1689; it is the work of Hieronymus Kohl, and originally graced a summer residence of the counts of Slavata.

Villa Portheim, now an art gallery

122 Kinský Villa

Letohrádek Kinských

Prague 5, Holečkova 2

Home of the Museum of Folk Culture.

The summer residence of the Kinský princes is an elegant **Empire villa**, designed by the Vienna architect Heinrich Koch around 1830. Since 1901 it has housed the department of the National Museum devoted to the folk art and culture of the Czechs and Slovaks. The Kinský Garden is an expansive landscape garden.

123 Hanau Pavilion

Hanavský pavilón

Prague 7, Letenské sady

A prominently sited example of cast-iron neo-Baroque.

The pavilion was made in the ironworks of Prince Wilhelm of Hanau for the jubilee exhibition of 1891, as a showpiece of material technology; the model was designed by Zdeněk Emanuel Fiala. After the exhibition the city council had it re-erected on the present site to serve as a café. It has been expertly restored to its pristine glory.

The Kinský Villa, a distinguished example of the Empire style on the slopes of Petřín Hill

The round chapel of St. Mary Magdalen at the foot of Letná Hill

The monumental domed building at the foot of **Letná Hill** (Nábřeží Edvarda Beneše 4-6) is the former Straka Academy, founded by Count Jan Petr Straka in 1710 for the sons of the Czech nobility. The present neo-Baroque structure dates from the end of the nineteenth century, and now houses the main government offices.

The early Baroque **rotunda** of St. Mary Magdalen, at the foot of the next bridge downriver (Čechův most), is a foundation of the "Cyriacs," the Holy Cross Knights of the Red Heart.

The prize-winning **Czech pavilion** for the Brussels World Fair, designed by J. Hrubý, F. Cubr, and Z. Pokorný, has found a new home at the far end of Letná Gardens, and a new function as the French restaurant Praha-Expo 58. From here, as from many other points on the paths that crisscross the slope, fine views are to be had across the river to the Old Town and the surrounding suburbs. The **Letná plateau** at the top of the hill is the venue of Labor Day gatherings, papal masses, circuses, and other large-scale events.

Proceeding northward into Bubeneč district we soon reach Stromovka park, which has evolved out of the old royal game preserve. On the southwest edge King Vladislav II had his **hunting lodge**, which

Rudolf II remodeled in the Renaissance style; from the seventeenth century until 1918 the governor, or viceroy, of Bohemia resided here. The present-day appearance of the villa is neo-Gothic.

Stromovka borders on the east with the exhibition grounds (**Výstaviště**), with pavilions designed by Antonín Wiehl for the jubilee exhibition of 1891. Today it is the site of a conference center, facilities for trade fairs, and various other attractions, such as a panorama of the battle of Lipany (Hussite wars, 1434), an amusement park, the Křižík fountain (son et lumière), and the **Lapidarium,** the National Museum's repository of historic stone relics from the eleventh to the nineteenth centuries. The Spirála Theater is the home of the Laterna Animata, a futuristic version of the Laterna Magika.

124 National Memorial
Národní památník
Prague 3, U památníku

Reputedly the largest equestrian statue in the world.

The hill known as Žižkov, or Vítkov, to the east of downtown Prague, was a favored vantage-point for the city's many besiegers. Today it is crowned by a massive **granite-faced cuboid mausoleum,** built between 1928 and 1932 to plans by Jan Zázvorka. The building houses the Tomb of the Unknown Soldier and the presidential vault. Czechoslovakia's first Communist president, the infamous Klement Gottwald, lay in state here for several years until the cadaver finally rejected the ministrations of the embalmers and went the way of all flesh, no doubt sparing the post-1989 generation an embarrassing dilemma. The 30-foot high statue of the Hussite leader Jan Žižka of Trocnov, by Bohumil Kafka, commemorates the one-eyed general's victory over Emperor Sigismund on 14 July 1420.

125 Troja Palace
Trojský zámek
Prague 7, U Trojského zámku 4

A major work of Bohemian Baroque, reminiscent of Renaissance villas in Rome, but with additional French-inspired features; houses the municipal gallery's collection of nineteenth-century Czech art.

Count Wenzel Adalbert of Sternberg, a member of the Bohemian/Moravian nobility and one of the wealthiest lords of the

realm, owned vineyards on the north bank of the Vltava a few miles out of town; here he decided to build himself a villa suburbana of the kind he had seen in Italy, somewhere he could retire to now and then. He found the right man for the job in Jean Baptiste Mathey, a painter and architect of Burgundian origin, who had himself spent twenty years in Rome and moved in the circles of Claude Lorrain and other artists. It is no surprise then to find Roman influences in Mathey's work for Prague, a notable example being the gazebo turrets on Toscana Palace (Hradčany) and on the lateral wings here at Troja.

The palace stands on an artificial terrace and is in direct line of sight of Prague Castle; the king and emperor would be constantly reminded that here dwelt a loyal, if very self-aware, subject. From the French garden – the first of its kind in Bohemia – a magnificent two-armed **staircase** (1685-1703) curves up to the Golden Hall on the first floor: this noble ascent was planned and adorned with statues by the Dresden sculptor Johann Georg Heermann, who was assisted by his nephew Paul. The vigorously dramatic, Berniniesque figures act out the Gigantomachy, the battle between the Olympian gods and the giants, the sons of the earth-mother Gaea. Since the days of the ancient Greeks the theme had served to symbolize the victory of law and order over a savage and chaotic primeval

Troja Palace is modeled on suburban villas in Rome

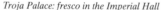

Troja Palace: fresco in the Imperial Hall

Staircase at Troja Palace

world; Sternberg's visitors would readily have seen the parallel with the victory of the Christians over the Turks. The busts of the four continents, elements, and divisions of the day on the outer balustrade were added by the Brokoff brothers, and the ornate terracotta vases on the terrace wall were sculpted by the Italian Bombelli. The heraldic emblems of the count and countess are much in evidence in the building: the star *(Stern)* stands for the Sternberg family, while hare and grapes represent Clara Bernhardina, daughter of an old Mecklenburg family with lands in Silesia, who before her marriage was countess of Maltzan. The frescoes (dated 1693) in the Imperial Hall, by the brothers Abraham and Izaak Godyn of Antwerp, glorify the House of Austria and its triumph over the Turks. The tapestry-like compositions at each end depict Rudolf I of Habsburg, who offers his horse to a priest who has to administer the last rites, and Emperor Leopold I after his victory before the walls of Vienna in 1683 – a Turk, probably Kara Mustafa Pasha, tumbles from the Roman temple of Janus pursued by the god of war and the furies. A Habsburg portrait gallery is arrayed along the sides, and further dynastic episodes are illustrated above: the wedding of Philip the Fair and "Mad" Joan of Castile and Aragon and, opposite, the abdication of Emperor Charles V in favor of his brother Ferdinand I.

The ceiling fresco radiates from the eye of God at its center; the allegory of Faith holds the chalice and the papal insignia. The apostles Peter and Paul kneel at the left edge, Sternberg (in an ermine cloak) and his wife at the right. Margrave Leopold III of Babenberg (St. Leopold) holds the model of Klosterneuburg Abbey and the flag of Lower Austria; King Jan III Sobieski of Poland (below), a representative of Hungary, and the lion of St. Mark's (right) allude to the Holy Alliance between the Empire, Poland, and Venice. Allegories of Justice and Victory preside above the fireplaces.

The frescoes in the other rooms and in the chapel were painted by Francesco Marchetti and his son Giovanni, of Trent.

Immediately to the west of Troja Palace lies the **zoo**, which has made a specialty of breeding Przewalski horses.

126 Břevnov Abbey
Břevnovský klášter
Prague 6, Markétská 28

Bohemia's oldest monastery, with a notable Baroque church by Christoph Dientzenhofer.

Adalbert (Vojtěch), the second bishop of Prague and one of the patron saints of Bohemia, founded the Benedictine abbey at Břevnov in 993, and under its aegis other monastic communities soon sprang up at various sites in Bohemia and Hungary. The first monks brought with them relics

Dramatic Berniniesque figures adorn the staircase at Troja Palace ▷

Břevnov Abbey

of SS. Alexius and Boniface from Italy; relics of St. Margaret of Antioch were acquired in the thirteenth century, since when the abbey has borne her name. The precinct is entered through a late Baroque **columned gateway** by Kilian Ignaz Dientzenhofer (1710), which is crowned by a statue of St. Benedict by Josef Hiernle of Landshut.

The High Baroque interior of Břevnov Abbey

The early Romanesque abbey church, the **crypt** of which is still extant, was replaced between 1709 and 1716 by a Baroque structure, designed by Christoph Dientzenhofer in the illusionistic style pioneered by Borromini in Rome. The **west and south facades** are accented by curvilinear gables. The **interior** is an aisleless space derived from a plan of four overlapping ovals; the vault is supported by diagonally set piers. There are definite echoes here of Banz Abbey, designed by Christoph Dientzenhofer's brother Johann. The vault frescoes were painted by Johann Jakob Stevens von Steinfels, who is known for his painting of the cupola at Waldsassen, just across the border in Bavaria; the themes are the Elevation of St. Adalbert, the church's patrons Alexius, Boniface, and Margaret, Bohemian Benedictines and patron saints, princes, kings, and popes. Also of artistic interest are the statues by Jäckel and the altarpieces by Brandl, which include a Death of St. Benedict and a Death of the Blessed Günther, a hermit who lived near Břevnov and is buried by the south wall of the church.

The choir was completed by K. I. Dientzenhofer, who also designed the monastery buildings. The **Prelates' Hall** (Theresian Hall) has a ceiling fresco painted in 1727 by Cosmas Damian Asam, one of the foremost late Baroque artists of southern Germany; the peacock in the scene was a moment ago, in roasted form, the centerpiece of a princely banquet; the Blessed Günther, not wishing to break his fast on such delicacies, has by earnest prayer procured its resuscitation.

127 Star Lodge
Letohrádek Hvězda
Prague 6, Obora Hvězda

Hunting lodge on an unusual plan, with a marvelously stuccoed ceiling.

The large park in the Liboc district was originally a **game preserve**, founded by Emperor Ferdinand I in 1530 and walled in between 1541 and 1563. The idea for a villa in the original shape of a six-pointed star came from the emperor's son, Archduke Ferdinand of Tyrol, who intended it to be a present for his wife, Philippine Welser of the Augsburg banking family. The detailed plans for the High-Renaissance structure were drawn up by Hans von Tirol and Bonifaz Wolmut, and realized around 1555 under the supervision of Giovanni Campione and Avostalis del Pambio. By 1560

Břevnov Abbey: the Prelates' Hall

they had decorated the ground-floor hall with an exquisite mantle of **stucco**, one of the earliest and best demonstrations of the technique in central Europe. The 334 individual panels depict scenes from mythology and ancient Rome: Aeneas and Anchises as forefathers of the emperors, Venus as mother of the Roman race (in the spirit of Raphael's Galatea), figures from the history of the Roman Republic (after Livy), Diana, Fortuna, and other gods, heroes, fabulous creatures, Cleopatra, and genre scenes reminiscent of Pompeiian frescoes.

Star Lodge today houses an exhibition on the battle of Bílá hora and a **museum** dedicated to the writer Alois Jirásek (1851-1930) and the artist Mikoláš Aleš (1852-1913), both of whom contributed with their work to the reawakening of the Czech national spirit.

165

Star Lodge is remarkable for the decorative scheme of its vaulting

128 St. Mary Victorious

Panna Marie Vítězná

Prague 6, Karlovarská 6

Typically Bohemian Marian shrine, with quadrangular ambulatory.

A little way to the north, a small stone pyramid stands on Bílá hora and reminds the world that this is the fateful "White Mountain," where the Catholic and Protestant armies met on 8 November 1620 in a battle that was to decide the course of Czech history for the next two hundred years. Two years later a chapel was erected to commemorate the battle, and a Servite monastery was founded a little to the east in 1628 (now the Velká Hospoda restaurant). The "Holy Precinct" was built by Italian architects on a pattern they knew from their homeland. The domed church was designed on a cruciform plan and completed in 1714. The frescoes are the work of Wenzel Lorenz Reiner, Cosmas Damian Asam (Assumption, in the cupola), and the latter's pupil Johann Adam Schöpf. The object of pilgrims' devotions, on the high altar, is the Madonna picture known as

"Maria de Victoria" (copy), which the aged Carmelite monk Dominicus a Jesu Maria carried in the van of the Catholic troops – so, it is believed, was their victory assured. Between 1730 and 1740 Johann

Star Lodge is built in the form of a six-pointed star

Anton Schöpf painted the walls of the ambulatory with thirty-nine depictions of other Marian shrines.

129 Zbraslav Palace

Zámek Zbraslav

Zbraslavské náměstí

Originally a Cistercian abbey, now showplace for the National Gallery's collection of nineteenth- and twentieth-century Czech sculpture.

Zbraslav (ancient Czech sagas tell of a knight so named) lies at the confluence of the rivers Berounka and Vltava, some six miles south of the city center. King Ottokar II had a hunting lodge here, which his successor, Wenceslas II, transformed in 1292 into the Cistercian abbey of Aula Regia ("Royal Hall"). The last members of the Přemysl dynasty were buried in the abbey church, which is now – rebuilt in an early Baroque style in the mid-seventeenth century – the parish church of **St. James**. The excellent altarpieces were painted by Giovanni Battista Piazzetta (the Assumption, on the high altar), Karel Škréta, and Peter Brandl.

The **monastery** buildings were burned down during the Hussite wars. Santin-Aichel, Bohemia's most versatile Baroque architect (see the Morzin and Thun-Hohenstein mansions), designed an elegant new complex, which Kaňka completed in 1724. The frescoes in the Grand Hall were painted by Reiner, the refectory by

Entrance to the shrine at Bílá hora

Palko (1762). After the suppression of the monastery in the reign of Joseph II, the property was converted into a palatial residence of the princes of Oettingen-Wallerstein.

Among the **sculptures** exhibited are fine works by Václav Prachner (*Vltava*), Václav Levý, Josef Václav Myslbek (1848-1922), the classic exponent of Czech realism (*Záboj and Slavoj, Music*), Jan Štursa, Stanislav Sucharda, Josef Mařatka, Bohumil Kafka, Bohuslav Schnirch, and František Bílek.

Forecourt of Zbraslav Palace

130 Karlštejn

24 miles southwest of Prague.
Ascent from village: 20 minutes,
guided tour: 1 hour

*A "castle shrine" without peer, its walls are
inlaid with precious stones; the imperial regalia
were once kept here.*

Here, far from the city's bustle, protected
by strong walls and tended by priests and
monks, the myth of the Holy Roman Empire was to find tangible expression. Such
was the vision of Charles IV, who saw himself as ruler by the grace of God, as much a
priest as a king; the imperial regalia, hallowed by Christian relics, were a token of
this divine vocation and deserved a worthy
home. In 1348 Arnošt of Pardubice, the
first Archbishop of Prague, laid the foundation stone of a castle that was never to
serve military purposes; it was only seven
years in the building, under the direction
of Matthias of Arras (master mason at
Prague cathedral), and the consecration
took place in 1355.

This "fortress of the Grail," command-
ingly sited on a cliff set back from the Berounka Valley, comprises three distinct
complexes: the imperial palace with the
burgrave's quarters adjoining at a lower
level, the intermediate Church Tower or
Lady Tower for the clergy, and the five-
story Great Tower containing the Chapel
of the Holy Rood about halfway up.

Only a few items of the Gothic inventory are today to be seen in the **imperial palace**: in the hall of the men-at-arms an Ecce
Homo triptych and a statue of St. Nicholas
(1380), in the dean's room chasubles, and
in the emperor's bedchamber a fine wood
carving of St. Catherine (c. 1400) and a dip-
tych by Tomaso da Modena. The tour proceeds via the audience chamber to the
Luxemburg Hall.

In the **Lady Chapel** in the central tower,
cleaning has brought to light parts of the
magnificent murals, depicting themes from
the book of Revelation and the "relic
scenes": Charles IV receives from the
hands of the French Dauphin and Louis I,

Karlštejn Castle

The "Kings' Wall" by Master Theoderich in the Chapel of the Holy Rood at Karlštejn (c. 1360)

king of Hungary, fragments associated with the Passion and incorporates them into a reliquary cross. The tiny chapel of St. Catherine was the **imperial oratory**, which only the emperor was allowed to enter; Charles spent whole days and nights here in prayer and meditation. The walls glimmer with semiprecious stones of Bohemian provenance; the boss of the vault is a gem from third-century Gaul. Murals in the Sienese style depict the Crucifixion, Charles and his third wife Anna of Schweidnitz being invested with worldly dominion by the Infant Jesus and the Virgin Mary, and (on the lintel of the door) Charles and Anna elevating the Cross (in similitude of Emperor Constantine the Great and his mother, Empress Helena).

The inner sanctum of Karlštejn is the sublime **Chapel of the Holy Rood**, in the Great Tower. For Charles IV and his ministers it must have been a quite otherworldly experience to gather here, the shimmer of hundreds of candles reflected in precious stones, gilt stucco, and stars formed of Venetian pâte de verre – as if they were in the "heavenly Jerusalem" of the Revelation of St. John, the emperor's favorite book. (Charles was well versed in theology, having studied at the Sorbonne in Paris and at the papal seat in Avignon;

his Byzantine brand of mysticism was no doubt influenced by the early Christian mosaics he had seen at Poreč in Istria.) The walls are studded with 2451 precious and semiprecious stones from Bohemia's hills: green chrysolite, purple amethyst, red, yellow, and black topaz, jasper, cornelian, onyx, agate. Gilt stucco originally covered the pews, picture frames, and floor, too. The 127 **panel paintings** by Master Theoderich represent milestones in the evolution of Bohemian and German art in the fourteenth century. His prophets, apostles, martyrs, church fathers, saintly virgins, popes, bishops, abbots, monks, knights, and sovereigns are beings of flesh and blood, stark, robust even, in their expressiveness. The pièce de résistance is a **Crucifixion** with SS. Mary and John. Behind the pictures are niches, where the crown jewels and relics were kept in caskets.

Only the emperor, the archbishop, and a very few privileged persons were allowed to enter the sanctuary beyond the screen – the lords and the other prelates heard mass at a respectful distance. Life at Karlštejn was governed by strict rule: banquets and other festivities would have been unseemly in such a holy place; and members of the fairer sex had to depart by nightfall.

Prague
Practical Tips

General Information

Before Departure

United Kingdom

Čedok, 17/18 Old Bond Street, London W1X 4RB. Tel. 071-491-2666.

United States

Čedok, 10 East Fortieth Street, New York, NY 10016. Tel. 212-689-9720.

In Prague

PIS – Pražská informační služba
(Prague Information Service), Praha 1, Na příkopě 20, Tel. 2 36 68 59; Praha 1, Staroměstské nám. 22, Tel. 26 36 91.

Čedok
Praha 1, Na příkopě 18, Tel. 2 12 71 11 (exchange office, airline tickets, public transport tickets)
Praha 1, Panská 5, Tel. 2 12 75 57 (accommodations)
Praha 1, Václavské nám. 24, Tel. 2 35 63 56 (sightseeing tours)
Praha 1, Bílkova 6, Tel. 2 31 82 55 (tours, excursions, theater tickets)
Pragotur, Hotel and Accommodations Service of the City of Prague, Praha 1, U Obecního domu 2, Tel. 2 31 72 81
American Express, Václavské nám. 56
Thomas Cook, Opletalova 1

Accommodations

Hotel Reservations

Čedok, reservation service, Praha 1, Nové Město, Panská 5, off Na příkopě
Pragotur, Prague hotel and accommodation service, Praha 1, Staré Město, U Obecního domu 2, near Powder Tower

***** Luxury Hotels

Alcron, Praha 1, Štěpánská 40
Intercontinental, Praha 1, nám. Curieových (near the Čech Bridge)
Esplanade, Praha 1, Nové Město, Washingtonova 19 (near main train station)
Jalta, Praha 1, Václavské nám. 45
Palace, Praha 1, Panská 12

**** (Category 1, A *)

Ambassador, Praha 1, Václavské nám. 5
Atlantik, Praha 1, Na poříčí 9
Atrium, Praha 8, Pobřežní
Diplomat, Praha 6, Evropská 15
Forum, Praha 4, Kongresová 1
International, Praha 6, Koulova 15
Olympik I, Praha 8, Invalidovna
Panorama, Praha 4, Milevská 7
Parkhotel, Praha 7, Veletržní 20

*** (Category 2, B *)

Axa, Praha 1, Na poříčí 40
Belvedere, Praha 7, M. Horákové 19
Beránek, Praha 2, Bělehradská 110
Centrum, Praha 1, Na poříčí 31
Evropa, Praha 1, Václavské nám. 25 (Art Nouveau hotel, Wenceslas Square)
Florenc, Praha 8, Křižíkova 11
Koruna, Praha 1, Opatovická 16
Olympik II Garni, Praha 8, Invalidovna
Paříž, Praha 1, U Obecního domu 1 (Art Nouveau hotel, near Powder Tower)
Sporthotel, Praha 10, Thorezova
Tatran, Praha 1, Václavské nám. 22
Ungelt, Praha 1, Štupartská 1
U tří pštrosů, Praha 1, Dražického nám. 12
Zlatá Husa, Praha 1, Václavské nám. 7

** (Category 3, B)

Adria, Praha 1, Václavské nám. 26
Bohemia, Praha 1, Králodvorská 4
Central, Praha 1, Rybná 8
Coubertin, Praha 6, Atletická
Cristal, Praha 6, José Martího 2
Erko, Praha 9, Kbely 723
Hvězda, Praha 6, Na rovni 34
Hybernia, Praha 1, Hybernská 24
Juniorhotel, Praha 2, Žitná 12
Juventus, Praha 2, Blanická 10
Kriváň, Praha 2, nám. I.P. Pavlova 5

Merkur, Praha 1, Tešnov 9
Meteor, Praha 1, Hybernská 6
Modrá Hvězda, Praha 9, Jandova
Moráň, Praha 2, Na Moráni 15
Opera, Praha 1, Tešnov 13
Praga, Praha 5, Plzeňská 29
Savoy, Praha 1, Keplerova 6
U Blažensky, Praha 5, U Blažensky 1
Union, Praha 2, Jaromírova 1

* (Category C)

Barbara, Praha 5, Uranová
Hlávkova Kolej, Praha 2, Resslova
Libeň, Praha 8, Rudé armády 2
Luník, Praha 2, Londýnská 50
Tichý, Praha 3, Seifertova 65
U Haštala, Praha 1, Haštalská 16
Vítkov, Praha 3, Koněvova 114

Botels and Motels

Botel Admirál B*, Praha 5, Hořejší nábřeží
Botel Albatros B*, Praha 1, nábřeží L. Svobody
Botel Racek B*, Praha 4, Dvorecká louka
Club Motel A*, Pruhonice, near Prague, on freeway E50, direction of Brno
Stop Motel B*, Praha 5, Plzeňská 215a

Car Camping

Caravan, Praha 9, Kbely, Mladoboleslavská 72
Caravancamp TJ Vysoké školy, Praha 5, Plzeňská
Kotva Braník, Praha 4, U ledáren 55
Sportcamp, Praha 5, V podhájí
Sokol Trója, Praha 7, Trojská 171
Sokol Dolní Počernice, Praha 9, Nad rybníkem

Private Rooms, Accommodation Service

AVE, main train station, Praha 2, Wilsonova 8, and Ruzyně Airport
Pragotur, Praha 1, U Obecního domu 2

Banks, Post Offices, Telephones

Money

The unit of currency is the Czech crown (koruna, Kč), which is made up of 100 haléř (h). Coins are in circulation in the denominations 10, 20, 50 h and 1, 2, 5, 10, 20, and 50 Kč. Bills are issued in the values of 10, 20, 50, 100, 200, 500, 1,000, and 5,000 Kč. Currently valid coins bear the inscription "Česka Republika," and bills have the words "korun českých." Shun tempting offers to change money on the street, where you are liable to be given old or forged bills.

But before changing money at an official *směnárna* it is well worth shopping around. Many of the street-corner booths charge commission of up to ten percent, and those that advertise a very low commission will probably give you less than the official rate. Your best bet is probably the Živnostenská Banka at Na příkopě 20, which pays the official rate less 1%. Note that some hotels and bed-and-breakfast establishments ask for payment in Western currency.

To change money back into a foreign currency you will need to present the receipt from the original exchange transaction. Importing and exporting Czech crowns is only permitted to a maximum of 100 Kč.

Post Offices

The main post office, open around the clock, is at Jindřišská 14 (near Wenceslas Square), Tel. 26 41 93. Mail can be sent poste restante to this address.

Parcel and EMS post is handled around the clock at Masarykovo train station (city center), Hybernská 13.

The basic postage rates are:

	Czech Rep.	Europe, overseas surface mail	Overseas airmail
Postcard	2.00	5.00	6.00
Letter to 10g	3.00	8.00	9.00
Letter to 20g	3.00	8.00	11.00
Letter to 30g	5.00	14.00	19.00
Letter to 40g	5.00	14.00	21.00
Letter to 50g	5.00	14.00	22.00

Telephones

Information: 120, 121
Information on area codes: 01 49
Alarm call service: 125
Telegram service: 127
Speaking clock: 112

As in most countries, calls made from a hotel are liable to be charged at a highly unfavorable rate.

Several types of pay phones are to be found around town. The orange booths only take 1 Kč coins (the price of a local call, or of one time-unit in intercity communication). To call abroad, look for a blue cabin that accepts coins in the values of 1, 2, 5, and 10 Kč, or a card phone; telephone cards (*telefónni karta*) can be purchased at kiosks in various values, e.g., 84 Kč for 80 units. The international access code is 00; for the UK, dial 00 44,

Charles Bridge is the place to pick up souvenirs of the Soviet era

for the US dial 001. A one-minute call to the UK uses up about 30 units, and a one-minute call to the US uses up about 60 units (there is no cheap period).

To call Prague from elsewhere in the Republic, dial 02; when calling from abroad, use your international access code + the country code 42 + area code 2.

Calls can also be booked at post offices, where a deposit is usually payable.

For credit card or reverse-charge calls you can dial your home-country operator direct (inquire about surcharge):
dial the code 004200, then

Canada: 0151	USA: AT&T 0101
UK: 4401	USA: MCI 0112

Information on international services: 0139
International directory inquiries: 0149

Emergencies

Emergency Services

Police: 158
Emergency doctor: 155, 156
Fire department: 150
Automobile breakdown services: Praha 1, Opletalova 21, Tel. 22 48 28
"Yellow Angels" (breakdown service): 154
Traffic accidents: 2 36 64 64

Emergency Medical Services

First aid: 155
Ambulance: 333
Emergency doctor
Praha 7, Dukelských hrdinů 21, Tel. 155;

outpatient clinics, Praha 1, Karlovo nám. 32
Emergency dental service
Praha 1, Vladislavova 22, Tel. 26 13 74
24-hour pharmacy
Praha 1, Na příkopě 7, Tel. 22 00 81
Eye specialists (Oční optika)
Praha 1, Mostecká 3, Tel. 53 11 18
Praha 1, Národní 37, Tel. 22 10 71
Veterinary clinic
Praha 10, Vršovice, Rybalkova 15, Tel. 25 21 39

Lost Property

Lost documents: Praha 3, Olšanská 2
Lost property: Praha 1, Bolzanova 5, Tel. 2 36 88 87

Consulates

UK: Praha 1, Thunovská 14, Tel. 53 33 47
USA: Praha 1, Tržiště 15, Tel. 52 66 41

Festivals and Special Events

January-March

The *Prague Winter,* a cultural festival week involving theater and concert performances, takes place every year in early January.

Since 1956, one week every March has been devoted to a festival of the works of contemporary Czechoslovakian composers: the *New Music Week* ("Týden nové tvorby").

April-June

Three months for jazz fans: in April, *Jazz Praha,* in the second half of May the *Salon for Traditional Jazz,* and in mid-June *Jazz on the Island* – modern Prague jazz on Slovanský ostrov (Slav Island).

The *Prague Spring* ("Pražské jaro") attracts international attention as a world-class music festival. It has been held every year since 1946, and traditionally opens on the anniversary of Smetana's death with a performance of his symphonic poem *Má vlast* (My Country) and closes with a performance of Beethoven's Ninth Symphony.

Concertino Praga in June: concerts by young musicians and soloists.

July-September

July is the month for theater and dance festivals.
1-8 July: *Theater Festival on Střelecký ostrov* (an island on the Vltava).

1-31 July: The *mime artists* of the Panoptikum Theater perform in the Reduta Club (Národni 20).

2-9 July: *International Festival of Modern Dance* in the Smetana Theater and Laterna Magika.

Mime performances also take place in August in the Disk Theater. And there is more jazz throughout August in the Reduta Club.

First week in September: *Pottery Market* on Kampa island.

October-December

The foundation of the Czechoslovak Republic is celebrated with public festivals in Hradčany and on Staroměstské náměstí on October 28th, and the anniversary of the 1989 democratic revolution is celebrated all over the city on November 17th. Every other year an *International Jazz Festival* takes place in October, and top jazz groups from all over the world also meet in Prague at the end of November and beginning of December.

Food and Drink

Carp has been a delicacy since the Middle Ages, when it was bred by the lords of Rosenberg in southern Bohemia's networks of lakes and ponds. *Prague ham* also enjoys a long-standing reputation. It is usually served with horseradish sauce and pickled gherkins (the best come from Znojmo in Moravia). The most famous item of Bohemian cuisine is of course the dumpling (*knedlík*), made in a long roll either from bread crumbs (*houskový*) or potatoes (*bramborový*) and served in slices to accompany roasts and goulash. The Czechs' staple fare is roast pork with dumplings and (slightly soured) cabbage; on special occasions they are very partial to roast goose.

The dumpling, with various kinds of fillings and custards, also features prominently on the dessert menu (it was one of the most enduring Bohemian contributions to the Habsburg empire, and is still today a standard feature of every Viennese coffeehouse).

Selected Dishes

Předkrmy (studené, teplé)	*Hors d'oeuvres (cold, hot)*
olejovky	sardines in oil
pražská šunka	Prague ham
rybí salát	fish salad
šunka v rosolu	ham in aspic
sýr	cheese
uherský salám	Hungarian salami
vejce	eggs
míchaná	scrambled
na měkko	softboiled
na tvrdo	hardboiled
plněná	stuffed
sázená	fried

Polévky	*Soups*
bramborová	potato
dršťková	tripe
houbová	mushroom
hovězí	beef
hrášková	pea
rajská	tomato
rybí	fish
s játrovými knedlíčky	with liver dumplings
s nudlemi	with noodles
s rýží	with rice
slepičí	chicken
zeleninová	vegetable
zelná	cabbage

Masité pokrmy	*Meat dishes*
hovězí	beef
skopový	lamb
telecí	veal
vepřový	pork
dušený	steamed, stewed
pečený	roast, baked
smažený	fried
uzený	smoked
vařený	boiled
bůček	belly
játra	liver
jazyk	tongue
klobása	sausage
kotleta	cutlet
ledviny	kidneys
maso	meat
párek	sausage
pečeně	roast
řízek	escalope
rostěná	grilled beefsteak
sekaná	meat loaf
svíčková	sirloin (in cream sauce)
žebírko	rib

Ryby	*Fish*
kapr	carp
platejs	plaice
pstruh	trout
sleď	herring
štika	pike
úhoř	eel

Drůbež	*Poultry*
husa	goose
kachna	duck
krocan, krůta	turkey
kuřátko, kuře	chicken

Zvěřina	*Game*
bažant	pheasant
divoký kanec	wild boar
jelen, srna	venison
zajíc	hare

Zelenina	*Vegetables*
brambory	potatoes
celer	celery
červená řepa	beetroot
cibule	onions
fazole (zelené)	beans (green)
houby	mushrooms
hrách	peas
hranolky	french fries
květák	cauliflower
mrkev	carrots
okurky	cucumber, gherkins
rajčata	tomatoes
žampiony	mushrooms
zelí (kyselé)	cabbage (sauerkraut)

Moučníky, Dezert	*Puddings, Dessert*
dort (nanukový)	gateau (with icing)
jablkový štrúdl/závin	apple strudel
koláč	cake
palačinka	pancake
pohár	fruit salad, sundae
šlehačka	whipped cream
švestkové knedlíky	plum dumplings
zmrzlina	ice cream

Nápoje / Beverages

Bezalkoholické	*Nonalcoholic*
čaj (s citrónem/ mlékem)	tea (with lemon/ milk)
kakao	cocoa
limonáda	lemonade
minerálka	mineral water
mléko	milk
sodovka	soda water
šťáva (hroznová/ jablečná/ pomerančová/rajská)	juice (grape/ apple/ orange/tomato)
voda	water
káva	coffee
alžírská	Algerian (with eggnog)
irská	Irish
překvapávaná	filtered espresso

turecká	Turkish, with grounds (as Czechs normally drink it)
vídeňská	Viennese (with cream)

Lihoviny	*Spirits*
borovička	juniper spirit
becherovka	herb liqueur
slivovice	plum spirit
zelený likér	peppermint liqueur

Pivo	*Beer*
lahvové/sudové	bottled/draught
světlé	light
tmavé/černé	dark

Víno	*Wine*
bílé/růžové/červené	white/rosé/red
suché/polosladké/ sladké	dry/medium/sweet
sekt, šumivé	sparkling

An English menu is available at many restaurants, though it sometimes shows quite different prices from the Czech menu! A modest cover charge is often made. Prices normally include tax and service, but it is customary to round up the bill (a tip of about 5% is quite adequate).

Prosím,	Please,
stůl na ... osoby	a table for ... persons
jídelní lístek	the menu
sůl/pepř/párátko	salt/pepper/ toothpick
ještě ...	another, some more ...
popelníček	ashtray
účet, platit	the bill
dobrý	keep the change
hotová jídla	quick dishes
jídla na objednávku	dishes cooked to order
Je tu volno?	Is this place free?
Pane vrchníku!	Waiter!
Slečno!	Waitress!

Bohemian, Moravian, and Slovakian Cuisine

Pezinok (in House of Slovakian Culture), Praha 1, Purkyňova 4
Halali-Grill, Hotel Ambassador, Praha 1, Václavské nám. 5
Jihočeské Pohostinství (southern Bohemian specialties), Praha 1, Na příkopě 17
Staropražská rychta (old Prague cuisine), Praha 1, Václavské nám. 7

U Fleků, a traditional beer hall

Waldštejnská hospoda (Waldstein restaurant), Praha 1, Valdštejnské nám. 7
Zunftsaal and "Masshaus" (Guildhall and Pint house), Hotel Intercontinental, Praha 1, nám. Curieových
U kalicha ("The Goblet"; specialties à la Schwejk), Praha 2, Na bojišti 12
Myslivna ("Hunting Lodge"), Praha 3, Žižkov, Jagellonská 21
Pálava (Moravian specialties and wine), Praha 3, Slavíkova 18
Bohemian Restaurant, Hotel Forum, Praha 4, Kongresová
Bohemia, Hotel Panorama, Praha 4, Milevská 7
Chodské pohostinství (western Bohemian specialties), Praha 5, Na Újezdě 5
Račanská vinárna, Hotel International, Praha 6, Koulova 15
Černý Kůň (Black Horse), Praha 1, Vodičkova 36
V podskalí, Praha 2, Podskalská 29

Gourmet Restaurants

Hotel Alcron, Štěpánská 40, near Wenceslas Square (Václavské nám.)
Hotel Ambassador, Václavské nám. 5
Hotel Esplanade, Praha 1, Washingtonova 19
Hotel Intercontinental (incorporating the Zlatá Praha restaurant, with a view of the Vltava), Praha 1, nám. Curieových 5
Hotel Jalta, Praha 1, Václavské nám. 45
Hotel International, Praha 6, Koulova 15
Praha-Expo 58 (pavilion from the World Exhibition in Brussels, 1958), French and Bohemian cuisine, Praha 7, Letenské sady (Letná Hill), view of the Vltava

Local and International Cuisine

Hotel Evropa, Praha 1, Václavské nám. 25
Hotel Palace, Praha 1, Panská 12
Obecní dům (Art Nouveau restaurant in the Civic Hall near Powder Tower), nam. Republiky 5
Hotel Paříž, Staré Město, U Obecního domu 1, near Powder Tower
Parnas, Staré Město, Smetanovo nábřeží 2
Savarin, Praha 1, Na příkopě 10, in Sylva-Taroucca Palace
Slovanský dům, Praha 1, Na příkopě 22, near Powder Tower
U červeného kola (The Red Wheel), Praha 1, Staré Město, Anežská 2/4
U krále brabantského (The King of Brabant), Malá Strana, Thunovská 15
Hotel U tří pštrosů (The Three Ostriches), Malá Strana, Dražickeho nám. 6
Opera Grill, Nové Město, Karolíny Světlé 35, near the National Theater
Botel Admirál, Praha 5, Hořejší nábřeží
U Barona, Praha 1, Pařížská 19
Pelikan, Praha 1, Na příkopě 7
Rotisserie, Praha 1, Mikulandská 6
Bellevue, Praha 1, Smetanovo nábř. 18

Terrace and Garden Restaurants

(Some of these are only open during the summer.)

Kajetánska, Hradčany, at the castle steps (Ke Hradu)
U Lorety (Loreto), Loretánské nám.
Café Poet, Bastion Garden of Prague Castle
Vikárka, Vikářská 6, north side of St.Vitus's Cathedral
Ve zlaté studni (The Golden Well), Malá Strana, U zlaté studně 4
Slovanský ostrov, on Slav Island in the Vltava, south of the National Theater

Vegetarian Restaurant

Vegetárka, Praha 1, Celetná 3

Poultry Specialties, Fondue

Hotel Jalta, Praha 1, Václavské nám. 45
Luxor, Praha 1, Václavské nám. 41
Svatá Klára, Praha 7, U trojského zámku 9

Seafood Restaurants

Baltik-Grill, Praha 1, Václavské nám. 43
Frionor, Praha 1, Vodičkova 34
Rybárna, Praha 1, Václavské nám. 43
Paroplavba, Praha 2, Podolské nábřeží (landing-stage)

Beer can also be enjoyed in the U Fleků garden

Vltavská Rybí Restaurace, Praha 4, Podolská 2
Rybářská Bašta (Fisherman's Bastion), Praha 10, U břehu 47
Reykjavik, Praha 1, Karlova 20

Bulgarian Restaurants

Mechana, Praha 1, Václavské nám. 29
Sofia, Praha 1, Václavské nám. 33

German Restaurants

Alex, Praha 1, Revoluční 11
Raabe-Diele (Hotel Flóra), Praha 2, Vinohradská 121

Jewish Restaurant

Kosher Restaurant (in an old synagogue), Maiselova 18

Cuban Restaurant

Habana, Praha 1, V jámě 8

Russian and Georgian Restaurants

Berjozka, Praha 1, Rytířská 31
Moskva, Praha 1, Na příkopě 29
Volha, Praha 2, Myslíkova
Thamada, Praha 3, Koněvova 228

Hungarian Restaurant

Budapest, Praha 1, Vodičkova 36

Vietnamese Restaurant

Thang Long, Praha 7, Dukelských hrdinů 48

Cafés

At the beginning of the eighteenth century, an Armenian named Deodatus Damajan founded Prague's first coffeehouse.

From the nineteenth century to the outbreak of the Second World War, cafés were meeting places for writers, artists, students, and politicians.
Arco, Hybernská 16, near Powder Tower. In the 1920s, this was a meeting place for literary figures such as Kafka, Werfel, Brod, Kisch, and Urzidil
Obecní dům, nám. Republiky 5, Art Nouveau café in the Civic Hall near Powder Tower
Slavia, Národní 1 (opposite the National Theater). A traditional café with a splendid view over the river
Evropa, Praha 1, Václavské nám. 25; Art Nouveau café in Hotel Evropa on Wenceslas Square
U zlatého hada (The Golden Snake), Staré Město, Karlova 18, opposite the Clementinum. The oldest café in Prague's old town
Malostranská kavárna, traditional Malá Strana café, Malostranské nám. 28
Kajetánska, Hradčany, at the castle steps (Ke Hradu), with a splendid view from the castle hill

Wine Cellars (vinárny)

All of Prague's south-facing slopes were once covered with vineyards. A district above Wenceslas Square is still called Vinohrady (Vineyards) today. Prague's wine cellars and restaurants serve a variety of home-grown wines, especially those from the Elbe valley (Mělník, Žernoseky) and southern Moravia (Bzeneč, Mikulov, Valticc, Hodonín, Znojmo).

Slovácká vícha, Staré Město, Michalská 6
U Golema, Staré Město, Maiselova 8
U pavouka (The Spider), Staré Město, Celetná 17
U Rudolfa II, Staré Město, Maiselova 5

U zelené žáby (The Green Frog), Staré Město, U radnice 8, near Malé naměstí. Prague's oldest wine tavern, with wines from Velké Žernoseky

U zlaté konvice (The Golden Pitcher), Staré Město, Melantrichova 20. Romanesque-Gothic vaulted cellar

U zlaté studně (The Golden Well), Staré Město, Karlova 3

U zlatého jelena (The Golden Stag), Staré Město, Celetná 11

Fregata, Nové Město, Ladova 3

Klášterní vinárna, in the former Ursuline convent, Nové Město, Národní 8

Mělnická vinárna, Nové Město, Národní 17

Obecní dům (Civic Hall), nám. Republiky 5, near Powder Tower

U Fausta (in the Faust Building), Karlovo nám. 4

Ve Františkanské Zahrady (The Franciscan Garden), Nové Město, Jungmannovo nám. 18, monastery near St. Mary of the Snows

U Piaristů (The Piarists), Nové Město, Panská 1

U Šuterů, Nové Město, Palackého 4

Znojemská vinárna, Nové Město, Václavské nám. 5

Lobkovická vinárna, Malá Strana, Vlasská 17. Wines from Mělník

Lví dvůr (Lion Court), Hradčany, U Prašného mostu 6, near the bridge to the Royal Garden

Makarská vinárna, Yugoslavian wines, Malá Strana, Malostranské nám. 2

U labutí (The Swans), Hradčany, Hradčanské nám. 11

U malířů (The Painters), Malá Strana, Maltézské nám. 11

U mecenáše (The Patron), Malá Strana, Malostranské nám. 10. One of Prague's most beautiful wine taverns

U patrona, Malá Strana, Dražického nám. 4, near Charles Bridge

U zlaté hrušky (The Golden Pear), Hradčany, Nový svět 3

Beer Halls, Pubs

Beer is the Czech national drink. Excellent beer is brewed in every part of the country, and the beers from Plzeň (pils) and České Budějovice (the original Budweiser) are world famous. All types of people meet in beer halls, both workers and intellectuals, as in the British pub. To go with the beer, sausage, ham, cheese and goulash are usually served, and sometimes other local specialties.

U Medvídů (The Litte Bear), Staré Město, Na perštýně 7. Budweiser beer

U zlatého tygra (The Golden Tiger), Staré Město, Husova 17. Original pils

U Fleků, Nové Město, Křemencová 11. Prague's most famous pub, with dark beer brewed on the premises. Has a garden, and in the evenings there is Czech cabaret.

U kalicha (The Goblet), Nové Město, Na bojišti 12. The usual haunt of the writer Jaroslav Hašek (1883-1923). This is where his novel's hero, the "good soldier Schwejk," wanted to meet his friends again after the war.

Scmíchovsky sklípek, Nové Město, Národní 31. Staropramen (strong beer)

Street musicians in Staré Město

U Bonaparta, Malá Strana, Nerudova 29. Smíchov beer

U černého vola (The Black Ox), Hradčany, Loretánská 2. Characteristic local bar with Velkopopovický kozel (strong beer)

U Glaubiců, Malá Strana, Malostranské nám. 5. Strong Smíchov beer

U Schnellů, Malá Strana, Tomášská 2. Original pils

U svatého Tomáše (St. Thomas's), Malá Strana, Letenská 12. Formerly a famous monastery brewery, today serving dark beer from Braník

Plzeňský Dvůr, Praha 7, Milady Horákové 59. Garden

U Sojků, Praha 7, Milady Horákové 40. Original pils

Language

German is the most widely understood foreign language in Prague, but many Czechs speak fairly good English. Nonetheless, it is highly advisable to learn a few of the most useful words and phrases; knowledge of the common courtesies can make all the difference to the kind of welcome one receives.

Pronunciation

Czech spelling is virtually phonetic, with the stress on the first syllable of a word. The acute accent and the little circle over the *u* mark a long vowel. The caret "softens" a consonant or adds a "y" sound before the vowel.

a as in "h*a*t"   á as in "f*a*ther"
e as in "b*e*d"   é as in "b*ea*r"
i as in "p*i*n"   í as in "f*ie*ld"
  (after *d, n, t*   (after *d, n, t*
  as in "*yi*ng")   as in "*yi*eld")
o as in "h*o*t"   ó as in "b*oa*rd"
u as in "b*u*ll"   ú,ů as in "r*u*le"
y as in "*a*byss"   ý as in "*Y*ves" or
          "s*lee*ve"
ě as in "*ye*t" (after *m* as in "lor*gne*tte")

The diphthongs *au, eu, ou* are combinations of the respective short vowels. The consonants are pronounced as in English, except:

c as in "*cz*ar"   č as in "*ch*ip"
ď as in "*d'y*ou"
g always as in "*g*as"
ch as in "lo*ch*"
j as in "*y*es"
ň as in "ca*ny*on"
ř as in French "a*r*gent" or "la*r*gesse"
s always as in "do*s*e"   š as in "*sh*op"
sh as in "i*s h*ot"
ť as in "las*t y*ear"
ž as in "mea*s*ure"

In agglomerations of consonants, a weak vowel sound as in "th*e*" is often heard before *l, m, r: čtvrt* [chtv(e)rt] "quarter," *vlk* [v(e)lk] "wolf," *sedm* [sed(e)m] "seven."

Some Common Words

ano	yes
ne	no
prosím	please
děkuji, děkuju	thank you
(mockrát)	(very much)
promiňte	excuse me (when addressing a stranger)
omlouvám	*se* I'm sorry
s dovolením	excuse me (may I pass?)

dobrý	good
výborný	excellent
dobrý den	good day
dobrý večer	good evening
dobrou noc	good night
na shledanou	good-bye
kde je	where is
nalevo, doleva	on / to the left
napravo, doprava	on / to the right
rovně	straight on
máte...?	have you...?
kolik to stojí?	how much is that?
to je drahé	it's too expensive
mluvte pomalu	speak slowly
napište	*to* write it down
nerozumím vám	I don't understand you
ještě jednou	once again, repeat
kolik je hodin?	what's the time?
kdy je otevřeno?	when does it open?
divadlo	theater
dům	house
hrad	castle
chrám	(large) church
klášter	monastery, convent
kostel	church
město	city, town
most	bridge
nábřeží	embankment
nádraží	station
náměstí	square
obchod	shop
ostrov	island
sady	public gardens
třída, ulice	street
ulička	alley
zahrada	garden
zámek	palace, mansion
starý	old
nový	new
malý	small
velký	large

Numbers

0	nula	10	deset
1	jed/en, /na, /no	11	jedenáct
2	dva, dvě	12	dvanáct
3	tři	13	třináct
4	čtyři	14	čtrnáct
5	pět	15	patnáct
6	šest	16	šestnáct
7	sedm	17	sedmnáct
8	osm	18	osmnáct
9	devět	19	devatenáct
20	dvacet	100	sto
30	třicet	200	dvě stě
40	čtyřicet	300	tři sta
50	padesát	400	čtyři sta
60	šedesát	500	pět set
70	sedmdesát	600	šest set, etc.
80	osmdesát	1000	tisíc
90	devadesát		

Cultural Events

Ticket Sales (Theater, Opera, Concert)

Čedok, Praha 1, Staré Město, Bílkova 6, Tel. 2 31 82 55
SLUNA, Praha 1, Panska 4/near Na příkopě, Tel. 22 12 06
SLUNA, Praha 1, Václavské nám. 28 (Wenceslas Square), Tel. 26 06 93
BTI (Bohemia Ticket International), Praha 1, Na příkopě 16, Tel. 22 78 38

Opera, Ballet

Národní divadlo (National Theater) and **Nová scéna** (New Stage), Praha 1, Nové Město, Národní 2-4, Tel. 20 53 64, 20 62 60
Státní opera (State Opera), Praha 2, Wilsonova 4, Tel. 26 97 46
Stavovské divadlo (Estates Theater), formerly Tyl or Nostitz Theater, Praha 1, Ovocný trh 6, Tel. 22 72 81

Theater, Mime

See above for National Theater, New Stage, and Estates Theater.
Laterna Magika (combining drama, music, mime, and film), Praha 1, Národní 4, Tel. 20 62 60
Divadlo Na zábradlí (Railings Theater; experimental drama, mime), Praha 1, Anenské nám. 5, Tel. 2 36 04 59
Divadlo Braník (mime), Praha 4, Branická 63, Tel. 46 05 07
Černé divadlo (Black Theater; dance, music, artistry, clowning), Praha 1, Pohořelec 28 and Vodičkova 39
ABC Theater (comedy), Praha 1, Nové Město, Vodičkova 28
E.F. Burian Theater, Praha 1, Na poříčí 26
Divadlo na Vinohradech (Vineyard Theater), Praha 2, nám. Míru 7, near St. Ludmila church
Realistic Theater, Praha 5, Štefanikova 57
S.K. Neumann Theater, Praha 8, Rudé armádý 34
Semafor Little Theater, Praha 1, Václavské nám. 28

Puppet Theater

Spejbl and Hurvínek (traditional play about a father, Spejbl, and his clever little son Hurvínek), Praha 2, Římská 45, Tel. 25 16 66
Jiří Wolker Theater, Praha 1, Staré Město, Dlouhá 39
Central Puppet Theater: *Theater U věže,* Praha 1, nám. Semovázné and *Theater Říše loutek,* Praha 1, Žatecká 1

Musical Theater

(Operetta, musicals)
Musiktheater in Karlín, Praha 8, Křižíkova 10
Folklore Theater at Klaróv, nábř. E. Beneše
Musiktheater, Praha 1, Opletalova 5
Divadlo Disk, Praha 1, Karlova 8, near the Clementinum

Concerts

The **Czech Philharmonic,** Czechoslovakia's oldest orchestra, has an outstanding reputation throughout the world.

Other orchestras, quartets, and trios: The Prague Symphony Orchestra, the Symphony Orchestra of the Czech Broadcasting Corporation, the Czech Chamber Orchestra, the Prague Chamber Orchestra, the Suk Chamber Orchestra, the Suk Trio (named after the violinist Josef Suk, a great-grandson of Antonín Dvořák), the Smetana Quartet, the Janáček Quartet, the Prague Madrigal Singers, etc.

Concert Halls (a selection)

Dvořák Hall in the Rudolfinum, Praha 1, nám. Jana Palacha
Smetana Hall in Obecní dům (Civic Hall), Praha 1, nám. Republiky 5
Palace of Culture, Praha 4, 5. května 65
St. Agnes's Convent (Mánes Hall), Praha 1, U milosrdných 17/Anežská
The Stone Bell (U Kamenneho Zvonu), Praha 1, Staroměstské náměstí 13
St. George's Basilica in Prague Castle
Foerster Hall (Foerstrova síň), Praha 1, Pštrossova 17
Atrium, Praha 3, Čajkovského 12

Particularly during the Prague spring and summer months, churches, monasteries, palaces, and villas also serve as elegant backgrounds for concert performances: St.Vitus's Cathedral, St.James in Staré Město, St.Nicholas and St.Thomas in Malá Strana, Villa Bertramka, Martinitz Palace in Hradčany, Strahov Monastery, the Knights' Chamber and Sala terrena of the Waldstein Palace, the Hall of Mirrors in the Clementinum, the Maltese Garden and Ledebur Garden in Malá Strana.

Cabaret and Variety

Alhambra, Praha 1, Václavské nám. 5
Jalta Dancing Revue, Praha 1, Václavské nám. 45
Letenský Zámeček, Praha 7, Letenské sady 371
Tabarin Družba, Praha 1, Václavské nám. 16

Elbe Landscape *by Josef Mánes (1862), in St. Agnes's Convent*

Tatran Bar, Praha 1, Václavské nám. 22
U Fleků, old-style Czech cabaret in
Prague's most famous pub, Praha 1,
Křemencová 11, near Charles Square
Varieté Praga, Praha 1, Vodičkova 30

Movies

Many movie theaters show foreign films
in the original version.

Museums, Galleries, Libraries

Most museums and collections are closed
on Mondays. The National Museum is
closed on Tuesdays, and the State Jewish
Museum in the former ghetto is closed on
Saturdays.

National Gallery Collections
*European art, nineteenth and twentieth-
century French art:* Šternberský palác,
Hradčanské náměstí 15. Daily except
Mon. 10 a.m.-6 p.m. [No. 15]
Old Czech art: Klášter svatého Jiří, Ná-
městí u Svatého Jiří 33. April to Nov. dai-
ly except Mon. 10 a.m.-6 p.m. [No. 10]
*Nineteenth and twentieth-century Czech
sculpture:* Zámek Zbraslav, Praha 5, Ke
Krňovu (6 miles south of Prague). Daily
except Mon. 10 a.m.-6 p.m. [No. 129]
Nineteenth-century Czech art: Klášter
svaté Anežky České, U Milosrdných 17.
Daily except Mon. 10 a.m.-6 p.m.
[No. 81]

Exhibition Halls of the National Gallery
Riding School in Waldstein Palace, Praha
1, Malá Strana, Valdštejnská 2 [No. 33]
Prague Castle Riding School, U Prašného
mostu, near the bridge to the Royal Garden [No. 13]

Prague Castle Collections
Works of art from the imperial
collections. *Castle Gallery:* second
courtyard. Daily except Mon., April to
Sept. 10 a.m.-5 p.m., Oct. to March
10 a.m.-4 p.m. [No. 2]
Cathedral treasury: Starý palác. Daily ex-
cept Mon., April to Sept. 10 a.m.-5 p.m.,
Oct. to March 10 a.m.-4 p.m. [No. 6]
Renaissance crafts: Mihulka. Daily except
Mon., April to Sept. 10 a.m.-5 p.m., Oct.
to March 10 a.m.-4 p.m. [No. 4]

National Museum
*Mineralogy, paleontology, zoology, prehis-
tory of the Czech and Slovak lands, numismatics:* Národní muzeum, Václavské
náměstí 68. Mon. and Wed. to Fri.
9 a.m.-5 p.m., Sat. and Sun. 10 a.m.-6 p.m.
[No. 94]
National history: Lobkovický palác,
Hradčany, Jiřská 3. Daily except Mon.
9 a.m.-5 p.m. [No. 12]
Ethnology: Náprstkovo muzeum,
Betlémské náměstí 1. Asia, Africa,
America. Daily except Mon. 9 a.m.-noon
and 12:45 p.m.-5:30 p.m., free admission
on first Fri. of month.
Physical education and sport: Muzeum
tělesné výchovy a sportu, Michna Palace,

Praha 1, Újezd 40. Daily except Mon. 9 a.m.-5 p.m.
National Museum of Technology: Národní technické muzeum, Praha 7, Kostelní 42. Daily except Mon. 9 a.m.-5 p.m.
Sculpture: Lapidárium, Praha 7, Výstaviště pavilion 422. Tues. to Fri. noon-6 p.m.; Sat., Sun., holidays 10 a.m.-12:30 p.m., 1 p.m.-6 p.m. [No. 123]
Smetana: Muzeum Bedřicha Smetany, Novotného Lávka 1. Daily except Tues. 10 a.m.-5 p.m. [No. 62]
Dvořák: Muzeum Antonína Dvořáka, Villa Amerika, Praha 2, Ke Karlovu 20. Daily except Mon. 10 a.m.-5 p.m. [No. 114]
Musical instruments: Velkopřevorský Palác, Praha 1, Lázeňská 2. Daily 10 a.m.-4 p.m., closed in winter. [No. 45]
Mozart and the Dušeks: Villa Bertramka, Praha 5, Smíchov, Mozartova 2. Daily except Mon. 10 a.m.-5 p.m. [No. 119]

Other Exhibitions
Aeronautics: Expozice letetstva a kosmonautiky, Praha 9, Mladoboleslavská (airfield). May to Oct. daily except Mon. 9 a.m.-5 p.m.
Arts and crafts: Uměleckoprůmyslové muzeum, 17. Listopadu 2. The world's largest glass collection. Daily except Mon. 10 a.m.-6 p.m. [No. 85]
Bílek: Bílkova villa, Praha 6, Mickiewiczova 1, near the Belvedere. Works by the sculptor František Bílek. Daily except Mon. 10 a.m.-noon and 1 p.m.-5 p.m. [No. 13]
Czechoslovak army and resistance movement: Muzeum odboje a Československé Armády, Praha 3, U Památníků 2. Daily except Mon. 10 a.m.-6 p.m.
Czech literature: Památník národního písemnictví, Strahovské nádvoří 1. Daily except Mon. 9 a.m.-5 p.m.; library daily except Mon. 9 a.m.-noon, 1 p.m.-5 p.m. [No. 25]
Ecclesiastical treasures: Loreta, Loretánské náměstí 7. Daily except Mon. 9 a.m.-12:15 p.m., 1 p.m.-4:30 p.m. [No. 21]
Folk culture: Národopisné muzeum, Praha 5, Holečkova 2. Reopens in 1994. [No. 122]
Gothic and Renaissance tiles: Dům Pánů z Kunštátu a z Poděbrad, Řetězova 3. Daily except Mon. 10 a.m.-6 p.m. [No. 58]
Ježek: Památník Jaroslava Ježka, Kaprova 10. Tues. 9 a.m.-noon and 2 p.m.-4 p.m.
Jirásek and Aleš: Muzeum Aloise Jiráska a Mikoláše Alše, Praha 6, Obora Hvězda. Daily except Mon. 10 a.m.-5 p.m. [No. 127]
Judaism in Prague: Státní židovské muzeum, Jáchymova 3; Close Synagogue,

The Vltava by night, with the National Theater in the background

Pinkas Synagogue, Old Jewish Cemetery, High Synagogue (textiles), Maisel Synagogue (metal artifacts). Daily except Sat. 9 a.m.-4:30 p.m., Old-New Synagogue closes Fri. at 3 p.m. [Nos. 86-92]
Komenský: Pedagogická muzeum J.A. Komenského, Valdštejnské náměstí 4. Daily except Mon. 10 a.m.-noon, 1 p.m.-5 p.m. [No. 32]
Military history: Vojenské muzeum, Hradčanské naměstí 22. May to Oct. 9:30 a.m.-4:30 p.m. [No. 16]
Modern art: Galerie moderního umění, Praha 7, Dukelských hrdinů 47 (opens 1995).
Modern Czech art: Městská Knihovna, Mariánské náměstí 1. Daily except Mon. 10 a.m.-6 p.m.
Municipal Museum: Muzeum hlavního města Prahy, Praha 1, Na poříčí 52. Daily except Mon. 10 a.m.-6 p.m. [No. 116]
Nineteenth-century Czech painting, European faience: Zámek Troja, Praha 7, U trojského zámku 1. Daily except Mon. 10 a.m.-5 p.m., Nov. to March Sat. 10 a.m.-5 p.m. only. [No. 125]
Philately: Muzeum poštovní známky, Nové Mlýny 2. Daily except Mon. 9 a.m.-5 p.m. [No. 96]
Police: Muzeum Policie, Praha 2, Ke Karlovu 1. Daily except Mon. 10 a.m.-5 p.m.
Vltava shipping: Podskalská celnice, Praha 2, Rašínovo nábřeží 412. April 15 to Oct. 15 Wed., Thurs., Sat., Sun. 10 a.m.-noon and 1 p.m.-5 p.m.
Vyšehrad: Nové Děkanství, Praha 2, K rotundě 10. Cemetery May to Sept. 8 a.m.-7 p.m., Oct. 8 a.m.-6 p.m., Nov. to Feb. 9 a.m.-4 p.m., Mar. and Apr. 8 a.m.-6 p.m.; museum daily except Mon. 9:30 a.m.-5 p.m. [No. 118]

Exhibition Halls (a selection)

Prague Municipal Gallery
Staré Město Town Hall, Staroměstské nám.
U kamenneho zvonu (The Stone Bell), Staroměstské náměstí 13
Kunštát-Poděbrady Palace, Romanesque rooms, Staré Město, Řetězova 3
Máncs Gallery (House of Art), Slovanský ostrov (Slav Island), Masarykovo nábřeží 250. [No. 105]
Čapek Brothers Gallery, Praha 2, Jugoslávská 20
Palác Kinských, Staroměstské náměstí 12. Graphic art, alternating exhibitions [No. 72]
Jaroslav Fragner Gallery, Staré Město, Betlémské nám. 15
Gallery D, Villa Portheim, Praha 5, Matoušova 9

Libraries

State Library of the ČFR, Praha 1, Clementinum, Mariánske nám.
French Library (part of the State Library), Praha 1, Štěpánská 35
State Technical Library, Praha 1, Mariánske nám. 5
City Library, Praha 1, Mariánske nám. 1
Library of the House of Russian Science and Culture, Praha 1, Rytířská 31

Bars, Nightclubs, Discos

Admirál, Praha 5, Hořejší nábřeží
Albatros, Praha 1, nábřeží L. Svobody
Barbara, Praha 1, Jungmannovo nám. 14 (dancing)
Barberina, Praha 1, Melantrichova 10
Cascade, Praha 1, Rybná 8
Embassy, Praha 1, Václavské nám. 5
Est-Bar, Praha 1, Washingtonova 19 (dancing, entertainment)
Galaxie, Praha 4, Kongresová 1
Havana Club Olympik, Praha 8, Invalidovna (dancing)
Interconti Club, Praha 1, nám. Curieových (dancing, entertainment)
International Club, Praha 6, Koulova 15 (dancing)
Jalta Club, Praha 1, Václavské nám. 45 (entertainment)
Krystal Bar, Praha 4, Palace of Culture, 5. května 65
Lucerna Bar, Praha 1, Štěpánská 61 (entertainment)
Luxor, Praha 1, Václavské nám. 41

Memfis Bar, Praha 7, Milady Horákové 19
Meteor Club, Praha 1, Hybernská 6
Monica, Praha 1, Charvátova 11 (dancing)
Olympia Grill, Praha 5, Šeříková 4
Park Club, Praha 7, Veletržní 20
Racek, Praha 4, Dvorecká louka
Solidarita, Praha 10, Soudružská 2
Tabarin Družba, Praha 1, Václavské nám. 16
Tatran Bar, Praha 1, Václavské nám. 22 (entertainment)
T Club, Praha 1, Jungmannovo nám. 17
Video-Disco Club, Praha 4, Milevská 7
Video-Disco Glasses, Praha 1, Václavské nám. 22

The most important shops for foreign visitors are located around Wenceslas Square (Václavské náměstí), Na příkopě, and Národní trída. Souvenirs and gifts of up to Kč 500 can be taken out of the country duty free. More information on customs can be obtained at travel agencies, Čedok representatives, and consulates.

Shopping, Prague style

Bohemian glass, porcelain

Bohemia Glas, Praha 1, Pařížská 2
Bohemia Moser, Praha 1, Na příkopě 12
Crystalex, Praha 1, Malé nám. 6
Diamant, Praha 1, Václavské nám. 3
Krystal, Praha 1, Celetná 26
Krystal, Praha 1, Václavské nám. 30

Jewelry, Bohemian garnets

Praha 1, Václavské nám. 9, 28, 47; Praha 1, Vodičkova 31; Praha 1, Národní 23 and 38; Praha 1, Jindřišská 10; Praha 1, Můstek metro station

Arts and crafts, folk art

Krásná jizba, Praha 1, Národní 36; Česká jizba, Praha 1, Karlova 12; Slovenská jizba, Praha 1, Václavské nám. 40; UVA, Praha 1, Na příkopě 25-27

Jewelry shops and souvenirs

Bijoux de Bohème, Praha 1, Staroměstské nám. 6; Praha 1, Na příkopě 12; Praha 1, Václavské nám. 47 and 53; Praha 1, Národní 25; Praha 1, ul. 28 října 15; Praha 1, Celetná 1; Praha 1, Na můstku 381; Praha 1, Michalská 11

Vltava bridges: Mánes Bridge, Charles Bridge (with the Old Town Bridge Tower and dome of St. Francis at left), and Bridge of the Legions with Shooters' Island

TUZEX shops (payment in foreign currency also possible; goods are exempt from export duty)
Praha 1, Rytířská 13 and 18 (antiques, gold, watches, jewelry); Praha 1, Na příkopě 12 (glass, porcelain); Praha 1, Železná 18 (glass, porcelain, spirits, Prague ham)

Antiquarian and other bookstores

Praha 1, Nové město, Dlážděná 5; Praha 1, Mostecká 22; Praha 1, Karlova 2 and 14; Praha 1, 28. října 13; Melantrich, Praha 1, Na příkopě 3; Albatros, Praha 1, Národní 49; U zlatého klasu, Praha 1, Na příkopě 23; Praha 1, Štěpánská 42; Praha 1, Vodičkova 21; Praha 1, Hybernská 34; Praha 1, Národní 9; Praha 2, Ječná 26

Antiques and Art Galleries

Praha 1, Mikulandská 7; Praha 1, Václavské nám. 60; Praha 1, Karlova 14; Praha 1, Uhelný trh 6; Praha 1, Na můstku 3; Praha 2, Vinohradská 45; Praha 1, Celetná 31 (coins and medals)
Dílo ČFVU (sales outlets for the Czech Art Foundation): Praha 2, Vodičkova 32; Galerie na Újezdě, Praha 1, Újezd 19; Prague Castle Gallery, Zlatá ulička u Daliborky; Gallery Center, Praha 1, 28. října 6; Galerie Na můstku, Praha 1, 28. října 16; Galerie Platýz, Praha 1, Národní 37; Galerie Karolina, Praha 1, Železná 6;

Galerie Zlatá lilie, Praha 1, Malé nám. 12; Praha 7, Milady horákové 22

Records and CDs

Praha 1: Celetná 8; Jindřišská 19; Jungmannovo 20; Václavské nám. 17 and 51; Vodičkova 41, Na příkopě 24

Sightseeing

The best way to explore the historic districts of Prague is definitely on foot, as motor traffic is prohibited in the most picturesque lanes and squares. For a first impression of the city one could hardly do better than follow the route that the kings of Bohemia traveled on the day of their coronation: the two miles or so of the *Royal Way* are crammed with the most splendid monuments of past epochs. Starting at Powder Tower, near the main train station, the historic route leads via Celetná, Staroměstské náměstí, Karlova, Karlův most, Mostecká, Malostranské náměstí, Nerudova, and Ke Hradu through the gates of Prague Castle to St.Vitus's Cathedral.

Guided tours by bus or on foot (with commentary in English) are organized by various agencies (see below), which also provide guides for individuals and private

Military band on Hradčanské náměstí

groups. Prague Information Service organizes tours of the National Theater and other buildings not normally accessible to the public. Guided tours of the Castle can be booked at the information office at Vikářská 2. Horse-drawn carriages can be rented on Staroměstské náměstí and Hradčanské náměstí.

Panoramic views of Prague can be enjoyed from various points on the castle hill, the Letná plateau, the gardens of the Malá Strana mansions, Smetanovo nábřeží, and Vyšehrad, and from towers such as those of St.Vitus's Cathedral, Staré Město Town Hall, the *rozhledna* on Petřín Hill, Charles Bridge, and the television tower in Žižkov (Mahlerovy sady).

There are plenty of *green spaces* for relaxation on the left bank of the river, as a glance at the map will show. The Vltava islands Kampa (south end), Slovanský ostrov, and Střelecký ostrov also offer opportunities to get away from the hustle and bustle. Not much more than a stone's throw from the densely built-up Staré Město is the Františkánská zahrada (Franciscan Garden), behind St.Mary of the Snows, just off Václavské náměstí, and east of the main station is the Riegrovy sady park. There is a botanical garden (Botanická zahrada) to the south of Karlovo náměstí (Na Slupi 16) and another in the Troja suburb in the north of the city (Nádvorní 134), not far from the zoo, which is famous for its breeding of Przewalski horses.

The observatory on Petřín Hill is open to the public most days; when Prague is suffering from its notorious smog, one should try the planetarium (Královská obora 233).

City Tours

Čedok, Praha 1, Bílkova 6, Tel. 2 31 88 55, 23 18 255
Historical Prague (3 hours): daily at 10 a.m., in summer also at 1:30 p.m.
Prague by night (5 hours, including dinner): May to Oct. 7 p.m.
Mini tour: every two hours, starting at 10 a.m. Staroměstské námestí – Loreto – Prague Castle – Malá Strana

Guided Tours

Tours of Prague for individuals and private groups: Pražská informační služba (Prague Information Service), Praha 1, Na příkopě 20/Panská 4, Tel. 22 43 1 11

Guided tours of the castle: Vikářská 2 (north side of St.Vitus's Cathedral)

Lookout Points

Petřín Hill lookout tower, with a mirror maze
April to Sept.   9 a.m.-6 p.m.
Oct.   9 a.m.-5 p.m.
Ascent by cable railway from Malá Strana, Újezd station.
Staré Město Town Hall Tower
April to Sept.   8 a.m.-6 p.m.
Oct. to March   8 a.m.-5 p.m.
Lesser Town Bridge Tower (Charles Bridge)
May to Sept.   10 a.m.-6 p.m.
April and Oct.   10 a.m.-5 p.m.
Old Town Bridge Tower (Charles Bridge)
9 a.m.-6 p.m.

Tower of St.Vitus's Cathedral: open during summer in fine weather
TV tower: 9 a.m.-10 p.m., restaurant 11 a.m.-4 a.m.

Botanical Garden

Botanická zahrada, Praha 1, Na slupi 16

16 March to 31 Oct.	10 a.m.-6 p.m.
1 Jan. to 15 March	10 a.m.-5 p.m.
Nov. and Dec.	10 a.m.-4 p.m.

Zoo

Praha 7, Troja

Oct. to March	9 a.m.-4 p.m.
April	9 a.m.-5 p.m.
May	9 a.m.-6 p.m.
June to Sept.	9 a.m.-7 p.m.

Observatory and Planetarium

Praha 1, Petřín 205
Observatory: Tues. to Fri. 2 p.m.-6 p.m. and 8 p.m.-10 p.m., Sat. and Sun. 10 a.m.-noon in addition.
Planetarium: Mon. to Thurs. 8 a.m.-noon and 1 p.m.-6 p.m., Fri. 8 a.m.-noon, Sat. and Sun. 9:30 a.m.-5 p.m.

Excursions

Most castles, etc., are open from April to September except on Mondays.
Český Šternberk: Gothic castle, seat of the illustrious Sternberg family (28 miles southeast of Prague)
Karlštejn: imperial castle (20 miles southwest of Prague) [No. 130]
Koněprusy: stalactite caves (28 miles southwest of Prague)
Konopiště: palace of Archduke Franz Ferdinand (25 miles southeast of Prague). Closed noon-1 p.m., Mon., and the day after public holidays

May to Aug.	9 a.m.-5 p.m.
Sept.	9 a.m.-4 p.m.
Oct. to April	9 a.m.-3 p.m.

Křivoklát: royal castle dating from Gothic times (29 miles west of Prague). Closed noon-1 p.m., Mon., and the day after public holidays

Feb. to April	9 a.m.-4 p.m.
May to Aug.	9 a.m.-6 p.m.
Sept.	9 a.m.-5 p.m.
Oct. to Dec.	9 a.m.-4 p.m.

Kutná hora: ancient silver-mining town, royal mint; St.Barbara's church, a showpiece of Bohemian Gothic (42 miles east)
Levý Hradec: seat of the Přemyslid rulers in the ninth and tenth centuries; archaeological excavations (9 miles north of Prague)

Art Nouveau hotel on Václavské náměstí

Lidice: memorial on the site of the village burnt down by the Nazis as a reprisal on 10 June 1942 (14 miles northwest of Prague)
Mělník: royal town, Lobkowicz palace, vineyards (24 miles north)
Nelahozeves: Renaissance mansion with an art gallery (medieval to Baroque), Dvořák's birthplace (museum) (19 miles north of Prague). Across the river lies Veltrusy (see below). April to Oct. 9 a.m.-5 p.m.
Poděbrady: famous spa town, Bohemian crystal glass manufactory, Renaissance palace and monument to the "Hussite king," George of Poděbrady (30 miles east)
Průhonice: botanical garden in the grounds of the former Sylva-Taroucca palace (10 miles southeast of Prague)
Terezín: site of the concentration camp Theresienstadt, memorial (37 miles northwest)
Veltrusy: Baroque mansion with large park (19 miles north). Closed noon-1 p.m., Mon., and the day after a public holiday.

April Sat. and Sun.	9 a.m.-4 p.m.
May to Aug.	8 a.m.-5 p.m.
Sept.	9 a.m.-5 p.m.
Oct. Sat. and Sun.	9 a.m.-4 p.m.

Zbraslav: Baroque palace and gallery containing nineteenth and twentieth-century Czech sculpture (6 miles south of Prague) [No. 129]

Sports

Golf

TJ Golf, Praha 5 (Motol), near Motel Stop, open all year

Horse Racing

Velká Chuchle State Racetrack, 7 miles from the city center. Take metro B to Smíchovské nádraží station; from there take bus no. 453

Indoor Swimming Pools

Podolí, Praha 4, Podolská 74
Klárov, Praha 1, nábř. E. Beneše 3
Výstaviště, Praha 7, Dukelských hrdinů 17
Motorlet Radlice, Praha 5, Výmolová 2

Outdoor Swimming

Občanská plovárna, Praha 1, nábřeží kap. Jaroše
Štvanice, Praha 7, Štvanice (Vltava Island)
Motol, Praha 5, Stará plzeňská
Lhotka, Praha 4, Novodvorská
Ďáblice-Ládvi, Praha 8 (heated water)

Tennis

Sparta ČKD Praha, Praha 7, Stromovka
Slavia Praha IPS, Praha 7, Letná, Kostelní
Dopravní podnik, Praha 7, Štvanice

Sports Halls and Stadiums

ČSTV Gymnasium, Praha 7, Za elektrárnou 49
Sparta ČKD Praha Gymnasium, Praha 7, Nad Královskou oborou 51
TJ Vysoké školy Praha, Praha 2, Na Folimance 2490
Areal Strahov, Praha 6
Evžen Rošický Stadium, Praha 6, Strahov
Dukla Praha, Praha 6, Dejvice, Na Julisce
Sparta ČKD Praha, Praha 7, Milady Horákové 98

Transportation within Prague

Most of Prague's sights are not easily accessible by car due to the extensive pedestrian zones and no-parking streets (wheel clamps are in operation). Leave your car in your hotel garage or at another guarded carpark: e.g., in the center, near Hlavní and Masarykovo stations, on Národní, náměstí Republiky, náměstí Jana Palacha, Karlovo náměstí; it is cheaper at the sub-urban metro stations Dejvická, Hradčanská, Pankrác, Radlická, and Strašnická.

Public Transport

Public transportation consists of trams, buses, subway (metro), and the funicular railway ascending Petřín Hill, and it runs between approx. 5 a.m. and midnight. Night trams and buses run at forty-minute intervals, the central interchange point being at Lazarská/Spálená.

Tickets cost 4 Kč each (2 Kč for children between 10 and 16) and are valid for a journey of any length on one vehicle, except on the metro, where tickets are valid for sixty minutes, including any change of line. The ticket (*jízdenka*) must be bought in advance (yellow machines, kiosks, hotels) and punched on boarding the vehicle (insert into the slot in the puncher with the arrow pointing down and the number grid facing you, and pull the slot toward you); in the metro, stamping machines are located at the entrance to the platforms (insert the ticket with the number grid face down). Books of twenty-five tickets can be purchased at a discount at transportation offices (at most metro stations): a book of standard tickets (*soubor jízdenek*) for 90 Kč, one of "ecological" tickets (*soubor ekologických jízdenek,* not valid for buses) for 75 Kč. The go-as-you-please tickets (*síťová jízdenka,* e.g., one day 30 Kč, five days 100 Kč) only represent a saving for the very frequent traveler.

Network maps are available at the DP information office at Palackého náměstí (vestibule of the Karlovo náměstí metro station), Mon. to Fri. 7 a.m.-6 p.m., Tel. 294682.

Taxis

Taxis can be hailed in the street or ordered by phone (20 29 51-60, 20 39 41-50, advance bookings 2 35 28 11, 2 36 58 75). The fare should not exceed 15 Kč per kilometer, but meters are often tampered with; in case of dispute, ask for a receipt (*stvrzenka*) and note the number of the cab.

Boat Travel

During the summer season boats ply along the Vltava between Slapy (south of Prague) and Roztoky (north); dinner and music cruises are also organized. Information is obtainable at the landing stage at Palackého Most (Tel. 29 38 03, 29 83 09).

Traveling to and from Prague

Documents

Citizens of the United Kingdom, Irish Republic, and United States do not require a visa. Nationals of other countries should inquire at the Czech embassy (visas may also be issued on the spot at Prague airport).

Customs

The usual regulations and allowances apply when personal belongings are brought into the Czech Republic; you can bring in gifts to the value of 3000 Kč. On leaving the country, a maximum of 200 cigarettes and one liter of spirits can be taken out duty-free. Exporting antiques (over 50 years old) without a permit is prohibited. Restrictions apply to certain other goods; inquire at the customs office at the point of entry or at Havlíčkova 11, Tel. 22 71 46. For currency regulations, see the section on Money above.

Automobiles

Foreign visitors can use their own cars in the Czech Republic for up to one year without any special formalities. The car should have a nationality sticker (e.g., GB, USA, CDN) and have third-party insurance coverage for the ČR. In most cases, a national driving license is sufficient.

The alcohol limit for drivers is zero. Speed limits are 60 km/h (37 mph) in built-up areas (designated by community name-boards), 90 km/h (55 mph) on country roads, 110 km/h (68 mph) on motorways, and 30 km/h (18 mph) at level crossings (often very bumpy). In case of accident the police should be called, and damage reported to the national insurance agency at Spálená 14-16.

Gasoline (benzín) and diesel fuel (nafta) are widely available, though lines often form at filling stations. Gasoline comes in the grades Special (93 octane) and Super (96 oct.); unleaded gasoline (Natural, 95 oct.) is not sold at all stations – in Prague, e.g., at the following (24-hour service): Praha 4, Újezd (motorway 1 to Brno); Praha 5 (Motol), Plzeňská (route 5 to Plzeň); Praha 7 (Holešovice), Argentinská (route 8 to Teplice); Praha 9 (Hrdlořezy), Českobrodská (route 12 to Kolín).
Services for foreign drivers:
Autoturist, Praha 1, Opletalova 21, Tel. 22 48 28

"Yellow Angel" Street Service, Tel. 154 (24-hour service). Stations in Prague: Praha 4, Macurova, Tel. 7 91 91 57, Praha 10 (Malešice), Limuzská 12, Tel. 77 34 55, and Praha 8, Lodžská 15, Tel. 8 55 83 81 (24-hour service).

Rail

Most international trains run to the main station (Hlavní nádraží); some arrive at Holešovice. Inland services also terminate at Libeň, Masarykovo, Smíchov, Vršovice, and Vysočany stations. The train is the cheapest mode of transport for excursions from Prague, though services are often infrequent, even on main lines.

Information

Prague's main train station (Praha Hlavní nádraži), Praha 2, Wilsonova (metro station), Tel. 2 36 38 24
Masarykovo train station, city center, Hybernská 13
Information office of Czech Railways (ČD): Passage Sevastopol, Praha 1, Na příkopě 31. Telephone inquiries: 2 35 38 36, 26 49 30.

Bus

There is an extensive network of local and long-distance bus routes. The *central bus station* is at Praha 8, Na Florenci (telephone inquiries 22 14 45, 2 36 49 10). Other bus stations are located near the metro stations at Anděl (Praha 5), Holešovice (Praha 7), and Roztyly (Praha 4).

Air Travel

The airport is at Ruzyně, Praha 6, approx. 12 miles northwest of the city center. The airport bus runs to the terminal at Revoluční 25.

Inquiries:

Ruzyně airport, Tel. 36 78 14
British Airways, Štěpanská 63, Tel. 2 36 03 53 (airport Tel. 36 77 31)
Czecho-Slovak Airlines, *tickets and reservations:* Praha 1, Revoluční 1, Tel. 21 46; *information:* Revoluční 25, Tel. 21 46, 2 31 73 95
Delta, Pařížská 11, Tel. 2 32 47 72

Index

Index

Index